Legal Issues in Biotechnology and Human Reproduction

LEGAL ISSUES IN BIOTECHNOLOGY AND HUMAN REPRODUCTION

Artificial Conception and Modern Genetics

Warren Freedman

Q

Quorum Books

New York • Westport, Connecticut • London

Library of Congress Cataloging-in-Publication Data

Freedman, Warren.
Legal issues in biotechnology and human reproduction : artificial conception and modern genetics / Warren Freedman.
p. cm.
Includes index.
ISBN 0–89930–635–7
1. Human reproductive technology—Law and legislation—United States. I. Title.
KF3771.F74 1991
344.73'095—dc20
[347.30495] 90–20709

British Library Cataloguing in Publication Data is available.

Library of Congress Catalog Card Number: 90–20709
ISBN: 0–89930–635–7

First published in 1991

Quorum Books, 88 Post Road West, Westport, CT 06881
An imprint of Greenwood Publishing Group, Inc.

Printed in the United States of America

The paper used in this book complies with the Permanent Paper Standard issued by the National Information Standards Organization (Z39.48–1984).

10 9 8 7 6 5 4 3 2 1

Contents

Preface

Modern biological science has brought forth many modern miracles, but none has achieved greater notoriety than artificial fertilization of the egg by the sperm in helping to solve infertility. Millions of American couples desire to procreate, or to employ the services of a surrogate mother, so as to commence the upbringing of a family. Interrelated to this natural human longing are the intricate legal relationships that must arise. Recent headlines proclaim that a surrogate mother who was paid handsomely for her services in giving birth to a child may still back out of the contract, or may seek revision of the contract, by either increasing the amount of her stipend or by refusing to tender the child she had carried for the nine-month period.

This book defines and delineates all aspects of the artificial relationship, and endeavors to reveal the legal rights and responsibilities of the parties. New concepts like cryopreservation, in vitro fertilization, banking of sperms and eggs, and patentable new organisms are delineated. The chapters look at artificial insemination and legal problems such as abortion, adultery, adoption, and ''baby selling.'' Chapter 6 deals with religion and morality in the creation of the new family. Several chapters discuss the legal liability of the physician, and others, the defense of nonpaternity, the common law marriage, pre- and postnatal injuries to the child, and so forth. There is even a look at the international aspects in Australia, Canada, England, Israel, and Italy, and a final chapter on forms of contracts and statutes affecting the creation of the new family.

Acknowledgments

Since my retirement as counsel and assistant secretary of Bristol-Myers Squibb Company ten years ago, I have devoted myself, for the most part, to the writing of legal treatises. In addition to this book, I have authored major texts in areas such as insurance, international products liability, the business tort of fraud and misrepresentation, toxic tort litigation, and hazardous waste liability. All of these writings were made possible by the research facilities of the law libraries at the Association of the Bar of the City of New York, Pace University in White Plains, N.Y., University of Connecticut in Hartford, and the Connecticut Supreme Court at Hartford.

The understanding and patience of my loving wife, Esther, a psychiatric social worker, contributed immensely to each work. I also acknowledge the assistance of my sons-in-law, Michael S. Stiebel of Hartford, Connecticut, and Richard Carmen of New York City, practicing attorneys in their respective states.

Legal Issues in Biotechnology and Human Reproduction

1

Introduction to the Biological Present and the Biological Future

1.1 INFERTILITY AND THE RIGHT TO PROCREATE

Infertility, defined as "failure to conceive after one year of regular coitus without contraception,"[1] creates a dire social, physical, and emotional crisis that affects perhaps 10 to 15 percent of all married couples in the United States.[2] Moreover, involuntary childlessness is on the increase.[3] Infertility is partly a result of stress factors related to the high divorce rate, the increase in single-person households, and the presence of male and female breadwinners in the family.[4] Male infertility has also been a prime factor in infertility,[5] as has the prevalence of sexually transmitted diseases, which cause infertility in both males and females.[6] William Shakespeare summed up the problem of infertility in *King Lear* with the curse on Goneril:

> Suspend thy purpose, if thou didst intend
> To make this creature fruitful.
> Into her womb convey sterility,
> Dry up in her the organs of increase,
> And from her derogate body never spring
> A babe to honor her!

Infertility or biologically dictated childlessness has been recognized since biblical days for its frustrations and even dangers.[7] The social incentives to procreation are identical with the social incentives that lead men and women to live in social groups and to accumulate property.[8] The right to procreate has been greeted by universal recognition even without the aid or encouragement of law, although in recent years sterilization, fornication, and some marriage laws have prevented some persons from reproducing.[9] There is no duty to procreate, but unfortunately laws and legal actions have too frequently been designed to "avoid" procreation. In Dandridge v. Williams (1970), the U.S Supreme Court opined that a state's failure to increase welfare benefits when additional children are born was not a penalty or a restraint on the right to procreate; it was simply a diminution of welfare benefits within the discretion of the state, and nothing more.[10] Forty-seven years earlier, the highest court, in Meyer v. Nebraska, stated that constitutional liberty included the right of an individual "to marry, establish a home and bring up children."[11] Marriage and procreation were deemed in Skinner v. Oklahoma to be among "the basic civil rights of man."[12] And in 1972 in Stanley v. Illinois,[13] the U.S. Supreme Court observed that "the rights to conceive and raise one's children have been deemed 'essential basic civil rights of man . . . ' more precious than . . . property rights."[14]

A 1988 report of the Congressional Office of Technology Assessment stated that Americans spent $1 billion in 1987 to combat infertility. On the average, childless couples spent from a few hundred dollars to $22,000 on infertility diagnoses and treatments.[15] More than 10 million Americans are struggling to have children; more and more women are waiting until the age of 35 or later to try to become pregnant, and more than 25 percent are failing.[16] According to one study,[17] infertility occurs one and a half times more often among blacks than among whites and is most common among black high school dropouts. Nearly 11 percent of married women, ages 20 to 24, are having trouble conceiving, compared with 3.6 percent only twenty years ago. Some researchers blame the surge on environmental factors like toxic chemicals and tobacco smoke. Sexually transmitted diseases are also a factor, plus such diseases as endometriosis (where the tissue that lines the inside of the uterus begins to grow outside the uterus) and, in the male, varicocele (where the swollen vein in the testicle causes higher temperatures that can destroy sperm production).[18]

Insurance benefits have generally not been available to cover medicines and surgical procedures for infertility.[19] Insurers balance the need to contain costs against the sometimes impossible financial burden to infertile couples. However, at least five states now require insurance carriers to cover infertility treatments, including in vitro fertilization.[20] The inertia and reluctance of insurance companies to provide coverage is similar to their initial resistance to cover heart and liver transplants, medical treatments that are generally covered today.[21] According to the Congressional Office of Technology Assessment, the average cost of diagnostic and medical treatments for infertility in 1988 was more than $2,500 per couple.[22] And with more than 37 million uninsureds, insurance coverage for in vitro fertilization has a low priority. Yet in 1987 about 40 percent of for-profit health insurance companies covered in vitro fertilization.[23] Insurers will usually pay claims for treatments that can be shown to heal an illness, such as treatment of endometriosis or efforts to remove tubal tumors, even if the goal is pregnancy.

It has been estimated that of the nearly 3.7 million babies to be born in 1990 in the United States, about 200,000 (about 18 percent) will owe their existence to infertility treatments.[24] There are nearly 200 infertility centers performing in vitro fertilization, although the technique is less than ten years old. Less than half of infertile couples who seek qualified medical assistance actually end up with babies.[25]

1.2 IN VIVO FERTILIZATION

It was not until the nineteenth century that medical science truly was freed from commercial casuistry to permit the development of sound biology and scientific pathology.[26] In the twentieth century the new disciplines made serious investigations into the facts of human infertility and sterility, not only by medical researchers and medical scientists but also by anthropologists, sociologists, and psychologists.[27] Coital intercourse, or in vivo fertilization, had always been beset by a myriad of impediments, including such physical factors as the low sperm count of the male, or oligospermia, the low motility and penetrability of the sperm, and the low compatibility with cervical mucus, for example. Social, economic, religious, political, psychological, and countless other factors have all played their respective roles either in infertility or in simply inadequate and unrewarding coital intercourse.

An alternative to in vitro fertilization had developed for the donation of embryos: in vivo fertilization and embryo transfer or embryo donation after uterine lavage.[28] The donor woman is artificially inseminated with the sperm from a husband of an infertile woman; after five or six days, the embryo is removed from the donor woman in a nonsurgical procedure, and the embryo is transferred into the uterus of the infertile woman.

This procedure has not achieved the popularity expected, probably due in part to the complicated medical procedures required.

1.3 IN VITRO FERTILIZATION

Of modern reproductive techniques, in vitro fertilization (IVF) has perhaps been the most prominent. IVF is defined as a process of reaction occurring in an artificial extracorporeal environment "as in a test tube or culture media."[29] Generally a physician performs a minor operation on the woman in order to remove an egg or oocyte from her ovary by inserting a small needle into the egg follicle, and then placing the egg in a shallow tube or "test-tube" containing the sperm and a special medium. For several days, the fertilized egg remains in incubation in the environment simulating the womb, and when it reaches the eight-cell embryo, or blastocyst, stage, coinciding with the normal time of implantation, the physician implants the fertilized egg or embryo back into the uterus of the mother. The first "test-tube" baby is believed to have been Louise Joy Brown who was born to Lesley Brown in England on July 25, 1978.[30] The world's first test-tube quadruplets were born in Australia on January 6, 1984.[31] The same year Dr. Cecil Jacobsen at the George Washington University Medical

School fertilized a chimpanzee egg IVF with chimpanzee sperm and implanted the fertilized egg into the uterus of a male chimpanzee, who later delivered a healthy baby chimpanzee by a cesarean section.[32]

IVF is clearly a humanitarian milestone and is supportive of the family since it enables a couple to achieve pregnancy.[33] The IVF technique bypasses damaged or blocked fallopian tubes and overcomes problems of ovulation and certain genetic disorders, as well as low sperm count.[34] Its success rate is high, judging by reports from Europe, Australia, the United States, and elsewhere.[35] New ultrasound-directed, nonsurgical aspiration methods make IVF an outpatient procedure. Even genetic screening can be performed on the in vitro embryo: one or more cells can be removed and screened for such maladies as Down's syndrome, and chromosomal testing can result in treating an embryo with a defect.[36]

There are, however, distinct disadvantages of attempting IVF with natural ovulatory cycles. Only one preovulatory follicle is available for aspiration of an egg, protracted monitoring is required to detect the hormonal surge, and the overall pregnancy rate is lower than with stimulated cycles where multiple follicles are available for aspiration.[37] In Del Zio v. Presbyterian Hospital, a 1978 federal district court jury in New York awarded prospective parents in an IVF procedure the sum of $50,000.[38] The "parents" claimed they endured great pain and suffering due to the deliberate destruction by the defendant of a potential embryo before fertilization had occurred.[39] There is, however, a 90 percent success rate for egg recovery, fertilization, and early embryonic cleavage.[40] As of 1986, more than 130 IVF programs existed in the United States, in major cities and even in small towns.[41] Pennsylvania[42] and Illinois[43] have statutes requiring the monitoring of the in vitro fertilization procedure, although in Illinois the physician's restricted liability is based upon custody of the woman's egg and presumably the man's sperm.[44] In many states, the legality of IVF as a medical procedure to overcome infertility is in question.[45]

Half of the infertility clinics in the United States in 1987 utilized the in vitro fertilization technique.[46] As one writer observed, "The IVF clinic represents the end of the road for most of the women here; each of us has a long history of disappointment verging on despair. Our pain is private; we keep it to ourselves. . . . I know, like every woman who waits in an IVF clinic, that anything less than 100% is failure."[47] In 1988 the U.S. Congress commenced a study toward regulation of or controlling "unscrupulous fertility clinics": more than half of the 169 clinics in the United States performing in vitro fertilization in 1987 never produced a baby.[48]

Pennsylvania is one of the few states that have statutes regarding IVF. It is designed to monitor the procedure by requiring the IVF clinic to file quarterly reports with the State Department of Health, describing the processes involved with the undertaking.[49] The Illinois statute is criminal in nature but does not directly prohibit the IVF procedure; it makes the physician who fertilizes a woman's egg outside her body the custodian of that tissue for purposes of the 1977 Child Abuse Act.[50] In short, in Illinois a physician who performs the IVF procedure without willful endangerment or injury to the embryo during the preimplantation period will not be prosecuted.[51] The Illinois statute grants custody to the physician and makes no provision for the parents to regain custody. In New York, in the unreported case of Del Zio v. Columbia Presbyterian Medical Center, the prospective parents of the IVF baby were compensated for emotional distress caused by the willful destruction of the embryo.[52]

Is IVF being oversold? Its national success rate is said to be only 15 percent.[53] To maintain uniformity and to improve IVF techniques, federal regulation has been recommended: all IVF laboratories would be certified, its personnel licensed, and its success rate verified.[54] However, it should be observed that IVF is most effective in surmounting tubal problems and endometriosis or sperm scarcity. Indeed, it may be the procedure of choice of only 5 to 10 percent of those seeking infertility treatment.[55]

1.4 EMBRYO TRANSFER

Another modern reproductive technique is embryo transfer (ET), which delineates the transfer of the fertilized ovum from its extracorporeal fertilization into the uterine cavity.[56] An embryo is the product of conception from the moment of fertilization to the end of the eighth week thereafter.[57] An artificial embryonation describes the process whereby the couple utilize a fertile woman who agrees to be inseminated with the man's sperm; four or five days after fertilization, the physician flushes out the embryo and implants it into the wife who will then carry the baby to term.[58] Embryo adoption, unlike egg adoption or artificial insemination,[59] refers to a situation where the embryo has genes from neither parent; if a woman has an ovarian or tubal problem and the husband is sterile, another woman is voluntarily inseminated by the sperm of a donor, and once fertilized, the embryo is flushed out after five days and implanted into the wife for normal maturation and birth.[60]

On February 3, 1984, the first human birth resulting from embryo transfer occurred; the baby, born to a woman in her thirties who had been treated for infertility, was genetically the product of the woman's husband and the egg donor.[61] Thus, the woman availed herself of the experience of pregnancy and childbirth through the embryo transfer. Her baby was genetically her husband's although she did not contribute the egg. Care in the selection of the ovum donor is of great importance; testing for diseases and chromosomal defects is mandatory. Should the mother die or some other unforeseen difficulty arise with respect to returning the fertilized egg to the mother's uterus, an embryo transfer could be made to another woman.[62]

The ET success rate is apparently higher than that for IVF methods with or without donated eggs.[63] In essence, ET mimics the usual way of having a baby: the woman who bears the child has the experience of pregnancy and childbirth. There are, however, at least two substantial physiological hazards that could accompany ET: tubal pregnancy in the recipient and a retained uterine pregnancy in the donor.[64] One solution is an abortion,[65] which appeared to be sanctioned in 1986 by the U.S. Supreme Court, as illustrated in Thornburgh v. American College of Obstetricians and Gynecologists:[66] "The States are not free, under the guise of protecting maternal health or potential life, to intimidate women into continuing pregnancies."[67] Years earlier the same Court, in Eisenstadt v. Baird,[68] observed: "If the right of privacy means anything, it is the right of the individual . . . to be free from unwarranted governmental intrusion into matters so fundamentally affecting a person as the decision whether to bear or beget a child."[69]

It has been suggested that a national deliberative organization on embryo status should be established that would be "free of the politics of the right-to-life and abortion debate."[70] This organization would focus on discrete problems, such as conditions for embryo research, for freezing and storage of embryos[71], and for embryo discard.[72] In July 1988 the U.S. Health and Human Services Department announced that it would reestablish an ethics committee to rule on applications for funds for fertility research involving embryos.[73]

Tubal ovum transfer, a new procedure, has been used to bypass blocked or damaged parts of the fallopian tubes. Eggs are retrieved as with IVF and moved past the blockage. ET is used when a woman's ovaries or fallopian tubes fail or when a genetic disorder or disease would otherwise be passed to the embryo.[74]

1.5 SURROGATE PARENTING

Surrogate parenting is a reproductive technique in which the surrogate mother provides both the egg and the gestation; she agrees to conceive the child, carry it to term, and then relinquish it to the couple or person providing the sperm.[75] In biblical days, Abraham and Sarah engaged Hagar to bear their son Isaac,[76] but Hagar was not a respectful surrogate mother, and eventually she and her son Ishmael were driven into the wilderness.[76] Surrogacy is still today a problematic experience, and there is little if any predictable legal guide for its rambling course.[77] The term *surrogate,* meaning "substitute," is perhaps misleading, for the surrogate mother is the person who actually bears and gives birth to the child via artificial insemination,[78] IVF,[79] or perhaps ET.[80] She is the gestational agent, to be sure,[81] and, if she is paid a fee, the practice is viewed as baby-selling,[82] and the arrangement may be void as against public policy, as demonstrated in the Michigan decision of Doe v. Kelly.[83] (For a contrary view, see the Kentucky decision of Surrogate Parenting Associates, Inc. v. Commonwealth of Kentucky ex rel. Armstrong.)[84]

The surrogate mother, it would appear, has the constitutional right to abort the child she is carrying, at least judging by the 1973 holding of the U.S. Supreme Court in Roe v. Wade.[85] No party to a surrogate contract or any other person involved in the arrangement can veto her right to abort.[86] After the birth of the child, the surrogate presumably terminates her parental rights, and the child is then available for adoption by the wife of the couple, subject to rebuttal of the presumption that the gestational or surrogate mother is the natural mother.[87] In Smith v. Jones, the Michigan court actually issued an interim order directing that the name of the ovum donor and not the name of the surrogate mother be listed as the natural mother on the birth certificate of the baby.[88]

Surrogate motherhood is costly, with a typical rate in 1987 of perhaps $15,000, plus medical and other expenses, including broker and attorney fees.[89] In Australia, a pioneer in the technique of freezing embryos, the frozen embryos of a wealthy Chilean couple killed in an air crash in 1983 were to be thawed and implanted in an Australian woman surrogate in 1988, according to the *New York Times*.[90]

In recent years state legislatures have introduced many bills dealing with surrogate parenting, some abrogating and others legalizing contracts with surrogate parents, thereby protecting the child born to the surrogate mother; other bills delineate the rights and responsibilities of all of the parties involved.[91] A number of states have drafted laws to regulate surrogate procedures or have legislative proposals prohibiting surrogate parenting.[92] For example, Nevada permits surrogate parenting for pay; in Arkansas a married couple contracting with an unpaid surrogate mother is accorded parental rights; but in Michigan surrogate contracts are void and subject the parties to a felony charge.[93]

The Uniform Status of Children of Assisted Conception Act was approved by the National Conference of Commissioners on Uniform State Laws on August 4, 1988.[94] The act offers two alternatives regarding surrogate arrangements: one for states desiring to permit but regulate surrogate parenting and the other for states seeking to void all such procedures. ''Assisted pregnancy'' is defined as any pregnancy resulting from fertilizing an egg of a woman with sperm of a man by means other than sexual intercourse or by implanting an embryo.[95] But assisted pregnancy does not include the pregnancy of a wife resulting from fertilizing her egg with the sperm of her husband. An enforceable surrogate contract must be in writing for approval by a court prior to conception; the couple must be married, and the surrogate mother can be single or married. But either party can repudiate the surrogate contract up to the date of conception; the surrogate mother then has an additional six months after conception to repudiate and keep the baby. The act limits the procedure to infertile wives or to those persons where there is a medical or genetic reason precluding the wife's pregnancy.

1.6 IMPLANTATION AND TRANSPLANTATION

Implantation and transplantation are modern reproductive techniques involving both the sperm and the ovum. In 1960 Jean Rostand argued that medical science was rapidly changing human beings and therefore the law affecting those human beings must be changed:[96]

> What would become of the notion of maternity if surgeons transplanted a fertilized ovum of a young embryo from one woman to another? If a woman bore a child that was not

genetically hers, who would be the real mother? Would it be she who carried or she who furnished the germ cell? As medical science develops further, there will come a time when a child can be produced from an ovum whose nucleus has been entirely removed and replaced by the nucleus of another person. The result would be that the real mother here would be the person who supplied the substitute nucleus. To further complicate things, this bastard nucleus can come from a person of *either* sex! This promises to play havoc with the domestic relations law of the future. Even "auto-adultery" will be possible, that is, self-fertilization by techniques employing an additional nucleus from the same woman, rather than from another person. This would produce a child that is not the child of any male! What the legal consequences of this will be are beyond conjecture. To further complicate the law of the future, "chemical adultery" is possible. Bacteria already can be changed by "directed mutation" by means of certain chemicals extracted from the chromosomes. If one extends this practice to human beings, certain hereditary characteristics of one individual can be transferred to the reproductive cells of another one, and the children would not be offspring of a particular couple but of the entire species of humanity.

Both implantation and transplantation undoubtedly will make possible "more visits to the courtroom than to the hospital."[97] This surge in litigation is predictable, for implantation and transplantation roam in a legal vacuum. Postimplantational ectogenesis, for example, may necessitate the development of an artificial placenta and artificial uterus, each with its attendant legal problems.[98]

Transplantation of organs has become accepted medical practice; the list of transplanted organs includes kidney, cornea, bone, tendon, liver, bone marrow, heart, pancreas, lung, skin, and bowel. Kidneys may be obtained from living donors; about a third of the more than 5,500 kidney transplants done in 1986 in the United States involved living donors. Organ transplantation is very expensive: a liver transplant may cost more than $300,000.

A court agreement in 1989 in the federal district court for the District of Columbia cleared the way for the first authorized human gene transplant in Foundation on Economic Trends v. Recombinant DNA Advisory Committee.[99] The settlement came in a lawsuit that challenged the planned use of a foreign gene in an experiment to be conducted on ten patients with melanoma.[100] Under the agreement the defendant must hold all deliberations and votes in open public session.

1.7 REPRODUCTIVE SCENARIOS

The various reproductive techniques encompassing collaborative or artificial reproduction may present a reproductive scenario, for example, that would allow a child to have perhaps five parents: "an egg donor, a sperm donor, a surrogate mother who gestates the fetus, and the couple who raise the child."[101] Additional "parents" may arise from the identity of the adoptive parents, the egg donee, the sperm donee, and the equitable or foster parents, to complicate the problem further.[102] Generally the rules for determining parenthood and legitimacy of children, as well as the rights and duties that flow from such status or relationship, are fixed by state law. Historically, these state laws have been predicated upon biological kinship, such as the legal presumption that a child born during wedlock to a married couple was the legitimate child of the wife's husband when the couple were regularly cohabiting as husband and wife.[103]

The Uniform Parentage Act seemingly meets the challenge of the new reproductive techniques in section 2 of the act: "The parent and child relationship extends equally to every child and to every parent, regardless of the marital status of the parents."[104] While this language abolishes illegitimate status of children, it also can serve as a legal guide for reproduction status when accompanied by the requisite of pretrial proceedings to establish paternity, where feasible.[105]

Other reproductive scenarios raise difficult questions as illustrated in the typical artificial insemination donor (AID) situation, where the sperm from a third party is combined with the ovum of a married woman who desires her husband to be deemed the father of the child.[106] The married woman and her husband are presumably the legal parents of the child, unless the husband's consent was withheld, as shown in In re Adoption of Young, a Pennsylvania decision precluding the natural mother's adopting the child.[107] The sperm donor may not be immune from legal obligations toward the mother and the child if the husband never consented to the AID situation.[108] In New York in Gursky v. Gursky, the husband's consent created against him an enforceable child support obligation and at the same time relieved the sperm donor of any legal obligation toward the mother or the child.[109]

Suppose the sperm of a third party is combined with the ovum of a married woman who agrees to give up the child to the sperm donor; the husband of the ovum carrier would be the presumptive legal father of the child if he consented to the reproductive practice. In any event, the court would probably be called upon to resolve the conflicting claims to the child. The sperm donor might have to resort to the adoption proceeding.[110] If he were married, presumably both he and his wife would have to adopt the child, if that be their wish. If the sperm of a third party is combined with the ovum of an unmarried person who agrees to give up the child to the sperm donor, the child might be deemed illegitimate, and the sperm donor would probably be deemed the legal father.[111] Where the sperm is combined with the ovum of an unmarried person who wants the child in a single-parent home, the child might be illegitimate and the sperm donor would be considered the legal, biological father.[112] The consent of the sperm donor would be necessary to allow the child to be adopted, according to Stanley v. Illinois, decided by the U.S. Supreme Court in 1972.[113] Child support and other obligations must take into consideration the welfare of the child.

Still another reproductive scenario might encompass the situation where the sperm of a married man is combined with the ovum of a donor and then the mixture is implanted in his wife's uterus (the IVF and ET situation).[114] The ovum donor would appear to be the mother if biology is the test of maternity, although the married wife did contribute her uterus for the development of the child. If the implantation is in the uterus of a woman other than the married wife, then the problem is compounded and beyond immediate solution, especially if the "other woman" is married and perhaps if the ovum donor is also married.

1.8 BANKING OF SPERM AND EGGS

The American Association of Tissue Banks (AATB), formed in 1976, is composed of medical practitioners and scientists with experience in cell, tissue, and organ banking. One of AATB's purposes, through its Reproductive Council, is to establish codes and standards for the collection, preservation, processing, and use of human sperm or semen.[115] AATB favors licensing of cryobanks, for example, and the promulgation by government of uniform standards. In New York City, donor semen must be tested by law for syphilis and gonorrhea; regulations disqualify any donor "affected with venereal disease, tuberculosis, brucellosis or who has any congenital disease or defect."[116] Human semen cryobanking began a period of growth in the early 1970s, and within a few years there were three major banks with eight branches located throughout the United States.[117]

The New York case of Zwerin v. Group Health Inc. involved a most unusual issue: can a cancer patient obtain compensation under a group health insurance policy for expenses related to sperm bank procedures prior to chemotherapy and compatibility tests on his sister, a potential donor for a bone marrow transplant?[118] The answer was "yes," but the court refused to extend insurance coverage to the sperm bank procedure, finding that it was an addition to the contract:

> The claim for recovery of the expenses relating to the sperm banking procedures undertaken by claimant as a defense of his cancer treatment was properly rejected by defendant under the clear terms of the policy.
>
> This procedure is not part of the actual treatment of claimant's illness or any of the other stated coverages of the policy. Additionally, the policy contains a specific exclusion for medical care *in excess of the care normally required for treatment of a condition* [emphasis added].
>
> The Court, in this instance, must adhere to the principle that unambiguous provisions in the contract must be given their plain and ordinary meaning. To adopt the claimant's position that the sperm bank procedures will enable him to have children in the future following chemotherapy is an addition to the contract and cannot be imposed by this Court. Under New York law, the second claim must be therefore dismissed.

1.9 CRYOPRESERVATION

Cryopreservation is the modern freezing technique for preservation of sperm and egg. Semen or sperm is generally frozen and preserved in liquid nitrogen at -196.5 degrees Centigrade. Freezing embryos is done at the two-, four-, or eight-cell stage of development since earlier-stage embryos are more difficult to freeze and later-stage embryos are too advanced to develop normally after thawing. Cryopreservation might actually improve a woman's chances for pregnancy because the thawed embryo can be inserted during a nonstimulated cycle, which is believed to enhance the embryo's chance for implantation. It appears that the fertilizing capacity of frozen sperm is approximately two-thirds of the fertilizing capacity of fresh sperm. But frozen sperm has the advantage of being on hand when required, as well as giving the purchaser a relatively wide choice of a donor's "preferred characteristics."[119] Cryopreservation of embryos has resulted in successful births after thawing embryos in the Netherlands and in Australia; in the United States the first birth of a child from a cryopreserved embryo was reported in Los Angeles on June 5, 1986.[120]

The ability to preserve sperm, egg, and embryo for later use by freezing has many consequences, including the thought that a twentieth-century embryo might be frozen until thawed in the twenty-second century. This technique of cryopreservation could rob a child of the chance to know his or her biological parents.[121] According to the *New York Times*, an infertile woman in Los Angeles became pregnant with triplets after two frozen embryos were implanted in her uterus. Her eggs had been removed from her ovaries surgically, mixed with her husband's sperm, and then implanted in her uterus.[122]

The frozen embryo process appears to be banned in certain states, including Minnesota, Michigan, and Illinois. Minnesota forbids experimentation on a living human conceptus, including those conceived *ex utero*, unless the experimentation is necessary to protect the health or life of the conceptus or unless scientific evidence has proved the experimentation to be harmless.[123]

In a divorce case, frozen embryos have become great topics of legal consideration: should an embryo be treated not as property but rather as potential life (if not life itself)? In Davis v. Davis, the Tennessee court in 1989 ruled that life begins at conception, and therefore all embryos are human beings and not property.[124] The court gave custody of the seven fertilized eggs to the wife despite the father's argument that he was being forced to become a father against his will.[125] The court treated the case like a custody dispute in which the overriding concern was the best interest of the child.[126] (According to the American Fertility Society, there are about 3,700 cryopreserved human embryos in storage in the United States.)[127]

On the other hand, the federal district court in Virginia in York v. Jones Institute ruled that the frozen embryo was property belonging to the couple whose genetic material created it.[128] The couple successfully moved the frozen embryo from a Virginia clinic to one in California where the couple planned to have it implanted.[129] (An ethics committee of the Virginia-based AATB is drafting rules for the handling and disposition of frozen embryos.)[130] California, in Moore v. Regents of University of California, ruled that a patient's extracorporeal bodily tissues and substances were his personal property and that he was entitled to any resulting profits from the use of his tissues.[131] A Louisiana statute defines an embryo created in vitro as a "person."[132] The issue is far from resolution.

1.10 CONSTITUTIONAL PROTECTION OF FAMILY PRIVACY

It is probable that the use of modern reproductive techniques is within the ambit of the right of privacy conferred and protected by the U.S. Constitution.[133] Freedom from unwarranted intrusion into one's body or one's person was the subject of the U.S. Supreme Court's 1965 decision in Griswold v. Connecticut,[134] which invalidated a state statute prohibiting the use of birth control, and its 1973 decision in Roe v. Wade,[135] sanctioning the right of a woman to decide whether to seek an abortion. These rights of privacy are sanctioned also by the state, which cannot abridge that fundamental right of the person to choose not to bear a child, although the state does have a compelling interest in protecting a viable fetus after the second trimester so as to restrain the woman's right to determine whether to terminate a pregnancy.[136] It is said that the core of procreative privacy is personal autonomy in choosing to obstruct conception and forestall childbirth. Indeed, "freedom of personal choice in matters of marriage and family life" is central among all protected liberties, according to Akron v. Akron Center for Reproductive Health.[137] Earlier the highest court, in Carey v. Population Services International, had declared that the "decision whether or not to bear and beget children is at the very heart of the cluster of constitutionally protected choices."[138] But there is a need to harness one's fecundity, as spelled out by the U.S. Supreme Court in the 1986 *Thornburgh* case.[139] Indeed, procreative privacy probably guarantees only the right of self-government or freedom of choice until the state's compelling interest in the viable fetus, for example, takes over. The Kentucky Supreme Court in 1986 refused to prohibit commercial surrogate parenting,[140] thereby according constitutional protection to "the decision whether or not to beget and bear a child."[141] Of course, it can be argued that deterring the commercialization of parenthood is one of the ponderous state interests that should be protected.

This procreational right of privacy must extend its constitutional protection to nontraditional family units and to alternative methods of reproduction.[142] For example, legislation prohibiting artificial insemination or other reproductive techniques to unmarried women would violate fundamental freedoms, including equal protection of the laws. As the highest court stated in Moore v. City of East Cleveland, "The Constitution prevents government from standardizing its children—and its adults—by forcing all to live in certain narrowly defined family patterns."[143] And in Planned Parenthood v. Danforth, the highest court opined that "constitutional rights do not mature and come into being magically only when one obtains the State-defined age of majority. Minors, as well as adults, are protected by the Constitution and possess constitutional rights."[144]

There are obviously severe limitations or restrictions on this right of privacy in the procreative field: consenting adults cannot publicly engage in homosexual conduct; parental freedom does not allow parents to place children at risk; and the right to abortion is limited by compelling state interest in protecting potential human life and preserving maternal health.[145]

Privacy law and its protections do not extend to homosexual conduct, according to the U.S. Supreme Court's 1986 decision in Bowers v. Hendrick.[146] By a 5–4 vote the Court ruled that the U.S. Constitution protects no "fundamental right to engage in homosexual conduct. . . . Proscriptions against that conduct have ancient roots. . . . The court is most vulnerable and comes nearest to illegitimacy when it deals with judge-made constitutional law having little or no cognizable roots in the language or design of the Constitution." The dissenters pointed out that the case delineated

The most comprehensive of rights and the right most valued by civilized man . . . the right to be let alone. . . . In a variety of circumstances we have recognized that a necessary corollary of giving individuals freedom to choose how to conduct their lives is acceptance of the fact that different individuals will make different choices. . . . Depriving individuals of the right to choose for themselves how to conduct their intimate relationships poses a far greater threat to the values most deeply rooted in our Nation's history than tolerance of non-conformity could ever do.[147]

It should be obvious that individual homosexual conduct involves such fundamental choices—among them, whether and whom to marry, whether to conceive a child, whether to carry a pregnancy to term. But the majority opinion contended that "none of the rights announced . . . bears any resemblance to the claimed constitutional right of homosexuals to engage in acts of sodomy that is asserted in this case."[148] The Court looked to history for reasons that the constitutional boundary should be so immutable—why the zone of privacy should not be extended to intimate relations between persons of the same sex—and concluded that condemnation of homosexuality has "ancient roots." The Georgia law at issue dated back to 1816, and all original thirteen states outlawed homosexual acts, as did all fifty states until 1961. (Since then, either by legislation or court decisions, private homosexual acts between consenting adults are no longer criminal in twenty-six states.) The privacy of one's home was delineated by the majority opinion:

Respondent, however, asserts that the result should be different where the homosexual conduct occurs in the privacy of the home. He relies on *Stanley v. Georgia* (1969), where the Court held that the First Amendment prevents conviction for possessing and reading obscene material in the privacy of his home: "If the First Amendment means anything, it means that a state has no business telling a man, sitting alone in his house, what books he may read or what films he may watch."

Stanley did protect conduct that would not have been protected outside the home, and it partially prevented the enforcement of state obscenity laws; but the decision was firmly grounded in the First Amendment. The right pressed upon us here has no similar support in the text of the Constitution, and it does not qualify for recognition under the prevailing principles for construing the Fourteenth Amendment. Its limits are also difficult to discern. Plainly, enough otherwise illegal conduct is not always immunized whenever it occurs in the home. Victimless crimes, such as the possession and use of illegal drugs, do not escape the law where they are committed at home. *Stanley* itself recognized that its holding offered no protection for the possession in the home of drugs, firearms, or stolen goods. And if respondent's submission is limited to voluntary sexual conduct between consenting adults, it would be difficult, except by fiat, to limit the claimed right to homosexual conduct while leaving exposed to prosecution adultery, incest, and other sexual crimes even though they are committed in the home. We are unwilling to start down that road.

In sharp contrast is the dissenters' view:

The behavior for which Hardwick faces prosecution occurred in his own home, a place to which the Fourth Amendment attaches special significance. The Court's treatment of this aspect of the case is symptomatic of its overall refusal to consider the broad principles that have informed our treatment of privacy in specific cases. Just as the right to privacy is more than the mere aggregation of a number of entitlements to engage in specific behavior, so too, protecting the physical integrity of the home is more than merely a means of protecting specific activities that often take place there.

The Court's interpretation of the pivotal case of Stanley v. Georgia (1969), is entirely unconvincing. *Stanley* held that Georgia's undoubted power to punish the public distribution of constitutionally unprotected, obscene material did not permit the state to punish the private possession of such material. According to the majority here, *Stanley* relied entirely on the First Amendment, and thus, it is claimed, sheds no light on cases not involving printed materials. But that is not what *Stanley* said. Rather, the *Stanley* Court anchored its holding in the Fourth Amendment's special protection for the individual in his home. The right of an individual to conduct intimate relationships in the intimacy of his or her own home seems to me to be the heart of the Constitution's protection of privacy. . . . We protect those rights not because they contribute, in some direct and material way, to the general public welfare, but because they form so central a part of an individual life. We protect the decision whether to marry precisely because marriage "is an association that promotes a way of life, not causes; a harmony in living, not political faiths; a bilateral loyalty, not commercial or social projects." Griswold v. Connecticut. We protect the decision whether to have a child because parenthood alters so dramatically an individual's self-definition, not because of demographic considerations or the Bible's command to be fruitful and multiply. And we protect the family because it contributes so powerfully to the happiness of individuals, not because of a preference for stereotypical households.

Only the most willful blindness could obscure the fact that sexual intimacy is "a sensitive, key relationship of human existence, central to family life, community welfare, and the development of human personality." Paris Adult Theatre I v. Slayton (1973). The fact that individuals define themselves in a significant way through their intimate sexual relationships with others suggests, in a nation as diverse as ours, that there may be many "right" ways of conducting those relationships, and that much of the richness of a relationship will come from the freedom an individual has to choose the form and nature of these intensely personal bonds.

In a variety of circumstances we have recognized that a necessary corollary of giving individuals freedom to choose how to conduct their lives is acceptance of the fact that different individuals will make different choices. For example, in holding that the clearly important state interest in public education should give way to competing claim by the Amish to the effect that extended formal schooling threatened their way of life, the Court declared: "There can be no assumption that today's majority is 'right' and the Amish and others like them are 'wrong'. A way of life that is odd or even erratic but interferes with no rights or interests of others is not to be condemned because it is different." Wisconsin v. Yoder (1972). The Court claims that its decision today merely refuses to recognize a fundamental right to engage in homosexual sodomy; what the Court really has refused to recognize is the fundamental interest all individuals have in controlling the nature of their intimate associations with others.

This 1986 U.S. Supreme Court decision took into consideration that eighteen states (Alabama, Arizona, Florida, Georgia, Idaho, Kentucky, Louisiana, Maryland, Michigan, Minnesota, Mississippi, Missouri, North Carolina, Oklahoma, South Carolina, Tennessee, Utah, and Virginia) had heterosexual and homosexual sodomy laws;[149] twenty-seven states (Alaska, California, Colorado, Connecticut, Delaware, Hawaii, Illinois, Indiana, Iowa, Maine, Massachusetts, Nebraska, New Hampshire, New Jersey, New Mexico, New York, North Dakota, Ohio, Oregon, Pennsylvania, Rhode Island, South Dakota, Vermont, Washington, West Virginia, Wisconsin, and Wyoming) had no sodomy laws. (Nevada, Texas, Kansas, and Arkansas had homosexual sodomy laws only.)[150] Thus, the 5–4 decision of the Court had the effect of significantly narrowing the conception of the right of privacy, despite the fact that more than half of the states had not concerned themselves with homosexuality and sodomy.[151]

The dissenting opinion of Mr. Justice Blackman focused at length on the majority's characterization of previous privacy cases as simply protecting family values: "We protect the decision whether to have a child because parenthood alters so dramatically an individual's self-definition, not because of demographic considerations or the Bible's command to be fruitful and multiply." He reasoned that because intimate sexual conduct is a means through which "individuals define themselves in a significant way," its protection is consistent with the Court's prior cases construing the right of privacy.[152] He argued that there is a spatial aspect to the right of privacy and thus that "the right of an individual to conduct intimate relationships in the intimacy of his or her own home is the heart of the Constitution's protection of privacy."

The majority view in Bowers v. Hardwick[153] indicated that rather than protecting an individual's freedom to make decisions fundamental to herself or himself, the right of privacy is limited to particular, traditional categories of private life. The decision is also significant in that it amounted to a symbolic rejection of the homosexual life-style in 1986.[154]

Privacy in family court is another fascinating aspect of the constitutional protection of family privacy. Proceedings in family court are generally closed to the public and almost always conducted beyond media scrutiny. In New York, for example, a 1986 court rule, entitled "Privacy of Proceedings in the Family

Court,'' strictly limits the presence of media representatives, agency officials, researchers, and attorneys who do not have a direct interest in the case, and it bars attendance by the general public.[155] Such exclusion, it is submitted, is built upon vulnerable underpinnings in that court proceedings are presumed to be open.[156] Discretionary court-imposed exclusion would appear to be impermissible, at least in quasi-criminal actions such as delinquency.[157] The Sixth Amendment to the Constitution does state that ''in all criminal prosecutions, the accused shall enjoy the right to a speedy and public trial.''[158] In the case of In the Interest of Dino, the Louisiana Supreme Court pointed out that a statute providing that the general public shall be excluded from juvenile adjudicatory hearings was ''unconstitutional insofar as it prohibits a juvenile from electing a public trial in adjudicatory proceedings based on criminal charges which would entitle an adult accused to have his trial conducted in public.''[159] A similar holding was seen in a 1971 decision of the Alaska Supreme Court.[160]

Beyond questions of propriety and good manners, legal protection of personal privacy is of biblical origin.[161] In Jewish law, the right to privacy is a vested right protected by injunction, restoration of the status quo, and the award of damages from the civil law. Interference with the right to privacy also has its criminal law character, to be countered by penal sanctions.[162]

1.11 A PATENTABLE NEW ORGANISM

In the growing field of modern reproductive techniques and genetic engineering, it is of interest to note that the U.S. Supreme Court authorized the patentability of genetically engineered microorganisms.[163] According to the Court, ''Respondent's micro-organism plainly qualifies as patentable subject matter. His claim is not to a hitherto unknown natural phenomenon but to a nonnaturally occurring manufacture or composition of matter—a product of human ingenuity 'having a distinctive name, character and use.' . . . [It is] a new bacterium with markedly different characteristics from any found in nature and one having potential for significant utility. His discovery is not nature's handiwork, but his own; accordingly, it is patentable subject matter.''[164] A California company recently obtained a patent application for the catheter used in the lavage in embryonic transfers.[165]

Clearly these and other patentable products must aid scientific progress with respect to the biological present and future. The drawback is commercialization, which can adversely affect the reproductive techniques, but the price of progress is sometimes expensive.

1.12 A WORD ABOUT EUGENICS

Prior to and during World War II, eugenics at the hands of Nazis received a bad name; eugenics was utilized to promote a superior race, and its focus was on selective breeding and forced sterilization, with a distinct class basis. Today eugenics has emerged as genetic engineering of one's own offspring. The new medical science offers prenatal testing to check for imperfections and diseases, although its success to date in finding cures for gene-linked disorders leaves much to be desired. Where gene research seeks to manipulate the gene pool, widespread criticism arises in many areas.[166]

The U.S. Senate in 1988 approved the first step of a $3 billion project advocated by the National Academy of Sciences to map every one of the 100,000 genes.[167] It is said that the 3,000-plus known genetic disorders hospitalize 12 million Americans a year at a cost of $2.35 billion.[168]

NOTES

1. See Benson, *Current Obstetrics and Gynecologic Diagnosis* 992 (5th ed., 1986) and note generally, 7 N. Ill. L. Rev. 1 (1986).

2. See National Ctr. for Health Stats., Vital & Health Stats., Ser. 23, No. 11, at 13–16, 32 (December 1982); also, *New York Times* (February 11, 1985), at A12, col. 3.

3. See *New York Times* (May 16, 1985), at A52, col. 6 and *New York Times* (April 7, 1985), at Al, col. 2; also, *Time* (September 10, 1984), at 50 and *Wall Street Journal* (October 12, 1984), at 1, col. 1.

4. See Mazor, "Barren Couples," 12 *Psychology Today* 101 (May 1979).

5. See Brody, "Infertility: Not Uncommon Male Problem, But Often Treatable," *New York Times* (March 20, 1985), at C21, col. 3.

6. See *Newsweek* (February 4, 1985), at 72.

7. Genesis: 16–17 recounts the story of Abraham and Sarah who were subsequently blessed with Isaac, the natural son of their old age.

8. See generally 58 Yale L.J. 457 (1949); also see Sumner and Keller, *The Science of Society* 406 (1927).

9. See 59 S. Cal. L. Rev. 939 (1986) at 956.

10. 397 U.S. 471 (1970).

11. 262 U.S. 390 (1923).

12. 316 U.S. 535 (1942).

13. 405 U.S. 645 (1972).

14. Id. at 651.

15. See *New York Times* (May 18, 1988), at A25

16. See *U.S. News & World Report* (October 5, 1987), at 58

17. Id. at 59.

18. Id. at 60–61. For general reading on the technical subject of infertility, see the following: *What We Know About Infertility: Diagnosis and Treatment Alternatives* by Robert Winston, (Free Press); *You CAN Have a Baby: Everything You Need to Know about Fertility* by Joseph H. Bellina and Josleen Wilson (Crown Publishers); *Give Us a Child: The Personal Crisis of Infertility* by Lynda Rutledge Stephenson (Harper & Row); *In Search of Parenthood: Coping with Infertility and High-Tech Conception* by Judith N. Lasker and Susan Borg (Beacon Press); *New Conceptions: A Consumer's Guide to the Newest Infertility Treatments* by Lori B. Andrews (St. Martin's Press); *The Infertility Book: A Comprehensive Medical and Emotional Guide* by Carla Harkness (Volcano Press);

and *The Miracle Seekers: An Anthology of Infertility* by Mary Martin Mason (Perspectives Press).

19. See *New York Times* (March 5, 1989) at E24.

20. See section 1.3 hereinafter.

21. Infra note 19.

22. Common diagnosis procedures include ultrasound or sonography (in which sound waves are used to detect blockages or irregularities in the reproductive organs) and laparoscopy (in which a tiny viewing scope is inserted into the fallopian tubes). Also infra note 15.

23. See *New York Times* (March 10, 1989), at A16

24. Arkansas, Maryland, Massachusetts, Hawaii, and Texas have taken liberal steps aiming at such coverage. See note 19.

25. See *Changing Times* (March 1989), at 73–78

26. See Malinowski, Introduction to Hogbin, *Law and Order in Polynesia,* lxviii (1934), and 58 Yale L.J. 457 (1949), at 458.

27. See Burgess and Cottrell, *Predicting Success or Failure in Marriage* 261 (1939).

28. See 251 J.A.M.A. 1171 (1984).

29. See *Stedman's Med. Dictionary* 723 (5th ed., 1982); also see generally 34 Clev. St. L. Rev. 311 (1986) at 312.

30. See *New York Times* (June 16, 1982), at 22, sec. 4, col. 1.

31. See ibid. (April 11, 1984), at 16, sec. 1, col. 4.

32. See Andrews, *New Conceptions* 261 (1984).

33. On the medical ethics, see Kass, ''Babies by Means of In Vitro Fertilization: Unethical Experiments on the Unborn?'' 285 New Eng. J. Med. 1174 (1971). Also see 220 J.A.M.A. 1346 (1987).

34. See 44 La. L. Rev. (1984), at pp. 1666–67; also 69 Va. L. Rev. 465 (1986).

35. See Wolf and Quigley, *Human in Vitro Fertilization and Embryo Transfer* (1984).

36. See Andrews, *New Conceptions: A Consumer's Guide to the Newest Infertility Treatments, Including In Vitro Fertilization, Artificial Insemination, and Surrogate Motherhood* 240 (1985).

37. See 17 Fam. L.Q. (Summer 1983), at pp. 203–4.

38. Unreported—F. Supp.—(S.D.N.Y., 1978).

39. See Grobstein, Flower, and Mendelhoff, ''External Human Fertilization: An Evaluation of Policy,'' 222 *SCI* 127 (1983); also 59 S. Calif. L. Rev 939 (1986).

40. Id.

41. See *New York Times* (May 4, 1986), at 8, sec. 4.

42. Pa. Stat. Ann. tit. 18, sec. 3213(e) (1983–1984).

43. Ill. Rev. Stat. ch. 38, sec. 81–26(7) (1983–1984).

44. See Smith v. Hartigan, 556 F. Supp. 157 (N.D. Ill., 1983).

45. See 21 Gonz. L. Rev. 395 (1985–1986) and 67 Geo. L.J. 1295 (1979).

46. See *New York Times* (May 18, 1988), at A25.

47. Note Davis, ''The Private Pain of Infertility,'' *New York Times Magazine* (December 6, 1987), at 106 et seq.

48. See *Hartford Courant* (June 2, 1988), at A3.

49. Sec. 3213(e), Pa. Stat. Ann. tit. 18.

50. Sec. 81–26(7), of Ill. Rev. Stat. ch. 38.

51. See Smith v. Hartigan, 556 F. Supp. 157 (N.D. Ill., 1983). Also note 21 Gonz. L. Rev. 395 (1985–1986), at 409.

52. Unreported dkt. 74–3558 (S.D.N.Y, April 12, 1978).

53. See *Time* (March 13, 1989), at 53

54. See *New York Times* (March 10, 1989), at A16, pointing out that the highest success rate was only 17 percent at Columbia Presbyterian Medical Center in New York City.

55. See *Changing Times* (March 1988), at 76.

56. See generally 17 Fam. L.Q. (Summer 1983), at 1 et seq. An ovum is the female germ cell, egg cell, or gamete; an oocyte is an immature ovum; and a zygote results from the union of a male sperm and a female ovum until it divides.

57. A conceptus is the sum derivatives of a fertilized ovum at any stage of development from fertilization until birth, including the extraembryonic membranes.

58. Infra note 32 at 261.

59. See Chapter 2.

60. See 34 Clev. St. L. Rev. 311 (1986).

61. See 44 La. L. Rev. (1984), at 1672.

62. See *New York Times* (January 29, 1982), at 17, sec., col. 1.

63. See Areen, King, Goldberg, and Capron, *Law, Science and Medicine* 1323 (1984); also note Utah L. Rev. 1 (1987).

64. See Utah L. Rev. (1987), at 8.

65. See section 7.7.

66. 106 S. Ct. 2169 (1986).

67. Id. at 2178.

68. 405 U.S. 438 (1972).

69. Id. at 453.

70. Infra note 40.

71. See sections 1.8 and 1.9.

72. See section 7.3.

73. See *New York Times* (July 15, 1988), at A10.

74. See *Changing Times* (March 1989), at 74.

75. See 59 S. Cal. L. Rev. 939 (1986), at 951.

76. Infra note 21.

77. See 18 U. Mich. J.L. Ref. 4 (Summer 1985).

78. See Chapter 2.

79. See section 1.3.

80. See section 1.4.

81. See 18 J.L. Ref. (Summer 1985), at 908.

82. See Chapter 5.

83. 106 Mich. App. 169, 307 N.W.2d 438 (1981).

84. 704 S.W.2d 209 (Ky., 1986).

85. 410 U.S. 113 (1973).

86. See section 7.4.

87. See 6 Whittier L. Rev. 789 (1984), at 794–97.

88. 169 N.W.2d 308 (Mich., 1986).

89. See 44 La. L. Rev. (1984), at 1655.

90. (December 5, 1987), at 35.

91. See generally Freed and Brandes, "Surrogate Parenting: Alternative Reproductive Techniques," N.Y.L.J. (March 30, 1989), 3, 7, 28.

92. See Note, 21 Fam. L.Q. 534 (Winter 1988).

93. See N.Y.L.J. (February 5, 1988), at 1.

94. Note, 15 Fam. L. Rev. 1023 (1989).

95. Infra note 91.

96. See Warren Freedman, *Society on Trial: Current Court Decisions and Social Change* (1965), at 77–78.

97. See 1987 Utah L. Rev. 1 (1987), at 12.

98. See 21 Ariz. L. Rev. 755 (1979) and 69 Va. L. Rev. 465 (1986).

99. Unreported—FRD—(D.C., January 30, 1989).

100. See *New York Times* (May 17, 1989), at A20.

101. See Andrews, "The Stock Market: The Law of the New Reproductive Techniques," 70 A.B.A.J. 50 (August, 1984), at 56

102. See Chapter 3.

103. See 69 Va. L. Rev. 465 (1986), at 489. Note Goodright v. Moss, 98 Eng. Rep. 1257 (K.B. 1777), the old English case precluding bastardy.

104. 9A U.L.A. 588 (1979); also, see Section 10. 2.

105. Section 10 of the act, 9A U.L.A. 66–601.

106. See Chapter 2.

107. 469 Pa. 141, 364 A.2d 1307 (1976).

108. See 69 Va. L. Rev. 465 (1986), at 490–91.

109. 242 N.Y.S.2d 406 (1963).

110. See section 4.4.

111. Infra note 178, at 493.

112. See 4 Harv. Women's L.J. 1 (1981).

113. 405 U.S. 645 (1972).

114. See sections 1.3 and 1.4.

115. See Sherman, *Banks for Frozen Human Semen: Current Status and Prospects in the Integrity of Frozen Spermatozoa* (1980).

116. N.Y.C. Health Code Article 21 (1959).

117. See Frankel, "Human-Semen Banking: Social and Public Policy Issues," 1 Man Med. 289 (Summer 1976).

118. Unreported—N.Y.S.2d—(Civil Ct., N.Y. County, May 25, 1989).

119. See Frankel, "Human-Semen Banking: Implications for Medicine and Society," 39 Conn. Med. 313 (May 1975).

120. See Mohr, Trounson, and Freeman, "Deep-Freezing and Transfer of Human Embryos," 2 J. In Vitro Fert. & E.T. 1 (1986); also infra note 75, at 950.

121. See 42 Fertility & Sterility 184 (1984); also 18 J.L. Ref. 872 (Summer 1985). Also see 247 J.A.M.A. 3235 (1982).

122. Id. at A10. Note that the world's first frozen embryo was in February 1985 when a Melbourne, Australia, woman delivered twins.

123. See Friedrich, "A Legal, Moral, Social Nightmare," *Time* (September 10, 1984), at 54; and also infra note 750 at 1081 fn. 13.

124. Unreported—S.E2d—(Tennessee, Dkt. E 14496, Blount County, September 22, 1989).

125. See *Hartford Courant* (September 22, 1989), at A4.

126. See *New York Times* (September 22, 1989), at A13; also see ibid. (April 22, 1989), at 1, 8.

127. See *New York Newsday* (August 6, 1989), at A3.

128. Unreported—F. Supp.—(Va., Dkt. 89–373-N, 1989).

129. See *Time* (July 24, 1989), at 63; also ibid. (March 27, 1989), at 42.

130. See Sherman, "Just Whose Embryo Is It, Anyway," N.L.J. (June 12, 1989), at 1, 22, 23.

131. 202 Cal. App. 3d 1230 (1988).

132. Infra note 130, at 23. See also Curriden, "Frozen Embryos, the New Frontier," A.B.A.J. (August 1989), at 68–72.

133. See Warren Freedman, *The Right of Privacy in the Computer Age* (1987).

134. 381 U.S. 479 (1965).

135. 410 U.S. 113 (1973).

136. Infra note 97 at 16. See Webster v. Reproductive Health Services, 109 U.S. 3040 (1989).

137. 462 U.S. 416 (1983), at 427. The Florida Supreme Court in In re T.W., unreported Dkt. 74, 143,—So.2d—(October 5, 1989), invalidated a Florida statute requiring parental consent for the abortion of an unmarried minor on the grounds that the statute violated the right of privacy provisions of the Florida Constitution. The parental consent statute had provided for a judicial bypass.

138. 431 U.S. 678 (1977), at 685.

139. Infra note 66.

140. See Surrogate Parenting Associates, Inc. v. Kentucky, 704 S.W.2d 209 (Ky., 1986).

141. Id. at 212.

142. See generally 1 Berk. Women's L.J. (1986), at 147, and 4 Harv. Women's L.J. 1 (1981), at 39.

143. 431 U.S. 494 (1977), at 506.

144. 428 U.S. 56 (1977), at 74. See 17 Colum. J.L. & Soc. Probs. 287 (1982), at 300.

145. See Dronenburg v. Zech, 741 F.2d 1388 (D.C. Cir., 1984), for example.

146. 106 S. Ct. 2841 (1986).

147. See *New York Times* (July 1, 1986), at 1, A19.

148. The case, a civil suit challenging the Georgia sodomy law, was brought by Hardwick, a homosexual who had been arrested in his Atlanta bedroom while having sexual relations with another man. The Georgia law defined sodomy as "any sex act involving the sex organs of one person and the mouth or anus of another."

149. Infra note 147, at A19.

150. Id.

151. For lower court opinion that was reversed, see 760 F.2d 1211 (11th Cir., 1985).

152. See Note, 100 Harv. L. Rev. 120 (1986), at 213–14.

153. 106 S. Ct. 2841 (1986).

154. Infra note 152 at 216: "The Court in *Hardwick* reconceptualized the right of privacy, choosing to characterize it as protecting decisions or conduct involved in only certain areas of private life—marriage, family, and procreation. In the Court's view, homosexual sodomy bears no relation to these categories, and therefore, its protection within the right to privacy is not required by precedent. In its earlier decisions, however, the Court had generally characterized the privacy right as a right of individuals in intimate association to decide important matters fundamentally affecting their lives and their relationships. . . . The Court in *Hardwick* thus rejected the underlying rationale of its earlier cases in favor of a formalistic approach: listing previously protected rights and concluding that the one claimed does not closely resemble those acknowledged rights.

A more sound approach would have focused on the personal, decisional aspects of the right claimed by Hardwick, thereby promoting the values of individual autonomy and freedom of choice. The essence of a privacy right that protects personal decisions is its protection of the right of individuals to define their own identities.''

155. Note Rule 205.04 of the Uniform Rules for the Family Court, Office of Court Administration, eff. January 1, 1986.

156. See Section 341.1 of the New York Family Court Act.

157. See generally Warren Freedman, *Press and Media Access to the Criminal Courtroom* (1988).

158. See generally Warren Freedman, *The Constitutional Right to a Speedy and Fair Trial* (1988).

159. 359 So.2d 586 (La., 1979), at 594–97.

160. See RLR v. State of Alaska, 487 P.2d 27 (Alas., 1971).

161. See Gavison, ''Should We Have a General Right of Privacy in Israel?'' 12 Israel L. Rev. 155–71 (1972).

162. See Rakover, *The Protection of Privacy in Jewish Law* (1970). See also 15 Israel L. Rev. 49 (1980).

163. Prince v. Massachusetts, 321 U.S. 158 (1944).

164. Id.

165. See 22 San Diego L. Rev. 1193 (1985), pointing out at 1201 that no state statute requires genetic screening of a sperm donor, for example.

166. See Chakrabarty v. United States, 447 U.S. 303 (1980).

167. See 44 La. L. Rev. (1984), at 1675.

168. See *Insight* (July 11, 1988), at 8 et seq.

2

Artificial Insemination: Its Role in the Scheme of Reproduction

2.1 HISTORICAL BACKGROUND

William Shakespeare in the *Merchant of Venice* opined, "It is a wise father that knows his own child." Artificial insemination (AI) may very well have been in the mind of the great Englishman who discerned a problem of filial identification when artificial means are introduced into the reproductive cycle. Artificial insemination is an ancient reproductive technique. As long ago as 222 A.D., according to one Talmudic document, a rabbi discussed the hypothetical status of a woman who unknowingly became impregnated by semen previously deposited in her bathing water. The rabbi concluded that she could not be blamed for giving birth, assuming that the semen had been satisfactorily preserved.[1] The first intentional act of donor insemination on record occurred in 1322 when warring Arab tribes stole into enemy camps and inseminated well-bred mares with semen from inferior stallions. In the sixteenth century, one Eustachius was reported to have performed an artificial insemination.[2] In 1799 artificial insemination was part and parcel of the practice of Dr. John Hunter in England, and Dr. J. Marion Sims of South Carolina performed the first AI operation in the United States in 1866. It was Dr. Sims who set the professional pattern for later generations of physicians by keeping separate the confidences of the semen donor and the patient-recipient.[3]

AI is an old reproductive technique (in contrast to the modern reproductive techniques described in Chapter 1). Under AI the woman visits her physician when she is about to ovulate. The physician introduces sperm into her vagina using a syringe that injects the sperm near the cervix or by inserting the sperm into a diaphragmlike cervical cap that the woman will wear for next four to six hours to achieve fertilization of the egg.[4] It is estimated that this procedure is the reproductive mode by which more than 250,000 Americans alive in 1980 had been conceived.[5]

One current variation on the artificial theme involves the lesbian family relationship, as portrayed in the *New York Post* (August 7, 1987):

> Consider the scene: a quiet Sunday as the nation sits becalmed before the television. Suddenly there appears on screen a chirrupy woman explaining the best way to pack sperm. Sperm is best packed, it seems, in a marinated artichoke jar—or a baby food jar. (A jar with a wide neck is the idea, should you be preparing to do your own sperm packing.) Next, you cover the jars with something nice and warming, our informant trills, "like a sock." . . . The above-noted woman—and sperm—appeared in "Lesbian Mothers," part of Public Television's Independent Focus film series. In it, we met as well a woman in a maternity dress who held hands with her lesbian partner while explaining earnestly, "how we got pregnant.". . . For the women appearing in this film had all been artificially inseminated: at home, since the male-dominated medical institutions are naturally not to be trusted. . . . One lesbian tells how during pregnancy she and her lover enrolled in a childbirth course. Which was, alas, run by a teacher who simply could not seem to grasp that one of the couples he was preparing for childbirth consisted of two women."[6]

AI had found another "family" relationship for its utilization against the infertile "marriage."

According to the U.S. Congressional Office of Technology Assessment in 1988, more than 172,000 women resorted to artificial insemination in 1987, and about 65,000 babies that year were born from this technique. Congressional concern centered about the potential transmission of infectious and hereditary diseases.[7]

In the Jewish religion, the child born of AI is legitimate, and there is no adultery or incest if there is no bodily contact between a man and a woman, according to the Talmud in reference to Leviticus 21:13–14. Indeed, according to Deuteronomy 23:3, only the child of an adulterous or incestuous relationship is illegitimate.

2.2 GENOTYPES OF THE CHILD

Modern reproductive techniques[8] embrace not only artificial insemination but in vitro fertilization, cryopreservation, prenatal diagnosis, elective abortion, and surrogate motherhood.[9]

In AI there are three genotypes, or three sources, from which the seminal fluid can be drawn: (1) AID (artificial insemination donor or artificial insemination heterologous), that is, the sperm is donated by a third person or donor; (2) AIH (artificial insemination homologous), that is, the sperm is donated by the husband; and (3) CAI (combined artificial insemination), that is, the sperm of the donor and the sperm of the husband are mixed together. The most frequently utilized procedure is AID, legalized in about twenty-nine states,[10] making the child born to the woman the legitimate child of her and her husband[11] However, in Grusky v. Gursky, the New York court held that the child who was the offspring of AID with the consent of the mother's husband was still not the legitimate child of the husband and that AID constituted adultery.[12] In 1974 the New York law was clarified by a statute dealing with the legitimacy of children born by artificial insemination[13] The New York statute provides that any child born to a married woman by means of artificial insemination, performed by persons duly authorized to practice medicine and with the written consent of the woman and her husband, shall be deemed the legitimate natural child of the husband and wife for all purposes. Note that the Uniform Parentage Act does create a presumption that the semen donor is not to be considered the biological father of the child:

§5 (Artificial Insemination)

(a) If, under the supervision of a licensed physician and with the consent of her husband, a wife is inseminated artificially with the semen donated by a man not her husband, the husband is treated in law as if he were the natural father of a child thereby conceived. The husband's consent must be in writing and signed by him and his wife. The physician shall certify their signatures and the date of the insemination, and file the husband's consent with the [State Department of Health], where it shall be kept confidential and in a sealed file. However, the physician's failure to do so does not affect the father and child relationship. All papers and records pertaining to the insemination whether part of the permanent record of a court or of a file held by the supervising physician or elsewhere, are subject to inspection only upon an order of the court for good cause shown.

(b) The donor of semen provided to a licensed physician for use in artificial insemination of a married woman other than the donor's wife is treated in law as if he were not the natural father of a child thereby conceived.[14]

The Uniform Parentage Act has been enacted in eight states: California, Colorado, Minnesota, Montana, Nevada, New Jersey, Washington, and Wyoming. AID is most useful where the wife is fertile and the husband is sterile or has cacogenic hereditary characters. Biologically, the child born of AID is not related to the husband, and therefore AID can be threatened with the wrath of the law. The procedure or technique was actually held adulterous in 1921 in the Canadian case of Orford v. Orford,[15] and in a 1948 Illinois decision, AID was also ruled adulterous and the husband was granted a divorce.[16] There are, however, limitations on the granting of a divorce for adultery in the AID situation, and these limitations can be interpreted favorably to AID, that is, where a husband's consent to the adulterous procedure vitiates adultery as a ground for divorce.[17]

In the 1948 New York case of Strnad v. Strnad, the wife suing for divorce admitted that her child was the product of AID.[18] She requested the court to preclude her husband from visitation rights over the child. But the court ruled that the child was the son of the father and the father's rights of visitation could not be denied. Ten years later, another New York court, in Matter of Abajian, refused to disturb the visitation rights of the husband because the children were conceived by AID:

To stigmatize them as children of an unknown father by means of artificial insemination of the mother is no more . . . than an attempt to make these innocents out as children of bastardy. And when a parent attempts such means, the law will still the lips of such a parent. This will be done even where artificial insemination is unlawful, for, on the last turn, it is the children who, when so revealed, must go through life in such obfuscation. For now, however, the respondent's wife's thrust at law, bluntly returned, may only serve to boomerang the conscience, since, regardless of the verity of respondent wife's claim in this respect . . . [she cannot be permitted] to litigate the attempted issue.[19]

But in 1956 in the Illinois case of Doornbos v. Doornbos, the court took a step backward when it held that AID "with or without the consent of the husband is contrary to public policy and good morals, and constitutes adultery on the part of the mother. A child so conceived is not a child born in wedlock and therefore is illegitimate. As such it is the child of the mother, and the father has no right nor interest (such as visitation) in said child."[20] The Illinois court, however, did indicate that AIH was "not contrary to public policy and good morals." A 1963 New York decision had echoed the same outmoded and distressing conclusion by holding that the child of AID was illegitimate under section 512 of the New York Family Court Act, defining a child born out of wedlock as "a child begotten and born out of lawful matrimony," even though here the husband had consented to the AID procedure.[21] However, the court refused to allow the husband to be "free of his obligation to furnish support for the child. . . . The husband's declaration and conduct . . . implied a promise on his part to furnish support for any offspring resulting from the artificial insemination."

Proponents of AID today point to several factors making it superior to adoption of children: the absence of any threat that the biological mother will return and claim her child; the fact that the child is biologically related to one of the parents; the outward appearance that the husband has successfully impregnated his wife; the parents' ability to experience pregnancy and birth of the child; and the child's physical resemblance to the parents.[22] There is also the underlying reason of overcoming the fear of transmitting a known genetic disease to the child.[23] Additionally, AID is used increasingly to provide a natural offspring to unmarried women and to women in a lesbian relationship.[24]

AIH poses fewer legal problems because the married woman is impregnated with the semen of her husband when normal copulation fails, perhaps due to various medical problems.[25] The child conceived through AIH is indeed the biological offspring of both the woman and her husband.

CAI enables a married woman to be artificially inseminated with a mixture of her husband's and a donor's sperm. The psychological advantage is that the husband can take the position that his sperm actually fertilized his wife's ovum.

AI is usually delineated in terms of utilization by married women, but there is increasing use of AI by unmarried women, although it would appear that a vast majority of physicians who perform AI may refuse to do so for unmarried women.[26] The lesbian "family" is a frequent recipient of the AI experience, notwithstanding.

2.3 DONOR SCREENING

AI must be concerned with donor screening. Since considerable AI takes place without physician intervention, the need of donor screening is all the more important.[27] Generally, when a woman approaches a physician or even a sperm bank, she is assured that the sperm donors are carefully screened by medical personnel. Indeed, physicians and sperm banks will be found negligent if it can be demonstrated that their actions fell below the required standards of care and these deviations were responsible for the disease or injury. These professionals are more likely to be concerned with the safety of the donated semen than with the efficacy of the donated semen. The possibility of transmitting infectious or genetic diseases by AI undoubtedly leads to careful scrutiny of screening procedures.

Courts consider the costs of screening tests, the scientific state of the art equipment, and the expected frequency of a disease trait in any particular donor population (such as testing black donors for sickle cell anemia). Another factor is blood compatibility; a sperm recipient might contract hepatitis as a result of insemination when the donor's blood was an Rh type incompatible with that of the recipient. The American Medical Association (AMA) in 1974 declared that "selecting and screening donors to control the transmission of infectious and genetic diseases insofar as current knowledge permits is ethically required."[28] It recommended obtaining a detailed and reliable medical and genetic history of the donor and his family. In the case of sperm banks[29] (which also pay for sperm from medical students), there has been an unwarranted tendency to expect medical students to screen themselves because of their knowledge of diseases and their symptoms.[30] But too frequently donor ignorance or the potential for financial motivation tends to decrease the thoroughness of self-evaluation.[31]

The quality of reproductive technology is a concern of the American Fertility Society, which in 1984 adopted minimum professional standards for training and experience on the part of practitioners.[32] The Reproductive Council of the AATB[33] also developed extensive guidelines for the proper screening of donors on the basis of a "personal, physical and genetic examination and history of individuals as well as an in-depth semen analysis which includes microbial screening."[34] Each sperm sample from the donor must be tested for gonorrhea with periodic analysis of the donor's blood for syphilis and hepatitis. AATB guidelines mandate rejection of a potential sperm donor if he is a carrier of any of nineteen specified disorders, if his risk of producing a child with a genetic defect is greater than 1 percent, if he is employed in a job involving chemical or radiation exposure, or if he is an alcohol or drug abuser.

One great difficulty even with donor screening is when the sperm donor subsequently seeks to be the legal father, as illustrated in In Interest of R.C.[35] Here the Colorado statute extinguished the rights of semen donors with respect to children conceived by artificial insemination, but the Colorado Supreme Court held that the statute was not applicable to the parental rights of a known semen donor who had agreed with the unmarried mother to be treated as the natural father of the child conceived.[36] The evidence revealed that the semen donor had set up a nursery in his house and had also established a college trust fund for the child. Thus, the preconception intent of the parties was relevant to the determination of parental rights.

In Los Angeles, a sperm donor was identified as the father of forty children.[37] This slender, blue-eyed, blond, age 39, living in northern California, had made many donations to a local sperm bank (about 300 between 1976 and 1984), for which he was paid almost $10,000. He then married and had children of his own. The story includes an interview with a psychologist who contends that a man should not donate sperm for more than three children, or about twenty-four donations, so as to avoid "such possibilities as unwitting incest in a small or even large town."[38] Another psychologist takes the position that the semen donor "should be known to the offspring. . . . No one considers the lifelong effect donor insemination will have on the feelings of the donor offspring. We're hearing about sperm banks rethinking their positions supporting anonymity. In Australia, Sweden, New Zealand, and England, for instance, all donors must now be registered and must be able to be known when necessary."[39]

2.4 INFORMED CONSENT

The highly emotional circumstances that accompany the experience of infertility and the distinct possibility of transmitting serious infectious and genetic diseases make it imperative that the informed consent of all parties to AI be obtained. Even the sperm donor's wife must be made a party to the informed consent procedure. Full disclosure of all known risks to the parties and to the prospective progeny is a prerequisite. It must be made clear that neither conception nor a "perfect" child can be guaranteed.

A physician's failure to inform and obtain informed consent about possible genetic defects that are at risk resulted in a successful malpractice suit in Becker v. Schwartz.[40] The highest New York court pointed out that the physician had not informed the couple of the type of testing that is available to determine if their fetus would be adversely affected. In Werth and Werth v. Nosenchuck, the Michigan court jury awarded a couple against their physician the costs of rearing the child until his eighteenth birthday, as well as damages for mental anguish, because the physician had given them insufficient information about the possibility of detecting Down's syndrome by amniocentesis, thereby depriving the couple of information needed to give informed consent to the AI procedure.[41]

In 1974 the U.S. Department of Health, Education and Welfare issued ''Protection of Human Subjects,''[42] detailing the elements of informed consent: (1) a fair explanation of the procedures to be followed and their purposes; (2) a description of any attendant discomforts and risks reasonably to be expected; (3) a description of any benefits reasonably to be expected; (4) disclosure of any appropriate alternative procedures that might be advantageous for the subject (such as information on the availability and higher success rate of fresh versus frozen semen); (5) an offer to answer all questions; (6) instruction that the person is free to withdraw his or her consent and discontinue participation at any time without prejudice to the subject; and (7) an explanation as to whether compensation and medical treatment are available if physical injury occurs and if so what it consists of.[43]

2.5 LEGITIMACY OF AI CHILDREN

The legitimacy of AI children is an issue that courts have grappled with over the years.[44] Notwithstanding the married status of the mother, some courts have held that a child born of AI is illegitimate. California has by statute made the AI child legitimate,[45] as has the Uniform Parentage Act.[46] Indeed, the U.S. Supreme Court has acted to establish, protect, and strengthen family life by invalidating as irrational and unjust laws that deny equal protection of the laws to illegitimate children.[47]

The California statute also forecloses any legal rights the illegitimate AI child may have against his biological father.[48] Similarly, an Oregon statute[49] states that the donor has no right, obligation, or interest with respect to a child born as a result of AI and that such a child has no right, obligation, or interest with respect to such donor.[50]; However, in Syrkowski v. Appleyard, the Michigan Supreme Court gave the sperm donor an opportunity for an order of filiation, declaring that his paternity of a child conceived by AI gave him such right.[51]

2.6 THE BIOLOGICAL PARENTAL RELATIONSHIP

Biology is said to control the allocation of parental rights and responsibilities, such as sharing the exclusive legal rights and obligations of support and rearing of children. But the biological model fails to accommodate changing social patterns, such as the unmarried mother and the lesbian family relationship.[52] Furthermore, such entrenched institutions as adoption services, foster families, and stepfamilies belie the notion that biology should control. Perhaps 25 percent of American children today are not living with both natural, biological parents. The Uniform Parentage Act has made the husband of the married woman and not the semen donor in AI the ''natural father of a child conceived thereby.''[53] This fiction is apparently consistent with the notion of the modern biological parent relationship.

In Scarpetta v. Spence-Chapin Adoption Service, the New York Court of

Appeals held that in the context of the creation of adoptive families, the biological parent retains for a time a legally cognizable interest in the child's placement.[54] Potential foster and adoptive parents appear to have no protectable interest in obtaining a child, that is, no constitutional right to become a foster or an adoptive parent.[55] Laws that require consent to the adoption of a newborn infant by the unwed mother but not by the unwed father are unconstitutional, according to the U.S. Supreme Court in Caban v. Mohammed.[56] The biological parentage must be respected. Some states require official notice to a court or governmental agency of the birth of a child conceived through AI.[57] The biological parent relationship continues to be the key to parenthood and all the accompanying rights and claims.

''Private ordering'' (a private contract between the parties) has somewhat altered that biological parent relationship.[58] The intent of the parties to the private contract should be controlling.[59] The parties should determine for themselves the allocation of parental rights and responsibilities for the resulting child. The caveat is that the private ordering must not violate public policy or any laws of the state. However, private arrangements concerning child-rearing and support obligations, for example, might not be upheld by the courts.[60] In Michigan, courts have denied private ordering where it violates public policy to allow payment for placement of children.[61]

2.7 REGULATION BY THE MEDICAL PROFESSION

It has been suggested that all forms of AI should be regulated by the medical profession itself. This would entail special legislation on the state level making it illegal to perform AI without the supervision of a licensed physician.[62] The same legislation might also state that the sperm donor would be deemed the legal father unless the donation was made to a licensed physician. Such legal complication would, it is argued, make the parties to the AI procedure more likely to resort to physician control. Regulation by the medical profession would ensure effective medical screening to protect the health and safety of the parties; genetic screening protecting the health of the child and precluding infectious diseases from both mother and child would also be ensured.

But donor insemination is not a complicated or complex medical procedure requiring medical expertise for its safe accomplishment. Once the sperm donor is located, the logistics of insemination are relatively easy; even a ''do-it-yourself'' kit may be available to guide the parties. Records of the identity and of the medical history of the sperm donor could be maintained, and these records could subsequently be made available to the child.[63] However, record keeping itself might discourage sperm donors, who generally seek anonymity. The problem persists whether or not the procedure is medically supervised.

Regulation by the medical profession might have the effect of placing too broad an authority in the hands of licensed physicians to restrict AI to perhaps married women and to bar such procedures for, say, unmarried women, low-income women, or lesbians[64] And professional medical standards for handling eggs, embryos, sperm donations, and other medical essentials have not yet been promulgated, so professional efforts at quality assurance have not yet resulted.[65]

2.8 STATE LAWS ON ARTIFICIAL INSEMINATION

Although no state has enacted a statute designed specifically to deal with the complex family law implications of AI,[66] more than half of the states have adopted some form of legislation dealing with donor insemination.[67] Georgia, Idaho, and Oregon have imposed criminal penalties for performing donor insemination without the supervision of a licensed physician.[68] Perhaps fourteen states delineate the involvement of a licensed physician in AI but do not prescribe criminal penalties where the procedure occurs without licensed physician involvement.[69] AI is encouraged by those state statutes that make the donor of the sperm not the legal father of the child unless the recipient of the sperm is the donor's wife.[70] In California "the donor of semen . . . to a licensed physician for use in artificial insemination of a woman other than the donor's wife is treated in law as if he were not the natural father of a child."[71] And in Connecticut, "a donor of sperm used in A.I.D. or any person claiming by or through him, shall not have any right or interest in any child born as a result of A.I.D."[72] Perhaps as many as eight states explicitly relieve the sperm donor of obligations to the child[73] The practical consequence is that sperm donors are more willing to donate sperm, even to single women, since the donors are protected from future liability for child support.

Probably the first AID statute was adopted in 1964 by Georgia.[74] The thrust of the legislation was to make the child born of AI "irrebuttably presumed legitimate." But only a physician licensed by the state was legally authorized to perform AID in Georgia; anyone else performing the procedure was guilty of a felony punishable by one to five years' imprisonment. The licensed physician performing the AID, having secured the written consent of the woman and her husband, is relieved from civil liability to them or to any child so conceived, except where negligence of the physician can be proved.[75] In Texas, the issue of the legitimacy of children born of AID was addressed by the requisite that the husband of the mother must have given written and notarized consent to the procedure.[76] In Louisiana, an onerous burden of proof is placed upon the child: "A child not entitled to legitimate filiation nor filiated by the initiative of the parent by legitimization or by acknowledgement . . . must prove filiation as to an alleged living parent by a preponderance of the evidence in a civil proceeding instituted by the child or on his behalf within the time limit provided."[77] In Succession of Levy the Louisiana appellate court permitted a child to prove filiation to his biological father even though the legal husband of the mother had not disavowed the child.[78] The result dealt a blow to the anonymity of the sperm donor in Louisiana.[79]

In New Jersey, a mother artificially inseminated herself with plaintiff's sperm by using a glass jar and a glass syringe. When the biological father sought visitation rights, the court in C.M. v. C.C.[80] granted his petition, and in a later action the same court mandated that the mother cooperate in changing the child's birth certificate, which had listed the father as "unknown."[81] Again, the thrust of the judicial approach was the legitimization of the child, despite the fact that no licensed physician was involved in the AID procedure.

Public policy may bar enforcement of an AI contract, as illustrated in Perry v. Atkinson.[82] Here the defendant, a married man, took plaintiff as his mistress, and she became pregnant. Plaintiff wanted to have the baby, but the defendant urged her to abort, promising that he would subsequently use AI to conceive a child with her. Plaintiff had the abortion, but defendant refused to keep his promise, which caused her to undergo extensive psychiatric treatment and to stop working temporarily. She sued for intentional infliction of emotional distress and for fraud. The California trial court granted defendant's motion for summary judgment on the claim of fraud, and the emotional distress claim was settled for $250,000. On her appeal, the California appellate court echoed the public policy argument that prevents enforcement of a contract like the promise to have an AI child. According to the court, the government cannot intercede in intimate relationships, which are cloaked in privacy matters; and second, California statutes specifically exclude suits for fraudulent failures to fulfill matrimonial functions. Indeed, if a married person is precluded from bringing the action, then a mistress is also precluded.

The Uniform Parentage Act[83] was promulgated in 1973 to establish the rights of illegitimate and legitimate children on equal terms and also to identify the person against whom these rights may be asserted.[84] The act defines the parent-child relationship in terms of a relationship that disregards the parents' marital status, although it provides for rebuttable presumptions of parentage.[85] The act sets forth the procedures for bringing a parentage suit under sections 6–24. Under section 5 of the act, the husband "is treated in law as if he were the natural father of a child conceived" if the husband and wife had consented in writing to have the wife artificially inseminated by a donor and if the insemination is performed by a licensed physician. This consent form must be filed with the State Department of Health and kept in a sealed file. The sperm donor who donates for a married woman other than his wife is deemed not to be the natural father of the child so conceived. Fewer than ten states have adopted the Uniform Parentage Act,[86] and California, Colorado, Washington, and Wyoming have declared that the donor is not the child's natural father, regardless of whether the donee is married or single.[87] Hawaii, North Dakota, and Ohio have passed versions of the act without any provision concerning AI, and the result is utter confusion, frustration of the parties' intentions, and open conflict with public policy.[88] The Washington version of the act permits the donor and the woman to "agree in writing that said donor shall be the father," which in effect authorizes the parties to change the rules by contract and complicate the matter of parentage.[89]

The selection of donors is apparently regulated by statute only in Oregon.[90] The Oregon statute requires that a licensed physician select the donor and that the donor must not offer his sperm for AI if he knows or should have known that he has a transmissible genetic defect or venereal disease.[91] Only New York City has a similar regulatory scheme in requiring the sperm donor to be tested for gonorrhea and in mandating a blood test to be performed to ensure Rh compatibility with the recipient of the sperm.[92] The ordinance also prohibits the use of sperm from a donor who has any other venereal disease or known genetic defect. There is a mandatory record keeping of the names and addresses of the parties and the results of the donor's physical examination, all to be kept in a confidential file.

2.9 FETAL RESEARCH

Fetal research has been restricted by many states intent upon observing religious, social, and economic shibboleths. At least half of the states have fetal research laws that prohibit nontherapeutic research with fetuses and embryos and also prohibit the use of experimental reproductive technologies.[93] Maine, Massachusetts, Michigan, North Dakota, Rhode Island, and Utah prohibit research involving living preimplantation embryos,[94] and such restrictive legislation undoubtedly precludes embryo cryopreservation,[95] for example. Research with embryos is essential to further progress in IVF and other forms of infertility treatment.[96] Indeed, such research could provide useful knowledge about birth defects, cancer, and a wide range of other health problems.[97] However, some state statutes have been construed as not restricting IVF or ET research or procedures,[98] on the ground that such research occurs prior to implantation of a fertilized ovum in the uterus and therefore prior to the creation of a fetus.[99] This view is perhaps supported by federal guidelines for fetal research that define *fetus* as "the product of conception from the time of implantation."[100]

Justification for limitations or restrictions on fetal research is found in society's attitude toward human life and society's respect for human dignity. Certain manipulations or changes may seem offensive since these manipulations or changes are done to living human cells that have the potential to become a person.[101] Limiting research maneuvering, it is argued, may be a meaningful way of demonstrating respect for human life. On the other hand, research limitations could arguably interfere with a fundamental right to procreate, although the U.S. Supreme Court in its 1976 decision in Maher v. Roe[102] did uphold a state's interest in prenatal, postconception life during the first two trimesters of pregnancy.[103]

Fetal research was dealt a severe blow by a 1979 Illinois statute[104] that stated that a physician who fertilized a woman's egg outside her body "shall with regard to the human being thereby produced, be deemed to have the care and custody of a child" for purposes of the Illinois child abuse act.[105] The statute was repealed in 1985 because physicians were unwilling to offer IVF under a statute equating embryos to children.[106] Earlier, in the 1983 case of Smith v. Hartigan,[107] the Illinois attorney general had agreed not to prosecute physicians conducting IVF if the physician did not willfully harm the embryo through abuse, mutilation, extermination, or destructive laboratory experimentation.[107] But the fear of prosecution still prevailed, and Illinois physicians did not conduct IVF. The 1985 repeal of the 1979 statute still forbade embryo research except for IVF procedures, which probably did not include embryo cryopreservation or embryo lavage after in vivo fertilization, techniques essential to continued research.

One aspect of fetal research has brought forth intense criticism: ''the selling of body parts'' in order to treat others' illnesses.[108] But many bioethicists, physicians, and attorneys favor the use of fetal remains, for example, to save the lives of others as consistent with societal values and constitutional laws. Fetal tissue can be derived from either spontaneous or induced abortions, and both are legal:

> Most current experimental therapies involve transplanting cells directly into adults from fetuses that have been aborted, either spontaneously or voluntarily. In vitro fertilization techniques create the possibility of breeding embryos in petri dishes so their cells can be used for research and therapy.
>
> But scientists may be able to avoid the highly charged question as to whether it is permissible to create human embryos just to destroy them. Already, they have developed the capacity to clone, or endlessly reproduce, certain fetal cells in a laboratory in immortal ''cell lines.''[109]

The U.S. Supreme Court in 1980 in Diamond v. Chakrabarty ruled that products of genetic engineering could be protected by patent, thus encouraging fetal research.[110]

2.10 LITIGATION AND ARTIFICIAL INSEMINATION

Litigation in the AI field has been minimal in the United States, although in Canada in 1921, Orford v. Orford was decided.[111] The Ontario court was faced with a suit for divorce in which the wife underwent AI in England without her husband's consent or knowledge. The court granted a divorce based on its determination that she had committed adultery—''not in the moral turpitude of the act of sexual intercourse, but in the voluntary surrender to another person of the reproductive powers or faculties of the guilty person; and any submission of those powers to the service or enjoyment of any person other than the husband or the wife comes within the definition of 'adultery'. Sexual intercourse is adulterous because in the case of the woman, it involves the possibility of introducing into the family of the husband a false strain of blood.''[112] This court decision is not consonant with subsequent scientific refinements and with changes in mores involving the infertility.[113]

The earliest court decision on AI in the United States was probably in 1945 in Hoch v. Hoch, where the husband sued his wife for divorce alleging her adultery because she had submitted to AID.[114] The evidence indicated that the wife had numerous male friends and that the husband was a World War II veteran. The Illinois court readily granted the soldier-husband his requested divorce. Three years later in 1948 in New York, Strnad v. Strnad dealt with the husband's visitation rights to a child conceived by AI during marriage and with the husband's consent.[115] It was the husband who sought a divorce alleging his wife's adultery; the wife argued that the child conceived was not her husband's and therefore he should be denied visitation rights. But the New York court, in granting the divorce, approved visitation rights for the husband because the child conceived by AID was still the son of the legal father, and the legal father had in fact consented to the procedure. The New York court spoke in terms of the fact that "the child has been potentially adopted or semi-adopted," and therefore the child was the legitimate offspring of the mother and the legal father.

Historically, the next decision was Ohlson v. Ohlson,[116] decided in 1954 in Illinois. Here AI was performed, but the performing physician could not conclusively state that the husband had not fathered the child, although there was little evidence of CAI.[117] Thus, the presumption of the child's legitimacy prompted the Illinois court to award the husband visitation rights; the child was deemed to have been born in wedlock. But in 1956 in Doornbos v. Doornbos, the Illinois Supreme Court opined that AID "with or without the consent of the husband is contrary to public policy and good morals, and constitutes adultery on the part of the mother. A child so conceived is not a child born in wedlock, and therefore is illegitimate. As such it is the child of the mother, and the father has no right nor interest (such as visitation) in said child."[118] Here the husband had consented to the AID procedure but failed to adopt the child in a legal proceeding. The court granted the wife's declaratory judgment that the husband was not in fact the child's father and had no right to the child. In dicta, the court stated that the AIH process, however, was "not contrary to public policy and good morals."[119]

The next historical divorce and visitation rights case was in 1958 in People ex rel. Abajian v. Bennett, decided in New York.[120] The visitation rights of the husband were not disturbed despite the divorced wife's utterance that both children were born to her as a result of AI. The New York court was primarily concerned about the welfare of the children:

> To stigmatize them as children of an unknown father by means of artificial insemination of the mother is no more . . . than an attempt to make these innocents out as children of bastardy. And where a parent attempts such means, the law will still the lips of such a parent. This will be done even where artificial insemination is lawful, for, on the last turn, it is the children who, when so revealed, must go through life in such obfuscation. For now, however, the respondent wife's thrust at law, bluntly returned, may only serve to boomerang the conscience, since, regardless of the verity of respondent wife's claim in this respect . . . [she cannot be permitted] to litigate the attempted issue.

Thus, the husband won continuance of the visitation rights he had obtained in a Nevada divorce decree. The court concluded that the wife's previous conduct, such as granting the husband rights in the divorce decree, demonstrated a recognition of her husband's rights to the children. In essence, she was estopped from asserting that her husband was not the father of the children.[121]

Strnad v. Strnad[122] was partially overruled in 1963 by the same New York court in Gursky v. Gursky,[123] which was decided on estoppel grounds. Mr. Gursky had consented in writing to his wife's receiving the donor's sperm and had even agreed to pay the costs of the entire procedure. The birth certificate listed him as the father of the child so conceived. When he later sought a separation and was countersued for annulment by his wife, he contended that he was not the father of the child. He pointed out that the marriage was not consummated. The New York Court ruled that because he had consented to the AI, he was estopped from claiming a lack of liability for the child's support. Ironically, the court decided that the child was illegitimate because there was a failure to comply with the New York adoption statute: "The State Legislature has exercised its power to modify the concept of illegitimacy in certain respects. . . . The fact that it has not chosen to deal with the question of legitimacy as it relates to children begotten and born through heterologous artificial insemination (A.I.D.) must be deemed to manifest a disinclination to modify . . . a concept which must logically result only in a determination adverse to the legitimacy of a child begotten by a father other than the husband of the mother."[124] It should be noted that the wife had been granted an annulment of the marriage, but nevertheless "it does not follow that the husband is free of the obligation to furnish support for the child. . . . The husband's declaration and conduct . . . implied a promise on his part to furnish support for any offspring resulting from the insemination" The court admitted that it was "constrained to hold that the child of the defendant wife is not the legitimate issue of the husband." The "equitable estoppel" here applied against the husband was based on the contention that the wife had relied on the word and deed of the husband, who changed his position; also her reliance to her detriment on her husband's implied promise to support the child must be respected.[125]

The holding of illegitimacy of the child in Gursky v. Gursky[126] was overruled by the New York court in its 1973 decision in In re Adoption of Anonymous,[127] although in its 1964 decision in Anonymous v. Anonymous[128] the court had reiterated its position on the illegitimacy of the child conceived by AID, yet holding the consenting husband liable for child support. The 1973 decision meant that AID children are legitimate, and there is not need for parents to adopt formally such a child. Support for this change of judicial ruling was found in public policy favoring legitimacy of children. Here a divorce of the parents after the child was conceived by AI raised the important issue when the wife's second husband wanted to adopt that child but the first husband refused to consent to the adoption. The court rejected the wife's argument that her first husband was not the biological father or the legal father: "A child born of consensual A.I.D. during a valid marriage is a legitimate child entitled to the rights and privileges of a naturally conceived child of the same marriage."[129] The court concluded: "It serves no purpose whatsoever to stigmatize the A.I.D. child; or to compel the parents formally to adopt."

In California in 1968 in People v. Sorensen, the California Supreme Court faced an interesting situation: a woman, after obtaining her husband's written consent to AI, subsequently obtained a divorce and declined support payments under the divorce decree.[130] When she became ill and began receiving public support, the state sued her husband for support. The court held the husband liable for support because he was the lawful father, thereby preventing the "obvious injustice that would result were a child artificially conceived excluded from the protection of the law intended to benefit all minors, legitimate or illegitimate. . . . In the absence of legislation prohibiting artificial insemination, the offspring of defendant's valid marriage to the child's mother was lawfully begotten and was not the product of an illicit or adulterous relationship."[131]

In the New Jersey case of C.M. v. C.C., which dealt with donor insemination of an unmarried woman who inseminated herself with her boyfriend's semen, the court opined that the semen donor was the legal father of the child and entitled to visitation rights.[132] The court observed that the couple intended to marry and that the semen donor was willing to assume the responsibilities of a father, prior to the unfortunate falling out of the relationship. However, the child was deemed to be illegitimate because the parents had never married.

In 1981 in K.S. v. G.S., the New Jersey Superior Court concluded that the husband who consented to the AID procedure was the child's lawful father.[133] In a subsequent divorce action, the husband agreed that he orally consented to the first series of AI attempts but that he later tried to stop the AID treatments because of the cost when the first successful insemination resulted in a miscarriage. The court refused to permit him to avoid liability for the support of the child so conceived: "Public policy considerations seeking to prevent children born as a result of A.I.D. procedures from becoming public charges or being bastardized require that a presumption of consent exist and that a strong burden be placed on one seeking to rebut the presumption. . . . Consent of the husband, once given, is presumed to be effective at the time when pregnancy occurs, unless the husband establishes by clear and convincing evidence that such consent has been revoked or rescinded. Defendant has not met that burden."[134]

In the 1985 New York case of Karin T. v. Michael T., the New York Family Court observed that the lesbian defendant had signed her name on the birth certificates of two AID children as "father" and accordingly ruled that she could not later deny her intention to provide support for the children.[135] She had caused the children to come into being by consenting to the AI of the children's mother. The court defined "father" or "parent" as simply one who brings forth offspring.

NOTES

1. See Warren Freedman, *Society on Trial: Current Court Decisions and Social Change* (1965), at 78–79.

2. See 58 J. Urban L. 459 (1981), at 460, n. 12.

3. Infra note 1, at 79.

4. See Williams, ''Differential Treatment of Men and Women by Artificial Insemination,'' 21 Tulsa L.J. 463 (1986), and Kritchevsky, ''The Unmarried Woman's Right to Artificial Insemination,'' 4 Harv. Women's L.J. 1 (1981), at 1, n. 3.

5. See Koerner, ''Medicolegal Considerations in Artificial Insemination,'' 8 La. L. Rev. 484 (1948), and Finegold, *Artificial Insemination* 5–7 (2d ed., 1976).

6. Id. at 21.

7. See *Hartford Courant* (August 10, 1988), at A3.

8. See 58 Yale L.J. 547 (1949), at 460.

9. See herein sections 1.3, 1.9, 2.1, 5.1, 7.2, and 7.7. Also, ''Reproductive Technology and the Law: The Future of Human Reproduction,'' 5 J. Hum. Rts. 71–95 (1987).

10. Alabama, Alaska, Arkansas, California, Colorado, Connecticut, Florida, Georgia, Idaho, Illinois, Kansas, Louisiana, Maryland, Michigan, Montana, Nevada, New Jersey, New York, North Carolina, Oklahoma, Oregon, Tennessee, Texas, Virginia, Washington, Wisconsin, and Wyoming.

11. See Freed and Brandes, ''Surrogate Parenting: Alternative Reproductive Techniques,'' N.Y.L.J. (March 30, 1989) 1, 3, 7, 9.

12. 242 N.Y.S.2d 406 (Kings County, 1963).

13. See sec. 73 of New York Domestic Relations Law (L. 1974, ch. 303, sec. 1).

14. 9A ULA 592 (1979). See also Section 10.2.

15. 49 Ont. L.R. 15 (1921).

16. Unreported Illinois Circuit Court, Cook County (1948). See Doornbos v. Doornbos, 23 U.S.L.W. 2308 (Ill. Circuit Ct., Cook County, 1954).

17. See Matchin v. Matchin, 6 Pa. 332 (1847); also 58 Yale L.J. 457 (1949) at 462.

18. 78 N.Y.S2d 290 (1948).

19. 184 N.Y.S2d 178 (1958).

20. Infra note 16; aff'd 139 N.E.2d 844 (Ill., 1956).

21. See Gursky v. Gursky, 242 N.Y.S2d 406 (1963).

22. See Finegold, *Artificial Insemination* (1976) at 23.

23. See 22 San Diego L. Rev. 1193 (1985) at 1196.

24. See Kern, ''The Fourteenth Amendment's Protection of a Woman's Right to Be a Single Parent Through Artificial Insemination by Donor,'' 7 Women's Rts. L. Rep. 251 (1983).

25. See generally Corson and Batzer, ''Homologous Artificial Insemination,'' 26 J. Reprod. Med. 231 (1981).

26. See Note, ''Reproductive Technology and the Procreation Rights of the Unmarried,'' 98 Harv. L. Rev. 669 (1985) at 670–71.

27. For example, see the case of C.M. v. C.C., 152 N.J Super. 160, 377 A.2d 821 (1977).

28. See ''Human Artificial Insemination,'' Report to the Judicial Council of the AMA to the House of Delegates, adopted June 1974.

29. See Section 1.8 hereinbefore.

30. See generally Titmuss, *The Gift Relationship: From Human Blood to Social Policy* (1971).

31. See generally Fiumara, ''Transmission of Gonorrhea by Artificial Insemination,'' 48 Brit. J. Venereal Disease 308 (August 1972).

32. 41 Fertility and Sterility 13 (1984).

33. See AATB, "Reproductive Council Addendum," Standards for Tissue Banking 25–32 (1984).

34. Id. at 38.

35. 775 P.2d 27 (Dkt. 1989 WL 57955, Colo., June 5, 1989); also see 760 p. 2d 501 (Colo., 1989).

36. See *Insight* (July 3, 1989) at 62.

37. See *Hartford Courant* (June 15, 1989) at F1.

38. Id. at F3.

39. Id.

40. 46 N.Y.2d 401, 386 N.E.2d 807 (1978).

41. Unreported—N.W.2d—(Mich., 1979).

42. 39 Fed. Reg. 18914 (May 30, 1974).

43. Id., 39 Fed. Reg. at 18917, and 43 Fed. Reg. 51559 (November 3, 1978).

44. See generally "Artificial Insemination and the Law," 1982 B.Y.U.L Rev. 935 (1982) at 966–73.

45. Calif. Civ. Code § 7005 (1982).

46. 9A U.L.A. 581 (1979). See Section 10.2.

47. See Trimble v. Gordon, 430 U.S. 762 (1976).

48. Infra note 45 at sec. 7005(b).

49. Ore. Rev. Stat. 109.239 (1981).

50. See 44 La. L. Rev. 1641 (1983) at 1673.

51. 362 N.W.2d 211 (Mich., 1985).

52. See Bartlett, "Rethinking Parenthood as an Exclusive Status: The Need for Legal Alternatives When the Premise of the Nuclear Family Has Failed," 70 Va. L. Rev. 879 (1984).

53. Infra note 44, sec. 5.

54. 28 N.Y.2d 185, 269 N.E.2d 787 (1971).

55. See Long v. Willey, 391 S.W.2d 301 (Mo., 1965).

56. 441 U.S. 380 (1979). See also 1987 Utah L. Rev. (1987) at 22–23.

57. See 69 Va. L. Rev. 465 (1983) at 500.

58. See 1 Berkeley Women's L.J. (1986) at 158–59.

59. See Sutton, "The Lesbian Family: Rights in Conflict under the California Uniform Parentage Act," 10 Golden Gate U.L. Rev. 1007 (1980).

60. See Ruddock v. Ohls, 91 Cal. App.3d 271, 154 Cal. Rptr. 87 (1979), and Fornier v. Lopez, unreported—P.2d—(Cal., 1979).

61. See Doe v. Kelley, 106 Mich. App. 169, 307 N.W.2d 438 (1981).

62. See 1 Berkeley Women's L.J.(1986) at 156.

63. See generally 44 La. L. Rev. 1641 (1984).

64. Infra note 62 at 158.

65. See 59 S. Cal. L. Rev. 939 (1986) at 1035.

66. See 69 Va. L. Rev. 465 (1983) at 482.

67. Ala. Code §26–17–21 (1985); Alas. Stat. §25.20. 045 (1982); Ark. Stat. Ann. §61–141(c) (1983); Cal. Civ. Code §7005 (1983); Colo. Rev. Stat. §19–6–106 (1978); Conn. Gen Stats. §45–69f to –69n (1980); Fla. Stat. Ann. §742.11 (1985); Ga. Code Ann. §74–101.1 and 74–9904 (1981); Idaho Code. §39–5401 to 39–5407 (1984); Ill. Ann. Stat. ch. 40, §1451–1453 (1985); Kan. Stat. Ann. §23–128 to 23–130 (1981); La. Civ. Code. Ann. Art. 188 (1985); Md. Est. & Trusts Code Ann. §1–206(b) (1974); Mass. Gen. Laws. Ann. ch. 46, §4B (1985); Mich. Comp. Laws. Ann. §333.2824(6)

and 700. 111(2) (1980); Minn. Stat. Ann. §257.56 (1982); Mont. Code. Ann. §40–6–106 (1983); Nev. Rev. Stat.§126.061 (1983); N. J. Stat. Ann. §9:17–44 (1983); N.Y. Dom. Rel. Law. §73 (1977); N.C. Gen. Stat. §49A–1 (1984); Okla. Stat. Ann. tit. 10, §551–53 (1985); Ore. Rev. Stat. §109.239. 109.243, 109.247, 677.355–70 (1983); Tenn. Code Ann. §68–3–306 (1983); Tex. Fam. Cod. Ann. §12.03(a) (1975); Va. Code. §64.1–7.1 (1984); Wash. Rev. Code §26.26.050 (1985); Wis. Stat. Ann. §767.47(9), 891.40(1) (2) (1981); and Wyoming Stat. Ann. §14–2–103 (1985).

68. See Ga. Code Ann. §74.101.1 (1981); Idaho Code §39–5407 (1984); Ore. Rev. Stat. §667.360 (1983).

69. See Alaska, California, Colorado, Connecticut, Minnesota, Montana, Nevada, New Jersey, New York, Oklahoma, Virginia, Washington, Wisconsin and Wyoming statutes, all delineated in note 67.

70. Infra note 50 at 1648.

71. Cal. Civ. Code sec. 7005(b) (1983).

72. Conn. Gen. Stat. sec. 45–69j (1981).

73. In addition to California and Connecticut, see note 67 for the statutes of Montana, Nevada, Oregon, Texas, Washington, and Wisconsin.

74. Ga. Code Ann. §19–7–21 (1982).

75. Infra note 66, at 483.

76. See 27 St. Mary's L.J. 927 (1986) at 953.

77. La. Civ. Code art. 209; see Fontenot v. Thierry, 422 So. 2d 586 (La. App. 1982).

78. 428 So. 2d 904 (La. App. 1983).

79. The marital status of the mother was immaterial in Malek v. Yekani-Fard, 422 So. 2d 1151 (La., 1982).

80. 377 A.2d 821 (N.J., 1977).

81. 407 A.2d 849 (N.J., 1979).

82. 240 Cal. Rptr. 402 (1987).

83. 9A U.L.A. 579 (1979).

84. 9A U.L.A. 581 (1979). See also Section 10.2.

85. See 46 Ohio St. L.J. 1055 (1985) at 1062.

86. California, Colorado, Illinois, Minnesota, Montana, Nevada, New Jersey, Washington, and Wyoming; see infra note 67 for statute citations.

87. Infra note 67.

88. See Haw. Rev. Stat. §584–1 to –26 (1976); N.D. Cent. Code §14–17–01 to –26 (1981), and Ohio Rev. Code Ann.§31111.01 to -.19 (1984)

89. Wash. Rev. Code §26.26.050(2) (1985).

90. Ore. Rev. Stat. §677 (1979).

91. See generally 22 San Diego L. Rev. 1193 (1985).

92. New York City Health Code, Art. 21 (1949):

Regulations Governing the Providing of Seminal Fluid for Artificial Human Insemination.

Regul. 1. A person from whom seminal fluid is to be collected for the purpose of artificial human insemination shall have a complete physical examination with particular attention to the genitalia at the time of the taking of such seminal fluid.

Regul. 2. Such person shall have a standard serological test for syphilis and a smear and culture for gonorrhea not less than one week before such seminal fluid is obtained.

Regul. 3. No person suffering from any venereal diseases, tuberculosis, or infection with brucella organisms, shall be used as a donor of seminal fluid for the purpose of artificial human insemination.

Regul. 4. No person having any disease or defect known to be transmissible by the genes shall be used as a donor of seminal fluid for the purpose of artificial human insemination.

Regul. 5. Before artificial human insemination is undertaken, both the proposed donor and proposed recipient shall have their bloods tested with respect to the Rh factor at a laboratory approved for serology by the Board of Commissioner of Health. If the proposed recipient is negative for the Rh factor, no semen shall be used for artificial insemination other than from a donor of seminal fluid whose blood is also negative for this factor.

Regul. 6. Where artificial human insemination is performed, the physician performing the same shall keep records which shall show:

(1) The name of the physician.
(2) The name and address of the donor.
(3) The name and address of the recipient.
(4) The results of the physical examination and the results of the serological examinations, including the tests for the Rh factor.
(5) The date of the artificial insemination.

Such records shall be regarded as confidential and shall not be open to inspection by the public or by any person other than the Commissioner of Health or such other persons as may be authorized by law to inspect such records. The custodian of any such records, the said Commissioner or any other person authorized by law to inspect such records shall not divulge any part of any such records, so as to disclose the identity of the persons to whom they relate except as provided by law.

93. See Ariz. Rev. Stat. Ann.§36–2302 (Supp. 1982–83); Ark. Stat. Ann.§82–436 to –441 (Supp. 1983); Cal. Health & Safety Code §25956 (West Supp. 1983); Fla. Stat. Ann.§390.001 (6), (7) (West Supp. 1983); Ill. Ann. Stat. ch. 38 §81, –32, –32.1 (Smith-Hurd Supp. 1983–84); Ind. Code §35–1–58.5–6 (1979); Ky. Rev. Stat. Ann. §436.026 (1975); La. Rev. Stat. Ann. §14:87.2 (West 1974) and La. Rev. Stat. Ann. §40:1299.35.13 (West Supp. 1984); Me. Rev. Stat. Ann. tit. 22 1593 (1980); Mass. Ann. Laws ch. 112§12J (Supp. 1983) Mich. Comp. Laws Ann. §§333.2685–2692 (1980); Minn. Stat. Ann. §145.421 to .422 (West Supp. 1982); Mo. Stat. §188.037 (Vernon Supp. 1983); Mont. Code Ann. §50–20–108(3)(1981); Neb. Rev. Stat. §28–242–346 (1979); N.M. Stat. Ann. §24–9 A–1. et seq. (1978); N.D. Cent. Code §14–02.02–01 to –02 (1981); Ohio Rev. Code Ann. §2919.14 (Baldwin 1982); Okla. Stat. Ann. tit. 63§1–735 (West Supp. 1982–83); Pa. Stat. Ann. tit. 18 §3216 (1983); R. I. Gen. Laws §11–54–1 (Supp. 1982); S.D. Comp. Laws Ann. §34–23A–17 (1977); Tenn. Code Ann. §39–308 (Supp. 1982); Utah Code Ann. §76–7–310 (Allen Smith 1978; and Wyo. Stat. §35–6–115 (1977)).

94. See Me. Rev. Stat. Ann. §1593 (1980); Mass. Ann. Laws ch. 112, §123 (1983); Mich. Comp. Laws §333.2685 to.2692 (1980); N.D. Cent. Code §14–02.2–01 to –02 (1981); R.I. Gen. Laws §11–54–1 (1982); and Utah Code Ann. §76–7–310 (1978).

95. See Section 1.9.

96. See Section 1.1.

97. See 24 W. Ontario L. Rev. 15 (1986).

98. See Section 1.4.

99. See generally 42 Fertility & Sterility 348 (1984).

100. 45 CFR §46.203(c) (1984). Note that there has been a ban on federal financing for transplants of fetal tissue from elective abortions. For decades, researchers have utilized fetal tissue for a wide variety of medical research, from birth defects to Parkinson's disease. See *New York Times* (November 19, 1989) at 1, 38:

There are no good figures on the number of fetuses used in research, but there are indications that it is substantial. Fetal tissue is widely used because it grows quickly and easily in the laboratory and because fetal cells in some ways resemble cancer cells, enabling scientists to look into what controls cell growth. Fetal tissue can also be used in direct experiments on the causes of birth defects.

The National Institutes of Health is financing more than 100 research projects that involve the use of fetal tissue; it spent $8.3 million on this research in the last fiscal year. In addition, privately financed research, often involving transplants of fetal tissue into animals and people, is carried out at places like the University of Colorado Medical Center in Denver and Hana Biologics, a company in Alameda, Calif.

While this research has gone on for some time, recent public attention has focused on the Bush Administration's announcement Nov. 1 that it would extend a 20-month-old ban on Federal financing of fetal tissue transplants. The ban was meant to head off what abortion opponents feared might be an enormous market for fetal tissue.

101. See 59 S. Cal. L. Rev. 939 (1986) at 982.
102. 432 U.S. 464 (1976).
103. See 51 S. Cal L. Rev. 1203 (1978).
104. Ill. Rev. Stat. ch. 38, §81–2617 (1983–1984).
105. Ill. Rev. Stat. ch. 23, §2354.4 (1981).
106. Ill. S.B. 890 (1985).
107. 556 F. Supp. 157 (N.D. Ill., 1983).
108. See N.L.J. (December 7, 1987) at 1 et seq.
109. Id.
110. 477 U.S 303 (1980).
111. 58 D.L.R. 25 (Ont., 1921).
112. See Warren Freedman, *Society on Trial: Current Court Decisions and Social Change* (1965) at 90–91.
113. See Section 1.1.
114. Unreported Ill. Cir. Ct., Cook Co., #44-C–8307 (1945).
115. 78 N.Y.S.2d 390 (1948).
116. Unreported Ill. Sup. Ct., #53-S–1410 (No. 1954).
117. See Section 2.2.
118. 12 Ill. App. 2d 473, 139 N.E.2d 844 (1956).
119. See Section 2.2
120. 15 Misc. 2d 260, 184 N.Y.S.2d 178 (1958).
121. See 46 Ohio St. L.J. 1055 (1985) at 1059.
122. Infra note 115.
123. 39 Misc. 2d 1083, 242 N.Y.S.2d 406 (1963).
124. Id. at 1087, 410.
125. See 17 St. Mary's L.J. 927 (1986) at 960.
126. Infra note 123.
127. 345 N.Y.S.2d 430 (1973).
128. 41 Misc. 2d 886, 246 N.Y.S.2d 835 (1964).
129. Infra note 127, at 435–36.
130. 68 Cal. 2d 280, 437 P.2d 495 (1968).
131. Id. at 289, 501.
132. 152 N.J. Super. 160, 377 A.2d 821 (1977).
133. 182 N.J. Super. 102, 440 A.2d 64 (1981).
134. Id. at 109, 68; also infra note 106 at 1061.
135. 484 N.Y.S.2d 780 (1985).

3

Dramatis Personae: General Rights and Duties

3.1 INTRODUCTION TO THE CAST OF CHARACTERS

In this remarkable drama of new reproductive technologies, the dramatis personae, or list of characters, is ever growing as the mystery of the brave new world unfolds. [1] It is already possible for a child to have five different ''parents'': (1) the woman who donated the egg; (2) the man who donated the sperm; (3) the woman to whose uterus the fertilized embryo is transferred so that she can carry it to birth; and (4) and (5) the man and woman who will receive and presumably raise the child.[2] In addition to these five persons, there are the adoptive parents; the equitable or foster parents, and the attending physician, along with other personnel, including a sperm bank that participated in the fertilization. To complicate the process are the twin concepts of secrecy and anonymity, which permeate the entire process.

The *New York Times* (October 2, 1987) carried a remarkable story from Johannesburg, South Africa, about a 48-year-old grandmother acting as a surrogate mother for her own three grandchildren. The grandmother was implanted with the her daughter's ova, which had been artificially inseminated with her son-in-law's sperm. Under South African law, the grandmother is the legal guardian of the three grandchildren, making her the first woman to carry successfully her daughter's transplanted embryos.[3] This successful surrogate embryo transfer must be distinguished from surrogate motherhood, where the child is not genetically related to both parents.[4]

3.2 THE DONOR OF THE SEMEN OR SPERM

To start the reproductive process, the semen or sperm of a male donor is the prerequisite. In truth, the male progenitor is not ''donating'' his semen or sperm for he is generally paid by the attending physician or by the sperm bank or by the parties themselves seeking artificial conception. It is the physician who generally selects the donor and maintains the secrecy of the donor's identity.

Male infertility[5] is a frequent cause for the use of a donor's semen or sperm; the problem can be oligospermia (a low sperm count), azoospermia (the absence of sperm), or a male genetic disease.[6] In case of oligospermia, the IVF procedure permits the donor sperm to be used as a backup in case the husband's sperm do not fertilize the egg after laparoscopy; in this event the situation is comparable to the CAI process,[7] and the husband with oligospermia might well be satisfied that his sperm actually fertilized the egg.

Donor insemination is also sought by unmarried women without male partners; they frequently plan to rear offspring alone or in a same-sex family. Where the physician is unwilling to inseminate the unmarried woman, the female procures semen from male friends and inseminates herself without screening for disease or adverse genetic factors.[8]

Embryo donation is not likely to occur on a large scale until cryopreservation and thawing of sperm, egg, and embryo are firmly established, especially in face of the logistical problems of coordination of donor and recipient menstrual cycles.[9] The supply of embryos for donation would increase with freezing and thawing successes; embryo discard would be curbed, and the moral and religious indignation accompanying embryo discard would wane.[10]

The legal rights of the donor of semen or sperm have generally not included any relationship with the conceived child (unless the donor is the husband of the woman whose egg was so fertilized).[11] However, in a recent California case, the donor of the sperm who filed a paternity suit was awarded visitation rights and declared to be the legal father of the child conceived.[12] Here a lesbian had inseminated herself with the semen from the plaintiff, whose identity she did not know until the paternity suit. After the child was born, plaintiff appeared to visit with the child, over the lesbian mother's objections. Since the mother had not engaged a licensed physician to inseminate her with the donor's semen, section 7005 (a) of the California Civil Code did not apply: "If, under the supervision of a licensed physician and with the consent of her husband, a wife is inseminated artificially with semen donated by a man not her husband, the husband is treated in law as if he were the natural father of the child thereby conceived." If the lesbian mother had been "married," her "husband" and not the donor would have been the legal father, provided that a licensed physician had performed the insemination. It should be noted that section 5 of the Uniform Parentage Act exempts the donor from any legal relationship to the child of a married woman.[13] The donor of the semen or sperm is absolved from any legal rights or obligations with respect to the child conceived.[14]

The male donor might well enter into a contract with the married couple, allowing him to have some rearing rights and duties in the offspring. Such agreements have been recognized where the recipient of the sperm is unmarried, perhaps to ensure a male-rearing parent for the offspring. Where the recipient of the sperm is married, such a rearing right would seriously interfere with normal family upbringing[15]. Indeed, the mere existence of rearing rights and duties in the offspring by the male donor would defeat the secrecy and confidentiality concept of the entire reproductive process and perhaps discourage the utilization of a donor's sperm in the first place. Where there is an intrafamilial donation of sperm, the procreative liberty and family autonomy might not be protected in the face of state laws against incest, for example. The state might also step in and hold the donor of the sperm financially responsible for the support of the child conceived where the mother is unmarried and is a public charge.[16]

3.3 THE DONOR OF THE EGG OR GAMETE

The female donor whose egg is fertilized by the sperm may consider herself the "mother" of the child conceived, but motherhood may be genetic, gestational, or social. The "rearing mother" is the gestating woman whose motherhood terminates with the birth of the child unless otherwise stated in the contract relationship between the parties. Where an artificial placenta is utilized, the extracorporeal gestator, not being a human being, can hardly be deemed a "mother."[17] The donor of the egg might be the genetic mother, if not also the social mother.

The use of donor eggs allows women with ovarian failure or premature menopause to gestate children. Egg donation became possible with the development of IVF and the ability of physicians to transfer the extracorporeal embryo to a physiologically receptive uterus other than that of the egg source. Donor eggs can be acquired from women undergoing ovarian stimulation as part of an IVF cycle or from women undergoing other abdominal surgery who agree to superovulation in order to donate eggs. There are health risks associated with these techniques and with ultrasound-guided transvaginal aspiration of eggs. Cryopreservation and successful thawing processes can ensure survival of eggs for subsequent fertilization.[18]

The legal relationship among donors of eggs, recipients, and offspring should parallel the relationship of sperm donation. Sperm donation statutes do not generally apply to egg donation since the "sperm" literally came before the "egg" historically in terms of development and practice. Just as the husband's consenting to the use of donor sperm assumes the donor's rearing rights and duties, so does the consenting wife (who may also be the gestational mother) take on rearing rights and obligations, terminating those rights of the donor of the egg. Contractual agreements allowing the donor of the egg to play some rearing role can be made to the same extent that a donor of sperm may be allowed rearing or visitation rights.

In Grenoble, France, in December 1988, it was reported that a woman without ovaries gave birth to a baby produced from her egg and her husband's sperm. The mother's egg had been fertilized in a laboratory dish by her husband's sperm, and the resulting embryo was frozen and implanted ten months later in her uterus.[19]

3.4 THE SURROGATE OR GESTATIONAL MOTHER

Surrogate motherhood is one of the many old reproductive techniques that have enabled infertile couples to have children. In biblical days, as set forth in the Old Testament, barren women were provided with sons by surrogate mothers. Sarah, in speaking to her husband, Abraham, said: "Behold now, the Lord has restrained me from bearing; I pray thee, go into my maid; it may be that I may obtain children by her."[20] And Rachel, the barren wife of Jacob, similarly remarked: "Behold my maid Bilha, go into her; and she shall bear upon my knees, that I may also have children by her."[21] Today surrogate motherhood is perhaps less personal but much more common as infertile couples seek to have children.

A surrogate mother is a woman who agrees to be artificially inseminated generally with the sperm of a man whose own wife is incapable of conceiving or carrying a child to term.[22] A surrogate mother might also be artificially inseminated with the sperm of a donor where the husband's sperm is incapable of fertilizing his wife's egg and/or where the wife is incapable of conceiving or carrying a child to term.[23] Generally the surrogate mother will enter into a formal contract relationship with the infertile couple to provide for her medical and living expenses in addition to a fee, which might range as high as $125,000.[24] The contract must endeavor to deal with all sorts of contingencies and eventualities, such as the surrogate mother's unwillingness to surrender the child after birth, the claims of the husband of the surrogate mother, the birth of a malformed child, or even the death or divorce of the infertile couple prior to birth of the child.

The behavior of the surrogate mother during pregnancy is of monumental concern to the contracting parents, who must include the vital language as to her behavior in the contract with her. The best interests of the unborn child mandate such concern when the surrogate mother does not abstain from tobacco smoking, alcohol consumption, drug ingestion, and sexual intercourse. Proper prenatal care is also imperative, and many states under the *parens patriae* doctrine demand protection of the unborn child.[25] Liability has been imposed on the surrogate mother for failure to act as a reasonably prudent person would under the circumstances presented.[26] Unfortunately, there has been no established standard applied particularly in instances of parents who negligently injure their children.[27]

The *New York Times* (September 16, 1987) reported that a Michigan surrogate mother had refused to surrender the twins whom she bore for an Arkansas couple under a properly drawn and executed contract and that the Michigan court, had, despite her breach of the contract, temporarily permitted her to retain custody but authorized the infertile couple to see the newborns twice a week.[28] The defense of the surrogate mother was coercion in having succumbed to seven inseminations of the legal father's sperm; also she argued that the contract itself violated the Thirteenth Amendment, which outlaws slavery. The famed Baby M case in 1987 in New Jersey,[29], upholding the validity of the contract, prompted New Jersey's Roman Catholic bishops to file an *amicus curiae* brief with the New Jersey Supreme Court opposing the practice of surrogate motherhood, which was therein delineated as promoting "the exploitation of women and infertile couples and the dehumanization of babies. . . . In short, it traffics for profit in human lives."[30] Israel, according to 1987 regulations of the Health Ministry, precludes a woman from "renting out" under contract her uterus to carry a fetus and then handing it over to another couple; also a fetus produced by IVF may not be implanted in a relative of the donor.[31]

Courts have honored family compacts for the relinquishment of parental rights in exchange for a promise to support the child or for a fee to the surrendering parent.[32] In Clark v. Clark the Maryland appellate court upheld a mother's promise to relinquish her son to the custody of his paternal grandfather in exchange for payments to her for her life.[33] Surrogate mothering here differs in that the child is already alive and the transaction is between blood relatives of the child, but the thrust of benefiting the child is the same unless the payments are disproportionate to the surrogate mother's expenses and the reasonable fee.

The state has in recent years taken a decided interest in these contracts for surrogate parenting. In Syrkowski v. Appleyard, the action was filed by a semen donor alleging that he had reason to believe that the defendant who had been artificially inseminated was pregnant with his child.[34] The AID physician supplied an affidavit in support of plaintiff's request for a filiation order declaring him to be the natural father, awarding him custody, having his name as father appear on the child's birth certificate, and letting the child bear his surname. The defendant surrogate mother did not oppose the petition, but the attorney general of Michigan intervened, contending that the court had no jurisdiction over the action under the Michigan Paternity Act because it involved a surrogate mother contract that was of doubtful validity.[35] The Michigan Court of Appeals agreed with the state that the defendant's husband who had consented to the AID should be deemed the child's father: "The issue raised . . . involved significant matters of State interest and public policy. . . . Family living and, more specifically, interest in the welfare of the child must continue to be of paramount importance to the people of this State." Thus, the validity of the surrogate mother contract was sacrificed to society's interest in promoting family living.[36] Indeed, it is contended that as of 1984, not a single state statute sanctioning surrogate mother contracts had been enacted[37]. One reason for this stricture or failure to recognize the surrogate mother contract is state policy against private adoption; the parents here are "adopting" a child not biologically their own.[38] If the child is not "adopted," the surrogate mother could be liable in tort for child abandonment.[39]

The validity of the surrogate mother contract was recently upheld in the New York decision in Matter of Baby Girl L.J.[40] Here the case involved the effort by a natural father and his wife to adopt a child pursuant to the surrogate agreement. Although the court first admitted to moral and ethical reservations regarding the contractual arrangements, it nevertheless acknowledged the reality of a child in being and the child's need to be reared by parents and not by the surrogate mother. The court ruled that the natural father and his wife were appropriate parents for the child and therefore granted the adoption. The surrogate mother's fee was found not to be prohibited by existing legislation.

In the New Jersey decision of Baby M,[41] that court took a different track, holding that "the laws of adoption, custody and parental termination were never intended to apply and do not apply to surrogacy. . . . The only rule of law by which this court may be guided is the application of the doctrine of a child's best interest in the exercise of its parens patriae jurisdiction."[41] The New York decision simply held that if any violation of New York adoption statutes were found in the terms of the surrogate contract, the court would find the surrogate agreement illegal.

To permit a surrogate mother to violate the contract, such as aborting the birth or retaining custody of the child at birth, would have a profound adverse effect upon the ability of infertile couples to procreate through surrogacy.[42] Infertile couples would be leery of entrusting their embryos to surrogates unless specific performance of the surrogate contract could be achieved or her role as a "trustee" of the embryo for the couple could be fully honored.[43] Indeed, prohibitions on surrogate contracts might be unconstitutional as infringing upon the procreative liberty of the infertile couple providing the embryo. In Surrogate Parenting, Inc. v. Kentucky, the Kentucky Supreme Court held that the surrogate contract did not violate the Kentucky statute against baby selling.[44]

The complications that can ensue from a surrogate motherhood situation have been dramatically set forth in the *Georgetown Law Journal* (1985). In early 1982, Judy, a married woman from Michigan, entered into a formal written contract with Alexander, a New York City accountant who was unable to have children with his wife. Judy agreed to be artificially inseminated with his sperm and to conceive and bear his child. As part of the arrangements, Judy agreed to forego sexual intercourse with her husband for a period of time to ensure that any child she might conceive would be a result of the artificial insemination. In 1983 Judy gave birth to a baby boy born with microcephaly, an abnormally small head that threatened to leave the child severely retarded. Alexander refused to allow medical treatment of even a staph infection until the physicians obtained a court order mandating medical treatment. Alexander then questioned whether the baby was his and subsequently refused to accept the impaired child. Judy and her husband contended that the baby did not belong to them and that, under the agreement, Alexander and his wife were responsible for the baby's care and custody. Blood tests confirmed that Alexander was not the biological father; Judy's husband then confessed that he had fathered a microcephalic child in a previous marriage and that the child, mentally retarded, had died in early childhood. Eventually the unwanted child went to live with Judy and her husband.[45]

Whether a surrogate contract could be so artfully drawn as to encompass these contingencies is problematical.[46]

3.5 THE BIOLOGICAL MOTHER AND THE BIOLOGICAL FATHER

It would appear that the identification of the biological mother and the biological father should be simple and uncomplicated. But where either or both parties are involved to some extent in the reproductive process, their identities are frequently lost in the shuffle between the semen donor, the egg donor, the surrogate mother, and perhaps the parents in place at any given point in time. In Matter of Ronald "FF," the New York Court of Appeals ruled that a man who believed he might be the father of a child but whose paternity was excluded by blood tests was not the biological father and he was not entitled to visitation rights under the "extraordinary circumstances" rule governing custody cases.[47] The court refused to interfere with "the mother's full custodial rights which include the right to determine who may or may not associate with her child."

Finding the biological father is not always good for the child, according to the Washington Supreme Court in McDaniels v. Carlson.[48] Here the young mother gave birth after having an affair with plaintiff while she was married to another person, who thereupon was sued by plaintiff to establish paternity. The trial court collaterally estopped the action because plaintiff had resided with the child's mother during the pendency of the dissolution action when plaintiff was declared to be the father and ordered to pay child support. But the high court reversed due to the "best interests of the child" and held that the mere filing of a paternity action does not automatically imply that the action is in the child's best interest. The court must also look at the recommendations of the guardian *ad litem* and all the pertinent facts in the record. The paternity determination of the biological father is not final until that moment, and the identity of the biological father not confirmed.

In a New York case, Matter of Adoption of Paula L., the petitioner adoptee applied to the surrogate's court to have her adoption records opened so as to obtain the medical history of her biological family.[49] She needed the information to diagnose a disease that she might have, and the medical history of the biological parents was essential. The court, seeking to protect the biological parents' identity, granted the application and ordered the appointment of a guardian *ad litem* to attempt to locate the biological parents and obtain their medical histories. The court observed:

> Two doctors have indicated that the disclosure of the medical history of petitioner's biological family is needed to properly diagnose and treat petitioner. The adoptive parents have joined in the application.
>
> The natural curiosity of an adoptee for information about her biological parents, standing alone, does not constitute the "good cause" required by law before an adoption file can

be unsealed and its confidential information revealed (Domestic Relations Law §114; Matter of Linda F.M., 52 N.Y.2d 236). The good cause requirement is fulfilled by a showing of physical or psychological medical need (Alma Soc. Inc. v. Mellon, 601 F.2d 1225, cert. den. 444 U.S. 995; Matter of Hayden, 106 Misc. 2d 849).

The papers submitted in support of this application established a prima facie entitlement to unseal the adoption file for the limited purpose of ascertaining whether it contained any helpful medical information while not revealing any information which would disclose the identity of the biological parents (Chattman v. Bennett, 57 A.D.2d 618). Unfortunately, the sealed file did not contain any medical records nor did it indicate the identity of the biological father. However, there is sufficient information about the biological mother to possibly ascertain her current whereabouts.

Surrogate Laurino established the useful procedure of appointing a guardian ad litem to protect the interests of the biological parents in proceedings to open adoption files (Matter of Anonymous, 89 Misc. 2d 132). Balancing the need of petitioner to know against the biological parents' right to remain anonymous if they so desire indicates that the best course to follow at this stage of the proceeding is to appoint a guardian ad litem to attempt to locate the biological mother and to make discreet inquiries as to whether she has any objections to furnishing her medical history and any information which she may have concerning the biological father. The guardian ad litem shall advise petitioner and obtain her consent before incurring any substantial expenditure of time and money in an attempt to locate the mother.

In Matter of Baby Girl T., there was an application by the biological mother to set aside her "extrajudicial" consent in this pending adoption on the ground that the consent was obtained as a result of "fraud, duress, coercion, lack of mental capacity, mistake and/or undue influence."[50] In addition, there was an application by the biological father that his consent was a prerequisite before this pending adoption could be consummated. The New York Family Court, Suffolk County, "tri-furcated the trial," and then expounded at length on the two basic issues:

(1) Article VII of the Domestic Relations Law (Section 109 et seq.) regulates and governs the procedures to be followed in all adoption proceedings commenced in this state. DRL 115(b) provides, inter alia, that a natural parent may consent to a private adoption of his or her child in one of two ways: by properly executing an extrajudicial consent form or by executing an adoption consent before a judge of a Court of competent jurisdiction. The latter becomes irrevocable upon its execution in the Court; the former is irrevocable 45 days after its execution. A revocation of an extrajudicial consent within the 45 day period will result in a custody hearing if the adoptive parents object to the revocation and/or return of the child. At such hearing, the natural parents and adoptive parents are in equality relative to their custodial claims, there being no superiority in the natural parent.

Although a natural parent may unilaterally (without reason) revoke his or her consent within the statutory period (and thereupon trigger a "best interests hearing"), a revocation may nonetheless be premised upon fraud, duress or coercion. Indeed, as DRL Sec. 115-b(7) specifically states: " . . . nor shall this section bar actions or proceedings brought on the ground of fraud, duress or coercion in the execution or inducement of an adoptive consent.

An adoption consent that is tainted by fraud, duress or coercion is void ab initio, tantamount to no consent at all. Thus, unlike the "unilateral" revocation, a revocation premised on fraud, duress or coercion preserves the superiority of parental rights, thereby requiring the return of the child, in the absence of extraordinary circumstances. See, e.g. Matter of Sarah K., 66 N.Y.2d 223."

Here, the revocation attempt by the natural mother was based upon both grounds. Susan claimed that fraud, duress, coercion, undue influence or mistake have vitiated the adoption consent dated February 18, 1989, and that revocation of the consent was timely and properly filed pursuant to DRL. Sec. 115-b. . . . While the existence of duress in the execution of an adoption consent may void same and result in the return of the child, such duress must be of the quality and nature that it overrides the parents' ability to make an intelligent and knowing decision to place their child for adoption. Indeed, an adoption consent executed under the cloud of duress is null and void. However, as was stated by then Nassau County Surrogate Bennett in Matter of T.W.C., NYLJ December 18, 1974, and restated by the Surrogate in Matter of E.W.D., 89 Misc. 2d 64 (1976):

"Contemplation of the surrender of one's own child is in many, if not all, cases a cause of emotional and mental stress. No statute has said that surrenders are valid only if executed free from emotion, tensions and pressures caused by the situation. No principle of law requires the rule.

"A balance of the interests of the persons concerned and of society weighs strongly against it." . . . The law requires a showing that external force was applied sufficient to deprive the parent of the ability to exercise free will. See, Commissioner v. Sandra G., 141 A.D.2d 821 (2d Dept. 1988). On this record, it cannot be said that Susan was subjected to such external pressure as would have removed her ability to make a free and uninhibited decision. Granted, she was under emotional stress; however, as indicated, such stress alone is insufficient to vitiate the adoption consent. Further, . . . the court does not find that Susan's denial or concealment of her pregnancy deprived her of the capacity to make a knowing decision to place her child for adoption.

It should also be noted that Susan T.'s revocation was allegedly also premised upon fraud in the inducement or execution of her consent. While these claims of fraud were not particularized or made clear at the trial, there was some reference to the hospital social worker and attorney Wool having "misled" Susan on February 18, 1989. Susan also claimed that she did not comprehend that upon the timely revocation of her adoption consent she would not automatically be entitled to the immediate return of her child.

As to social worker Palermo, there was no evidence of her making false representations to Susan during any of their meetings. As previously noted, the court believes that Ms. Palermo was somewhat confused herself, but confusion and fraud are two different things. Indeed, the establishment of one has nothing to do with the other. . . . Under the circumstances, this court does not find that Susan's consent must be set aside due to fraud or mistake. Having already determined that duress, coercion and lack of capacity were not established, the court must view Susan's revocation as a unilateral one only, thereby calling for a best interest hearing pursuant to DRL 115-b.

And (2) Separate and apart from the issue of the validity of Susan T.'s adoption consent is the issue of whether the consent of the biological father, Richard C. is required herein.

Given that the child was born out of wedlock and placed with the adoptive parents almost immediately after her birth, the provisions of DRL Sec. 111(d) are controlling.

That section states that the consent to adoption of a father of a child born out of wedlock is required only if:

such father openly lived with the child or the child's mother for a continuous period of six months immediately preceding the placement of the child for adoption; and (ii) such father openly held himself out to be the father of such child during such period; and (iii) such father paid a fair and reasonable sum, in accordance with his means, for the medical, hospital and nursing expenses incurred in connection with the mother's pregnancy or with the birth of the child.

The legislative intent behind the bill that became DRL Sec. 111(1)(d) was to adhere to the U.S. Supreme Court's opinion in Caban v. Mohammed, 441 U.S. 380, which "accords protection to fathers who 'participated in the rearing' of the child, who had established a substantial relationship with the child, or who have 'manifested a significant parental interest in the child'." The bill "provides a reasonable, unambiguous and objective standard to guide agencies and courts" (Sen. Pisani, memorandum in support of the bill, as sponsor, 1980 NY Legis Ann. at 243).

The precise, albeit difficult issue, before the court is whether the biological father, Richard G., has satisfied the requirements of DRL Sec. 111(1)(e), thus requiring his consent to this adoption.

The evidence at trial in this regard was not seriously disputed. There is no question that Richard did not live with the child or with Susan T. for a continuous period of six months immediately preceding the February 18, 1989 placement of the child. Further, Richard did not openly hold himself out as the child's father during such six month period. Finally, the evidence is clear that Richard did not pay a fair and reasonable sum for medical, hospital and nursing expenses incurred as a result of Susan's pregnancy and the birth of the child. Thus, on these facts alone and literally construing the statute, there has been a failure of actual proof as to Richard's strict compliance with the three criteria set forth in DRL Sec. 111(1)(e). . . . Most significantly, there is simply no persuasive evidence in the record before us to demonstrate that the natural father in this case made every effort to establish a substantial family relationship or that any such purported efforts were thwarted by improper behavior on the part of the natural mother. . . . Thus, in the final analysis, Richard was prevented from fulfilling the requirements of the statute, not by physical barriers, not by maliciousness, but by the situation itself and by Susan's unusual withdrawals from reality. As noted, supra, the court believes that Susan knew of her own pregnancy at some level of comprehension, but she failed to accept same. The court cannot fault Richard in this regard, and we cannot accept the notion that Richard should be penalized and prejudiced for something that he could not control. If fault must be ascribed in this case, it must rest with Susan, who exclusively controlled the pregnancy, as well as its disclosure to Richard. Having failed to provide Richard with any opportunity to participate in her life and in the pregnancy, Susan must be found to have acted wrongfully vis-a-vis Richard and his own parental rights.

Under the circumstances, the court finds that Richard's consent to this adoption is required.

3.6 THE ADOPTIVE PARENTS

Adoptive parents are playing a significant role in the modern reproductive processes in spite of the exceptional high costs of adoption.[51] In 1987, fees for adopting healthy infants ranged from $5,000 to $12,000, and the market was sparse for the 2 million couples seeking to adopt the 50,000 or more babies available each year. The prime reasons for the low supply of adoptable babies are single mothers' keeping their babies, greater availability of legal abortions, liberalized views toward contraceptive use, successful counseling of troubled families, and the fading of the social stigma formerly associated with illegitimacy.[52] Today adoptions are arranged through private agencies, public agencies, or independently, without an agency.

The rights of adoptive parents are not always secure, although the Nebraska Supreme Court in Gaughan v. Gilliam tied the knot securely.[53] Here an unmarried 16 year old who had given birth to a healthy child signed adoption papers with the defendants but later changed her mind and filed a writ of *habeas corpus* to regain custody of her child from the adoptive parents. The trial court decided that, although the child's father had voluntarily consented to the adoption, the plaintiff mother had not voluntarily signed the consent and had acted to revoke it within a reasonable period of time. But the Nebraska high court reversed: absent threats, coercion, fraud, or duress, a properly executed relinquishment of parental rights and consent to adoption signed by the natural parent voluntarily, knowingly, and intelligently was valid. The defendant adoptive parents had had custody of the child for one and a half years prior to plaintiff's change of mind. The court found that plaintiff's relinquishment and consent were voluntarily executed, and the rights of the adoptive parents were secured.

On the other hand, the Utah Supreme Court in 1987 recognized the right of an Indian mother to reclaim her child from the adoptive parents.[54] The federal Indian Child Welfare Act of 1978 stated that only an Indian court has jurisdiction to decide the issue. It appears that although the biological mother did not seek the return of her child for two years after adoption, she was then only 18 years of age, unmarried, and unemployed and was not represented by a lawyer when she signed the adoption papers.

The religion of the adoptive couple is also an issue, as illustrated in the New York case of Matter of Anonymous, decided by the surrogate's court, Westchester County, New York, May 17, 1989, where the local couple were ordered to return the infant they were seeking to adopt to the child's birth mother after it was learned that the couple withheld from the birth mother their religious affiliation. The birth mother, an unwed Lutheran, learned that the adoptive mother was Catholic and the adoptive father was Jewish. The court rejected the argument of the adoptive couple that the birth mother's attempt to revoke her consent to the adoption was based on religious bigotry, which should not be sanctioned by a court of law. The court pointed to Article 6, section 32 of the New York Constitution and to section 373 of the New York Social Services Law, which lay out the state's public policy requiring, where practical, that children be adopted by persons of the same religious faith as the child's birth mother. Accordingly, "a particular religion which in other contexts would be inherently suspect and subject to constitutional attack is a reasonable requirement for the birth mother's choice of adoptive parents in private adoptions.'' According to the court, ''Religious matching statutes not only reflect a socio-psychological attempt to match children and parents that are best suited to each other but in a broader and equally significant sense embody an application of the fundamental rights of a parent to control the upbringing of a child . . . . Allowing a biological parent to impose conditions on the religious activity and denomination of the adoptive parents, merely respects the parent's free exercise right.''

The New York court observed that the willful withholding of the adoptive father's religion ran contrary to the wish of the birth mother that the child be raised as a Christian. Indeed, the adoptive couple's conduct was intended to ''convey a false impression to the birth mother that both adoptive parents were Christians and that theirs was a Christian home. The birth mother relied upon the fraudulent acts to her detriment.'' The court concluded:

> Religious matching statutes not only reflect a sociopsychological attempt to match children and parents that are best suited to each other but in a broader and equally significant sense embody an application of the fundamental rights of a parent to control the upbringing of a child. The Supreme Court has recognized on numerous occasions that the relationship between parent and child is constitutionally protected (Wisconsin v. Yoder, 406 U.S. 205, 231–233 (1972); Stanley v. Illinois, 405 U.S. 645, 651–652 (1972); Meyer v. Nebraska, 262 U.S. 390, 399–401 (1923). Moreover it is now firmly established that ''freedom of personal choice in matters of family life is one of the liberties protected by the Due Process Clause of the Fourteenth Amendment (Quilloin v. Walcott, 434 U.S. 246, 255 (1978) citing Cleveland Board of Education v. LaFleur, 414 U.S. 632, 639–640 (1974).
>
> Religion is not an issue that lends itself to quantitative analysis. One's perception of the issue reflects an individual's moral values more than societal norms. It is significant that religion is the only criterion affecting the qualification of the adoptive parents that is statutorily proscribed.
>
> Allowing a biological parent to impose conditions on the religious activity and denomination of the adoptive parents, merely respects the parent's free exercise right. Permitting the biological parent to specify that adoptive parents be active members of the same religion is a reasonable extension of this right and should be given effect. . . .
>
> . . . The constitutionality of New York's religious matching statute (SSL 373(7) is clearly established (Matter of Dickens v. Ernesto, supra). A condition which requires that both parents be of the same religion is a legitimate and enforceable preference within the purview of this section.

3.7 THE EQUITABLE PARENTS

''Notwithstanding the fact that the husband is not the biological father of a child born during the marriage, the husband may acquire rights of paternity under the theory of 'equitable parent,' '' declared the Michigan Court of Appeals in Atkinson v. Atkins, decided on June 8, 1987.[55] Thus the court recognized the concept of ''equitable parents'' and thereby expanded the rights of adults who raise children not biologically their own. In the case, the husband was unaware until he was in the midst of a divorce proceeding that he was not the biological father of a boy born during his marriage. Accordingly, as an equitable parent, he was entitled to possible rights of custody, visitation, and support, based upon the following factors: (1) he wanted parental rights with respect to the child; (2) he and the child mutually acknowledged the parental relationship, or the mother "must have cooperated in the development of such a relationship" before the divorce complaint was filed; and (3) he agreed to take on the obligation of child support. It should be observed that the plaintiff husband was "the only father" the child had known; furthermore, plaintiff husband had been actively involved in the child's life even after the separation and divorce. Forbidding him to have custody rights or visitation rights would not be in the child's best interests, according to the court.

Equitable parentage differs from paternity by estoppel in that the latter involuntarily imposes obligations, while the former voluntarily imposes obligations. In either event, both doctrines give broader legal rights to those persons serving in the capacities of parents even though they are not biological parents in any sense.[56]

3.8 THE ATTENDING PHYSICIAN AND OTHER MEDICAL PERSONNEL

Artificial insemination and other modern reproductive techniques raise interesting questions as to the liability of the person or persons performing the process.[57] Less than a quarter of the states appear to mandate that only a licensed physician or medical personnel working under his or her supervision can perform such genetic processes.[58] Generally single women and lesbian women wishing to create a family unit artificially are barred from using the services of licensed physicians and other medical personnel, most of whom object to doing so on moral grounds.[59] The U.S. Supreme Court in its 1977 decision in Maher v. Roe recognized the right of a state to exclude nontherapeutic abortions from the federally funded Medicaid programs.[60] Accordingly, physicians employed by a state might well refuse to administer the reproductive process to unmarried or lesbian women. Section 20–214 of the Maryland Health and General Code (1982), for example, states that neither an individual physician nor a hospital may be required to perform artificial insemination and that such refusal will not result in either civil liability or disciplinary action.[61] Such legal discrimination apparently does not constitute medical malpractice.[62] Laws that create or establish extremely high standards of care for physicians and other medical personnel may also make it unlikely that physicians and other medical personnel will offer such reproductive services to everyone, unmarried or lesbian or other sexual orientation.

The attending physician and other medical personnel are frequently fearful of liability for simply performing the artificial reproduction, as illustrated by Smith v. Hartigan.[63] Here the attending physician had determined that Mary Smith was unable to conceive because of irreversibly damaged fallopian tubes and that IVF was the only possible solution to her and her husband's desire for a baby. However, the state of Illinois apparently prohibited the procedure, and therefore all parties were fearful of the legal consequences. The statute in question stated that "any person who intentionally causes the fertilization of a human ovum outside the body of a living human female shall, with regard to the human being thereby produced, be deemed to have the care and custody of a child." [64] Plaintiffs argued that the statute was unconstitutional in that it violated the First, Fourth, Ninth, and Fourteenth Amendments. State officials, in defending the action, pointed out that "the attempt to conceive and bear a child using the procedure and under the circumstances described in the complaint and supporting documents is entirely permissible under Illinois law."[65] The defense contended that the only prohibition under the Illinois statute is the "duty imposed by the provision . . . to refrain from willfully endangering or injuring a conceptus." The federal district court for the Northern District of Illinois sided with defendants, although the court agreed that "plaintiffs are proper parties to raise the constitutional challenge." Nevertheless, the court found no true case or controversy in the constitutional challenge to the Illinois statute:

> It is clear that the in vitro provision does not prohibit absolutely the act of causing in vitro fertilization. When it is argued that in vitro fertilization is prohibited for the Smiths, it is so only because their physician will not perform the procedure because of what he perceives to be a threat of prosecution under the State's regulation of that process. . . . The court cannot turn from nor disregard the defendants' interpretation of the statute. . . . Under the circumstances of this case on this record, the court agrees with defendants that it would be inappropriate for this court to render any decision on the constitutionality of the in vitro provision at this time. Accepting defendants' interpretation of the statute and their conclusion that the procedure plaintiffs wish to use is not prohibited by the statute and relying on defendants' representation that plaintiffs will not be prosecuted if they proceed with in vitro fertilization according to the procedure set forth by Dr. Lipchez, the court concludes that a case or controversy does not exist here.

3.9 THE BANK FOR SPERM, EGGS, AND EMBRYOS

Sperm banks, egg banks, and embryo banks are generally not licensed or otherwise regulated by the states, although some statutes dealing with clinical laboratories might equally apply to such banks.[66] For example, Georgia's licensure statute[67] defines a clinical laboratory to include "tissue banks which store human or animal tissues designed to be used for medical purposes in human beings."[68] In Illinois, the liability statute would appear to encompass the banks for sperms, eggs, and embryos as it does the blood banks; the statute states that

> the procuring, furnishing, donating, distributing, or using human whole blood, plasma, blood products, blood derivatives and products, cornea, bones, or organs or other human tissue for the purpose of injecting, transfusing or transplanting any of them in the human

body is declared for the purposes of liability in tort or contract to be the rendition of a service by every person, firm or corporation participating therein, whether or not any remuneration is paid therefor, and is declared not to be a sale of any such items and no warranties of any kind or description nor strict liability shall be applicable thereto, except as provided in Section 3.

Section 3 provides that those engaged in rendering the services warrant that they have exercised due care and followed professional standards of care "according to the current state of the medical arts."[69] Indeed, it would appear that the states have generally failed to provide regulatory mechanisms for the newly expanding techniques of reproduction. There is a strong need to integrate not only these banks for sperm, eggs, and embryos but also the new reproductive techniques into the existing statutory schemes.

3.10 SECRECY AND ANONYMITY FOR THE PARTIES

The secrecy of the sperm donor and surrogate mother is the general rule in this collaborative reproduction. Nevertheless, the interest of the offspring in knowing the genetic and gestational roots frequently is in conflict with the rule. Some banks for sperm, eggs, and embryos will show the recipients photographs of the sperm donor, for example, but maintain as confidential the identity of the person. Yet the need to disclose genetic defects, if any, or the need to locate siblings for a vital bone marrow or kidney transplant, for example, make it imperative that there be some relaxation of the rigid rule favoring secrecy and anonymity.[70]

Surrogate practices, however, involve more contact among the participants due to the need for some ongoing relationship.[71] There is also a substantial investment of money and time in the surrogate practice, as well as the distinct likelihood of a lawsuit should anything go wrong.[72]

The adopted child, like the child born of AI or IVF, has no constitutional right to learn of his or her genetic or gestational roots, according to the Second U.S. Court of Appeals in a 1979 decision in Alma Society, Inc. v. Mellon.[73] And disclosure of the adoption could lead to liability for breach of confidentiality, as illustrated in Humphers v. First Interstate Bank of Oregon.[74] Furthermore, disclosure policies might conflict with the desires of the collaborators to maintain privacy.[75]

3.11 SEXUAL DECEIT IN INTERPERSONAL RELATIONSHIPS

As in all other aspects of life, deceit is frequently practiced in the sexual interpersonal relationship of men and women, with consequent pain and suffering of the innocent person.[76] An unwanted pregnancy or a defective offspring that results from the deceit practiced by the noninnocent person has not always prompted the courts to recognize liability, despite the interest of the state in preventing and deterring deceitful conduct.[77] The state should also be concerned with the welfare of the child, who may well become a public charge.

Typically, where sexual deceit results in the birth of a child, the innocent woman will sue the father to establish paternity and will seek damages encompassing medical expenses, her emotional distress, her economic loss, and financial support for raising the child. Under the Uniform Parentage Act, the father of a child born out of wedlock is liable for the expense of the mother's pregnancy and delivery, as well as for support, education, and funeral expenses of the child, whether or not it is born alive.[78] The act, like the typical paternity statute, does not provide compensation for emotional distress or pain and suffering. A successful tort action against the noninnocent person for emotional distress or pain and suffering or diminished economic capability is frowned upon by many courts, especially where a healthful baby is born of the sexual deceit.[79] Courts do not want to treat a healthy baby as a damage element in a suit between the parents; the lawsuit itself might connote parental rejection and therefore be emotionally detrimental to the child. The Wisconsin Supreme Court in Reich v. Medical Protective Co. was also loathe to recognize such damages in a medical malpractice situation and took occasion to declare:

> To permit the parents to keep their child and shift the entire cost of its upbringing to a physician who failed to determine or inform them of the fact of the pregnancy would be to create a new category of surrogate parent. Every child's smile, every bond of love and affection, every contribution by the child to the welfare and well-being of the family and parents is to remain with the mother and father.[80]

Even *Restatement (Second) of Torts* in section 920 recognized this truism by providing for a deduction for "the value of the benefit conferred" where the defendant "has conferred upon the plaintiff a special benefit to the interest which was harmed" in calculating the damages due to "defendant's tortious conduct."

Where the father is the innocent person—the woman deceived him into having unprotected sexual intercourse by misrepresenting that she was using some form of birth control—the father's counterclaim in the paternity will generally not succeed.[81] The judicial reasoning is that there would be unwarranted governmental intrusion into the individual's right of privacy if relief were to be granted.[82] Furthermore, the father's claim would be against public policy because the claim would have a negative impact on the welfare of the child.[83] The father's counterclaim will not succeed unless he agrees to provide support for the child.[84] An independent tort action for deceit, on the other hand, by the husband might succeed, although it is questionable whether the separate tort action will withstand a motion to dismiss when the deceit cause of action arose out of the same transaction or occurrence that gave rise to the paternity suit.[85]

NOTES

1. See generally 1 Berkeley Women's L.J. 140 (1986), and 18 J. Law Ref. 866 (Summer 1985).
2. See Andrews, "The Stork Market," 6 Whittier L. Rev. 789 (1984) at 791.
3. At A9.
4. Note Section 3.4.
5. See Section 1.1.
6. See 59 S. Cal. L. Rev. 939 (1986) at 1004.
7. See Section 2.2.
8. See 11 N.Y.U. Rev. L. & Soc. Change. 193 (1983).
9. See Section 1.9.
10. Infra note 6 at 1010.
11. See for example, Cal. Civ. Code 7005(b) (1982).
12. Infra note 1 at 141.
13. 9A U.L.A. 592 (1979). See also Section 10.2.
14. See 184 J. of Law Ref. (Summer 1985) at 897.
15. Infra note 6 at 1005.
16. See Hughes v. Hutt, 500 Pa. 209, 455 A.2d 623 (1982) on imposition of child support obligations; also In re Pamela P., 443 N.Y.S.2d 343 (1981).
17 See Law Med. Health Care (October 1984) at 194.
18. Infra note 9.
19. See Hartford Courant (December 7, 1988) at A20. Also, see *New York Times* (January 18, 1988) at 1 et seq.
20. Genesis 16:2.
21. Genesis 30:3.
22. See 20 Colum. J.L. & Soc. Probs. 1 (1986) at 2.
23. Other possible reasons for surrogate motherhood might be the wife's genetic defects, which could be passed on to the child, or where the wife's pregnancy might pose a great danger to her health or mental well-being, or where the wife has a business career that cannot withstand interruption even for the birth of a child.
24. See Annas, "Making Babies without Sex: The Law and the Profits," 74 Am. J. Pub. Health 1415 (1984) at 1416. Also note Syrkowski v. Appleyard, 122 Mich. App. 506, 333 N.W.2d 90 (1983), rev. 420 Mich. 367, 362 N.W.2d 211 (1985).
25. See Prince v. Massachusetts, 321 U.S. 158 (1944), for example, where the highest court restricted parental rights; also note Jefferson v. Griffin Spalding County Hospital, 274 S.E. 2d 457 (Ga., 1981).
26. Note, 34 Cleve. St. L. Rev. 311 (1986) at 310.
27. See Grodin v. Grodin, 301 N.W.2d 869 (Mich., 1980); Miller v. Leljedal, 455 A.2d 256 (Pa., 1983); and note 10 Suffolk U.L. Rev. 582 (1976).
28. At A21 (Huber v. Yates).
29. 525 A.2d 1128 (N.J., 1987).
30. See *New York Times* (July 19, 1987) at 28.
31. See *Jewish Week* (New York) (July 22, 1987) at 11.
32. Infra note 15 at 894.
33. 122 Md. 114, 89 A. 405 (Md. App., 1913).
34. Infra note 24.

35. Mich. Comp. Laws sec. 333.2824(6) (1980).

36. See generally 69 Va. L. Rev. 465 (1986) at 481.

37. See 44 La. L. Rev. (1984) at 1655.

38. Note, La. Civ. Code art. 1895.

39. See Commonwealth ex rel Teitelbaum v. Teitelbaum, 50 A.2d 713 (Pa., 1947).

40. 132 Misc. 2d 972 (1980).

41. Infra note 29.

42. Infra note 6 at 1014.

43. See Parker, "Motivation of Surrogate Mothers," 140 Am. J. Psychiatry 117 (1983).

44. 704 S.W.2d 209 (Ky., 1986).

45. 73 Geo. L.J. 1283 (1985) at 1285–86.

46. See 5 Cardozo L. Rev. 713 (1984); 16 U. Rich. L. Rev. 467 (1982); and 17 Willamette L. J. 913 (1981).

47. 70 N.Y.2d 141 (July 1987).

48. 738 P.2d 254 (Wash., June 11, 1987).

The *New York Times* (November 23, 1989) at A20 reported that a Sebring, Florida, couple had been given the wrong baby at the hospital nearly eleven years before, and that one Mays had to respond to his 11-year-old daughter that he was not her "biological father." The child was assured that while she now has another family, she could stay with Mays and call him "Daddy." The other family (with seven siblings ranging from 6 to 21 years of age), agreed not to seek custody of the child even if genetic tests proved that she was their daughter. The psychological harm to the child was the paramount issue in the recognition that the hospital had negligently switched babies.

49. Unreported—N.Y.S.2d—(Bronx County Surrogate, September 27, 1988).

50. Unreported—N.Y.S.2d—(Suffolk County Family Court, November 7, 1989).

51. See *New York Times* (August 9, 1987) at F9.

52. See Bowal, "Surrogate Procreation: A Motherhood Issue in Legal Obscurity," 9 Queen's L.J.5 (1983) at 9–10. Also, note 7 N.Ill. L. Rev. 1 (1986) at 1.

53. 401 N.W.2d 687 (Nebr., 1987).

54. See *Insight* (July 13, 1987) at 58.

55. 408 N.W.2d 516 (Mich., 1987).

56. See N.L.J. (July 6, 1987) at 3.

57. See 44 La. L. Rev. (1984) at 1649.

58. For example, see Conn. Gen. Stats. §45–69 (g) (1981); Nev. Rev. Stat. §126.061 (1983); and Okla. Stat. Ann. Tit. 10, §553 (1988–1984).

59. See C.M. v. C.C., 377 A.2d 821 (N.J., 1977).

60. 432 U.S. 464 (1977).

61. Infra note 57 at 1060.

62. See generally 34 Va. L. Rev. 822 (1948).

63. 556 f. Supp. 157 (N.D. Ill., 1983).

64. Ill. Rev. Stat. ch. 38, §81–26(7) (1981).

65. Infra note 63 at 160.

66. Infra Section 1.8.

67. Ga. Code. Ann. §31–22–1(2) (1982).

68. See generally 69 Va. L. Rev. 465 (1986).

69. Ill. Ann. Stat. ch. 111 ½, §5102 (2).

70. See Lifton, *Twice Born: Memoirs of an Adopted Daughter* (1975).

71. See 59 S. Cal. L. Rev. 939 (1986).
72. See Chapter 4.
73. 601 F.2d 1225 (2d Cir., 1979), cert. denied 444 U.S. 995 (1979).
74. 696 P.2d 527 (Ore., 1985).
75. Infra note 71 at 1017; see also 34 Rutgers L. Rev. 451 (1982).
76. See generally Ill. L. Rev. (1986) at 824 et seq.
77. See generally Freedman, *The Right of Privacy in the Computer Age* (1987).
78. See Section 10.2.
79. See Barbara A., 145 Cal. App. 3d 369 (1983).
80. 219 N.W.2d 242 (Wis., 1974).
81. Infra note 76 at 831.
82. See Pamela P., 59 N.Y.2d 1, 449 N.E.2d 713 (1983); for lower court opinion, see 443 N.Y.S.2d 343 and 451 N.Y.S.2d 766 (1982).
83. Id.
84. Also see Stephen K., 105 Cal. App. 3d 640 (1980).
85. See 20 Am. Jur. 2d, sec. 13, 15 (1965)

4

Some Legal Issues and Problems

4.1 THE CRIME OF ADULTERY

The new reproductive technologies have not been free from charges of criminal wrong on the part of participants. In the 1921 Canadian case of Orford v. Orford, the Ontario Supreme Court opined that a wife's submission to artificial insemination without her husband's consent constituted adultery.[1] An English court in 1948 ruled that artificial insemination homologous (AIH),[2] wherein the husband's sperm was mixed with the sperm of a donor, still constituted adultery, and the court granted the wife an annulment of the unconsummated marriage.[3] In the 1956 Illinois case of Doornbos v. Doornbos, the court ruled that AID with or without the husband's consent constituted adultery and the child so conceived was illegitimate.[4] A Scottish court in 1958 granted a husband a divorce because of his wife's alleged adultery. It appears that the couple separated in May 1954, the wife gave birth to a child in June 1955, and her defense was that the child was conceived through AID. Lord Wheatley, writing for the Scottish court, reasoned that "unilateral adultery is possible, as in the case of a married man who ravishes a women not his wife." However, he did have misgivings when he stated that "self-adultery is a conception as yet unknown in the law" and held that AID, even without the husband's consent, was not the equivalent of physical contact proscribed in adultery, noting that adultery is concerned with the means and not necessarily the end result. However, since the wife refused to disclose particulars of her alleged AID, the court granted the husband a divorce on the basis of the wife's adultery.[5]

It is self-evident that, if the wife is guilty of adultery for participating in an AI program, the married sperm donor has also committed the crime of adultery.[6] The attending physician and other medical personnel[7] can emerge as co-

conspirators to adultery, liable both criminally and civilly in tort.[8] In the 1924 English case of Russell v. Russell, Lord Dunedin of the House of Lords reviewed a proceeding for divorce in consequence of adultery, and the sole issue was whether a husband or wife is permitted to give evidence of nonintercourse after marriage to bastardize a child born in wedlock.[9] The wife had admittedly conceived a child without penetration by any man. Lord Dunedin pointed out that it was immaterial whether the sperm came at the orifice and not within the vagina, for the act was still adultery under English law.

In the United States the crime of adultery generally requires sexual penetration by an adulterer measured by the realistic criteria of rape.[10] Yet legal writers in the 1940s persisted in describing artificial insemination as "contrary to accepted standards of legitimacy and adultery."[11] Today there is little discussion of adultery in our liberalized, freer society. A child custody dispute between two women after the breakup of the lesbian relationship raised no issue of adultery, even though the child was sired through AID by one woman who used semen from the brother of the other woman.[12] However, it has been argued that a fertilized egg is a human being and the failure to reimplant it should be considered murder.[13]

4.2 PREGNANCY TERMINATION

In Del Zio v. Manhattan's Columbia Presbyterian Medical Center, the chief of obstretrics and gynecology, after fertilization but prior to implantation, destroyed the resulting specimen without the consent of the donors.[14] His intentional act was based on his professional decision that the procedure was not properly conducted and that implantation would result in the mother's contracting peritonitis, a potentially fatal disease.[15] The New York jury nevertheless awarded the plaintiff $50,000 for her emotional distress, with nominal damages to her husband for his loss. Wrongful death damages, however, have generally been awarded only for viable or quick fetuses.[16] In Curlender v. Bio-Science Laboratories, the California court recognized a right of the resulting child born with Tay-Sachs disease to claim damages for pain and suffering during his lifetime and for pecuniary loss resulting from impaired functioning due to the disease; the medical testing laboratory here was found negligent for improperly performing genetic testing.[17] In Scales v. United States, a child was born defective due to the mother's having contracted German measles during her pregnancy; the defendant physicians had failed to test the mother for the pregnancy when she had the measles.[18] The child recovered damages for pain and suffering, lack of potential employability and payments for child care and treatment.[19]

The U.S. Supreme Court in Roe v. Wade had recognized the right of a mother to terminate her pregnancy in the early stages.[20] Subsequently in 1989 in Webster v. Reproductive Health Services, the highest court sanctioned reasonable restrictions by the state.[21] Courts in general have recognized, nevertheless, the parental right to maintain wrongful life actions where the mother has not terminated her own pregnancy and injury occurs to the child.[22] Even the surrogate mother has the right to decide whether to abort the child she is carrying.[23] However, the strong emotional attachments involved make it mandatory that the contract with the surrogate mother be drawn to embrace every possibility, including dispute resolution and remedial measures.[24]

4.3 DISCARD OF UNWANTED EMBRYO

The U.S. Supreme court in its 1986 decision in Thornburgh v. American College of Obstretricians and Gynecologists had occasion to remark: "The States are not free, under the guise of protecting maternal health or potential life, to intimidate women into continuing pregnancies."[25] In 1983 in Akron v. Akron Center for Reproductive Health, Inc., the Court had invalidated a range of municipal regulations on abortion procedures as hindering a woman's fundamental right to choose to have an abortion.[26] Discard of unwanted embryo would appear to be consonant with these mandates; there is no law that requires that all fertilized eggs and all preimplantation embryos, for example, be transferred to a uterus.[27] However, it is medically certain that polyspermic eggs are likely to miscarry or lead to an early neonatal death,[28] and therefore discard of such embryos would be warranted, as would the discard of other embryos to avoid the birth of a severely handicapped child, once the genetic makeup of the embryo is identified.[29] The necessity for discard of unwanted embryos also arises where the embryos are frozen and the couple dies before the embryos are thawed or where the couple changes their mind and insists on discard rather than donation. Couples may refuse transfer of an embryo on genetic grounds following pretransfer genetic screening techniques such as where one cell of a cleaving embryo is removed, examined, and found faulty. It should be noted that the standard IVF regimen stimulates the ovaries to produce multiple eggs, and since recovered eggs vary in maturity, they may not all fertilize or cleave; discard of some unwanted embryos is to be anticipated.

On the other hand, as delineated in Commonwealth v. Edelin, the woman's right to remove the fetus from her body does not give her the right to control disposition if it emerges alive, even if survival will lead to an unwanted genetic link that may cause the mother suffering and psychological discomfort.[30] In 1976 the U.S. Supreme Court in Planned Parenthood of Central Missouri v. Danforth struck down a statute specifying the standard of care that physicians doing abortions must exercise with respect to the fetus because the provision "impermissibly required the physician to preserve the life and the health of the fetus, whatever the stage of pregnancy."[31] Discard of unwanted embryos has been struck a mortal blow by the most modern medical approaches for detecting fetal disorders: the chorionic villus sampling procedure in which a sample of tissue is removed from the uterus to detect a variety of genetic defects, including Down's syndrome, as early as nine weeks into pregnancy, and the alphafetoprotein test, a blood test that can indicate the possibility of nervous system defects and mental retardation without posing a danger to the fetus.[32]

In summary, the rights of embryos are not violated by discard; imposing an unwanted biological offspring on a person is not only unwarranted but is an abuse of constitutional rights of the party or parties compelled not to discard the unwanted embryo. It should be noted that medical science has progressed to the point where tests of fetuses have risen sharply with the development of new methodology such as the chorionic villus sampling[33] and the alpha-fetoprotein test.[34] An ultrasound probe through the birth canal provides sampling at six weeks rather than nine or ten weeks.[35] (Chorionic sampling causes miscarriages in about 1 of 130 women, and amniocentesis causes miscarriages in about 1 of 300 women.)

Discard of unwanted embryo obviously does not involve such legal terms as *wrongful birth*, *wrongful life*, and *wrongful conception* because there has not been a birth.[36] Wrongful birth is an action brought by parents of an unhealthy or abnormal child against the physician for his or her negligence.[37] Wrongful life is an action brought by or on behalf of an unhealthy infant against the physician for his or her negligence.[38] And a wrongful conception or wrongful pregnancy claim is an action brought against the physician for negligent sterilization, for example.[39] Most courts are loathe to recognize a wrongful life claim due to public policy and the difficulty of calculation of damages. Wrongful conception and wrongful birth claims are more commonly recognized, although damages may vary considerably.[40]

4.4 ADOPTION

Adoption may be defined as the creation of a family relationship not by biological means, but by means of legal authority and sanctions.[41] Under section 110 of the New York Domestic Relations Law, for example, adoption is that "legal proceeding whereby a person takes another person into the relation of child, and thereby acquires the rights and incurs the responsibility of parent in respect of such other person."

Historically, adoption was a frequent and observed practice in ancient times. The early Greeks were adept at the intracacies of adoption, and in Roman times the role of the Genitor, the biological parent, and the role of the Pater, the foster parent, were distinct; each played a role in Roman society. Under Hebrew law, there was no provision for the creation of this parental relationship, but the voluntary assumption of the parental care of another's child was well known; for example, Abraham took his nephew Lot as his own son, and Mordecai took Esther into his home as a daughter. The first adoption law in the United States was enacted in Massachusetts in 1851, and by 1940 every state had passed legislation prescribing court proceedings for adoption.[42]

The child born of artificial conception will obviously be "adopted" by parents, although the limits of existing state adoption law may not be sufficient to handle such contemporary efforts to produce or procure children of artificial conception for adopting parents. State legislatures must act in order to avoid the kind of a crisis that confronted England in a case where the infant girl, the product of a breached surrogate mother contract, was ''impounded'' by a British court.[43] Adoption statutes must anticipate and define inheritance rights by and from an adopted child with regard to both natural and adoptive parents.[44] The recent New York decision in Matter of Etheridge that adopted children have ''no cognizable interest'' in the estate of their natural parents who die without wills may be a step in that direction.[45] The New York Court of Appeals in Matter of Ragone in 1983 had ruled that the rights of the adopted son to inherit from and through his natural parents terminated upon the making of the order of adoption.[46] Networks of child placement agencies operated or regulated by the states must work efficiently; adoption agencies must provide mechanisms for insulating adopted children and adoptive parents from the natural parents so as to integrate the child fully into the adoptive home.[47]

Wrongful adoption was the issue in Burr v. Board of County Commissioners where the adoptive parents alleged that they were fraudulently misled, to their detriment, by a county employee's material misrepresentations concerning the child's background and physical condition.[48] Apparently, the county test records indicated that the child might have low intelligence and was at risk of disease; furthermore, the county employee had represented that the child's mother was an unwed 18 year old living with her parents, when in fact her mother was an inmate of a state hospital. The jury returned a verdict in favor of the adoptive parents in the sum of $125,000, and the Ohio Supreme Court affirmed.

In People ex rel. Anonymous v. Anonymous, the New York Appellate Division, Second Department, upheld a lower court decision to return a baby to its biological parents eighteen days after its ''would-be adoptive parents'' had assumed custody.[49] Two months before the baby was born, its unmarried mother and father had appeared in court and signed papers consenting to the adoption. Two days after giving birth, the mother signed additional papers authorizing the hospital to release the baby for adoption. But sixteen days later, the natural mother and father changed their minds and wanted the baby for themselves, and the New York appellate court agreed: ''Although Domestic Relations Law, Sections 111 and 115-b neither expressly prohibit nor approve execution of a prebirth consent to adoption, we are persuaded that the statutory provisions do not authorize taking of a consent from the biological parent prior to the birth of the child to be adopted.''

Mere emotional distress or mistake is not sufficient ground in New York to permit withdrawal of consent to an adoption.[50] However, in Matter of Baby Boy L., a New York court held that the adoption forms ''are defective on their face'' and furthermore: ''Compounding the normal stresses confronting a young mother without resources were the seriously defective consent agreement, the questionable referrals made by Dr. Pellitieri, and the grossly inadequate time and attention given her by Attorney DiPalma necessary to familiarize her with the nature and consequences of her signing the documents.''[51] The court concluded by permitting the consent to be revoked and by denying the petition for adoption.[52]

4.5 "BEST INTEREST OF THE CHILD": PLACEMENT, VISITATION RIGHTS, AND CUSTODY RIGHTS

In examining the bundles of rights and obligations placed upon persons associated with the product of artificial conception, the paramount issue is generally what is in the best interest of the child. The New Jersey Supreme Court in D.Y.F.S. v. A.W. observed that "the standard must reflect the constitutional significance of the interest being protected," and the court focused on the possible harm to the child as the determinant justifying placement, and perhaps even visitation rights and custody rights.[53] One approach is to determine who is "better" able to provide for the child, as perhaps delineated in In Baby M.[54] The U.S. Supreme Court in Santosky v. Kraemer spoke in terms of the child's constitutional right to maintain a full, healthy relationship with both parents.[55] The next year the Court in Lehr v. Robertson recognized a difference between the mother's role and that of the father: the father's rights attached only after he had developed a postbirth relationship with the child.[56]

Visitation rights and custody rights are volatile areas where emotions frequently outweigh reason, and the courts are perplexed by the weight of their responsibilities. In Matter of Bennett v. Jeffries the New York Court of Appeals considered the grounds for terminating parental custody by reference to the "best interests of the child:" "Intervention by the State in the right and responsibility of a natural parent to the custody of her or his child is warranted if there is first a judicial finding of surrender, abandonment, unfitness, persistent neglect, unfortunate or involuntary extended disruption of custody, or other equivalent but rare extraordinary circumstances which would drastically affect the welfare of the child. It is only on such a premise that the courts may then proceed to inquire into the best interest of the child."[57] In Matter of Ronald "FF," the same court ruled in 1987 that visitation rights may not be granted to a "biological stranger" where the child was born out of wedlock and the mother is in proper custody of the child: "Nothing in this record establishes any basis for interfering with the mother's full custodial rights, which includes the right to determine who may or may not associate with her child."[58] The highest New York court agreed that "visitation is a sub-species of custody, but the difference in degree in these relational categories is not so great and so fundamental that rules like the *Bennett* rule, which have been carefully crafted and made available only to custodial disputes, should not be casually extended to the visitation field. Thus, we expressly decline to do so."

In 1958 in People ex rel. Abajian v. Bennett, the New York court had examined in a divorce proceeding the question of custody rights and visitation rights of the children whom the wife, for the first time, claimed had been born to her as the result of artificial insemination.[59] The court promptly estopped her from that claim but ruled that the estoppel did not render her unworthy as a mother so as to require modification of the divorce decree to grant custody and visitation rights to the husband. Five years later in Gursky v. Gursky, another New York court ruled that a child conceived by artificial insemination with the husband's consent mandated that the husband be liable for the support of the child if the husband is to enjoy any rights of visitation and custody.[60]

In December 1988 a presidential advisory group recommended that the federal government not support efforts to allow homosexuals to adopt children: "It is also preferable to place a child in a family with a similar racial background; transracial adoption should be a permissible method of providing a loving permanent home."[61] Yet in the California case of Matter of Brian Todd Batey, the California Superior Court awarded the custody of a 16-year-old boy to the male lover of his deceased father.[62] On the other hand, in the Arizona case of Matter of the Appeal in Pima County Juvenile Action B–10489,[63] the appellate court upheld a trial court's decision declaring a bisexual man ineligible for adoption.[64] In Opinion of the Justices, the New Hampshire Supreme Court reviewed the state's foster parent law and found enough of a possible risk, "not immediately disprovable by contrary evidence."[65] But in the South Carolina case of Stroman v. Williams, the court gave a lesbian mother the right to raise her child.[66] The parents' homosexuality was insufficient to deny custody in Alaska,[67] Indiana,[68] Massachusetts,[69] and New Jersey.[70] But Kentucky,[71] Missouri,[72] North Carolina,[73] North Dakota,[74] Oklahoma,[75] and Virginia[76] appear to have ruled against custody of children by homosexuals.

4.6 LIABILITY FOR SAFETY OF CRYOPRESERVATION

Cryopreservation is an essential ingredient in the modern reproductive techniques, and therefore the safety of cryopreservation is at the core of potential liability for all participants. It has been estimated that between 30 and 50 percent of embryos used do not survive the freezing process.[77] However, in the course of the natural reproductive process, only 31 percent of fertilized ova actually survive to the point of childbirth.[78] Indeed, statistics do not explain why those engaged in the cryopreservation process should or should not be held liable for the errors of their ways or for strict liability regardless of fault. It would appear that liability, if any, must be predicated upon fault, for the liability of cryopreservation banks would undoubtedly rest on the same platform as blood banks, which are involved in a "service" and therefore are not subject to strict products liability. Blood banks by statute and by court decisions perform a "service" and do not manufacture or sell a "product," which would subject them to strict liability.[79] However, in Cunningham v. MacNeil Memorial Hospital, the Illinois court in 1970 imposed strict liability on the hospital, despite the absence of a technique for identifying the hepatitis virus in the donor blood product.[80]

The cryopreservation bank appears to have statistics going for it: embryos that survive the deep freeze may actually have a better chance of survival than do newly fertilized eggs obtained by in vitro fertilization.[81] Babies born from frozen embryos do not appear to suffer any more increased risk of abnormalities than do infants conceived naturally.[82]

Is there a constitutionally protected right to semen, to eggs, or to embryos? It is doubtful whether any law has developed on this issue, although in Georgia Lions Eye Bank, Inc. v. Lavant, the Georgia Supreme Court upheld a Georgia statute that authorized removal for transplantation of the corneal tissue of decedents if no objection was made by the decedent in his life or by next of kin after death.[83] The court expressly held that there is no constitutionally protected right in a decedent's body and that the state legislature had the power, in the interest of the public welfare, to authorize the corneal removal procedure. Summary judgment motions in favor of the eye bank and the hospital should have been granted, according to the court.[84]

4.7 PARENT-CHILD IMMUNITY FROM LIABILITY

The parent-child immunity concept denies the minor child a cause of action for personal injuries inflicted upon the child by its parent or parents.[85] The rationale behind the immunity rule was to preserve the family relationship rather than to permit it to disintegrate by virtue of disputes entitling victims to compensation. There are, however, many exceptions to the immunity rule: (1) where the family relationship does not actually exist or when the child is emancipated;[86] (2) in automobile negligence cases where the injuries were caused by the parent or parents;[87] (3) where the parent tortfeasor's negligence resulted in the death of the child;[88] (4) where the parent or parents lacked custody and control of the unemancipated child at the time of the tortious act;[89] (5) where the negligence of the parent or parents entailed a breach of a duty primarily owed to the general public;[90] (6) where the injuries occurred while the parent or parents were not engaged in parental activities;[91] and (7) where the parent or parents are covered by liability insurance.[92] It would appear that these many exceptions may constitute an abrogation of the parent-child immunity rule.[93]

The surrogate mother and the child have a unique relationship in the sense that the surrogate mother is liable for her tortious conduct that results in injury to the child, as illustrated by Smith v. Brennan.[94] Here the New Jersey Supreme Court ruled: "Justice requires that the principle be recognized that a child has a legal right to begin life with a sound mind and body. If the wrongful conduct of another interferes with that right, and it can be established by competent proof that there is a causal connection between the wrongful interference and the harm suffered by the child when born, damages for such harm should be recoverable by the child."[95] It would appear that since the surrogate mother enters into a business contract to carry the infant for the contracting parents, she must bear a higher standard of care than a mother in the traditional child-bearing role. It is the business of surrogate motherhood that carries the onus of liability; the surrogate mother exercises no parental duties and assumes no parental responsibilities for the child after birth.

4.8 STERILIZATION

Much to the horror of patients' rights advocates, Iowa in February 1988 became the tenth state to authorize sterilization of mentally retarded persons. In Matter of Matejski, the Iowa Supreme Court took that eventful step, even though an Iowa statute providing for such action had been repealed eleven years earlier.[96] The decision came in the case of the legal guardians of their 33-year-old mentally retarded daughter. A bitter dissenting opinion asked the question: "At what level of mental retardation can sterilization be compelled? . . . In taking this first wide leap, the majority commits itself to eventual resolution of a twisted conglomeration of attendant social and ethical issues. . . . Future litigants, faced with unanswered questions of great social and ethical dimensions, or with missing ingredients of a vague application process, will continue to press us for determinations we are singularly unfit to reach."[97]

Other states taking similar positions include Alaska,[98] Indiana,[99] Massachusetts,[100] and New Jersey.[101]

In Custodio v. Bauer, the California court faced a plaintiff who sought to recover damages (medical expenses, the physical pain of the surgery, the mental anguish incident to the pregnancy, and the economic loss caused by the unwanted child) when an unsuccessful sterilization operation resulted in the birth of the unwanted child.[102] The court found compensable damages: "Where the mother survives without casualty there is still some loss. She must spread her society, comfort, care, protection, and support over a larger group. If this change in the family status can be measured economically, it should be as compensable as the former losses." Note that the general rule is that there can be no recovery by the parents following a normal delivery of a normal, healthy child, even though the child is unwanted. The Michigan Supreme Court in Troppi v. Scarf recognized a cause of action for wrongful pregnancy, although the birth of a normal, healthy child is not an item of damages.[103]

Medical insurance policies do not cover reversals of voluntary sterilizations for either men or women.[104] In Marsh v. Reserve Life Insurance Co.,[105] the Louisiana appellate court expressly held that the insured's elective surgery to reverse a voluntary tubal ligation was excluded from coverage since it did not result from an injury or sickness, nor was it medically necessary as required by the insurance policy.[106] An insured's vasectomy expenses were not covered in Reuss v. Time Insurance Co., although the health insurance policy covered expenses due to sterilization.[107]

4.9 GENETIC ENGINEERING

Genetic engineering, the deliberate alteration of an organism's genetic material, is an intensely complicated process and goes far behind the scope of this brief introduction.[108] The Genome Project[109] is bold effort to decipher the entire human genetic code, probably "the biggest, costliest, most provocative biomedical research project in history."[110] Yale University School of Medicine Genetics Laboratory uses recombinant DNA technology to test individuals, families, and unborn babies for three inherited disorders: fragile-X syndrome, a cause of mental retardation; Duchenne and Becker muscular dystrophy; and an enzyme deficiency that can cause death in infancy.[111]

Injuries and death resulting from such genetic engineering require compensation either at the hands of the government or under a tort system of liability against nongovernment tortfeasors. Given the unique and potentially catastrophic dangers posed by genetic engineering, overlapping regulatory regimes make sense.[112] The private tort system can work in tandem with governmental regulation.

It is interesting to note that DNA has been utilized in Great Britain for crime detection by genetic fingerprinting.[113] An Englishman was convicted on a rape charge on the basis of complex genetic samples of DNA that yield patterns as distinct for each individual as fingerprints. The samples of DNA can be taken from all kinds of biological material, including saliva, hair, skin, semen, and blood. DNA genetic fingerprinting is also useful in paternity cases, for testing can be made of blood and other biological samples.

Given the potential dangers posed by genetic engineering, federal governmental regulation in the public interest makes sense.[114] But "for the foreseeable future, there is no prospect that any conceivable purely administrative scheme can adequately protect public safety and the environment. Hence, tort reform is required, including a system of rebuttable presumptions designed to ease plaintiffs' burden in proving causation, financial responsibility requirements such as mandatory insurance, and a standard of joint and several strict liability. This proposal for regulating DNA releases could serve as an important model for future regulation of emerging technologies by harnessing the knowledge and expertise of entrepreneurs to serve the public interest."[115]

NOTES

1. 58 D.L.R. 251 (Ont., 1921).
2. See Section 2.2.
3. See L. v. L. (1949), 1 All. E.R. 141 (P Ct., 1948).
4. 139 N.E.2d 844 (Ill., 1956).
5. MacLennan v. MacLennan, 1958 Sess. Cas. 105 (Scot Outet House); see generally 69 Va. L. Rev. 465 (1983). Note of Connecticut Gen. Stats. defining adultery as a misdemeanor: "any married person is guilty . . . when he engages in sexual intercourse with any person other than his spouse."
6. Id. at 492.
7. See Section 3.8.
8. See 58 Yale L.J. (1949) at 462.
9. 13 Brit. Rul Cas. 246 (H.L. App. Cas.).
10. See Nider v. Commonwealth, 131 S.W. 1024 (Ky., 1910), for example.
11. See 34 Va. L. Rev. 822 (1948) at 824.

12. See *USA Today* (April 29, 1983) at 2A, col. 4.

13. See 46 U. Cinn. L. Rev. 725 (1977) at 756–57.

14. Unreported (Dkt 74–3558)—F. Supp.—S.D.N.Y., 1978).

15. See *Newsweek* (July 31, 1978) at 70.

16. See Bonbrest v. Katz, 65 F. Supp. 138 (D.C., 1946), and see 44 La. L. Rev. (1984) at 1670.

17. 106 Cal. App. 3d 811 (1980).

18. —F. Supp.—(W.D. Tex., 1981), rev. on other grounds 685 F.2d 970 (5th Cir., 1982), cert. denied 103 S. Ct. 1772 (1982).

19. See 44 La. L. Rev. (1984) at 1640.

20. Id.

21. 108 S. Ct. 2722 (1989).

22. See Becker v. Schwartz and Park v. Chessin, 46 N.Y.2d 401, 386 N.E.2d 807 (1978).

23. See (1986) N. Ill. U.L. Rev. 1 (1986) at 30–31.

24. See 7 Am. J.L. Med. 323 (1981) at 345.

25. 106 S. Ct. 2169 (1986) at 2178.

26. 462 U.S. 416 (1983); see generally 1987 Utah L. Rev. 1 (1987).

27. See 59 S. Cal. L. Rev. 939 (1986) at 977.

28. See Uchida and Freeman, "Triploidy and Chromosomes," 151 Am. J. Obstet. & Gynec. (January 1985) at 65.

29. Infra note 27.

30. 359 N.E.2d 159 (Mass., 1976).

31. 428 U.S. 52 (1976).

32. See *New York Times* (September 22, 1987) at C1 et seq.

33. See *New York Times* (September 22, 1987) at C1 and C10, where chorionic villus sampling is shown to examine "cells cut from the projections on the membrane around the fetus. An alternative to amniocentesis, which examines cells from amniotic fluid, it detects chromosomal disorders such as Down's syndrome. The chorionic villus test's advantage is that it is performed earlier in pregnancy, allowing for an earlier, safer abortion should the woman make that choice. While its risk is uncertain, experts believe the test may cause spontaneous abortion close to 1 percent of the time, comparable to the risk of amniocentesis."

34. Id. The alpha-fetoprotein test, which requires a blood sample, "is being offered to pregnant women regardless of their age. Abnormal levels of the protein indicate possible neurological disorders such as spina bifida or genetic disorders such as Down's syndrome. But the results are not conclusive. A suspicious blood test is followed up with a sonogram and then amniocentesis, which can confirm the disorders. Critics worry that the blood test will lead to unnecessary use of amniocentesis, with its hazards for healthy fetuses."

35. See *New York Times* (December 24, 1988) at B8.

36. See Hilton and Ream, "Duty to Unborn Children," *For the Defense* (September 1988) at 2–6.

37. See Haymon v. Wilkerson, 535 A.2d 880 (D.C. App., 1987).

38. See Siemieniec v. Lutheran General Hospital, 512 N.E.2d 691 (Ill., 1987).

39. See Morris v. Sanchez, 746 P.2d 184 (Okla., 1987).

40. See note 36 at 6.

41. See Freedman, *Societal Behavior: New and Unique Rights of the Person* (1965) at 233 et seq.

42. Id. at 236–37.
43. See *Manchester Guardian Weekly* (January 13, 1985) at 1.
44. See Section 3.6.
45. Unreported—N.Y.S.2d—(July 15, 1987).
46. 58 N.Y.2d 866 (1983).
47. See generally 69 Va. L. Rev. 465 (1980) at 512.
48. 491 N.E.2d 1101 (Ohio, 1987). Also note Case Comment (November-December 1987) at 45.
49. 534 N.Y.S.2d 706 (June 20, 1988).
50. 66 N.Y.2d 223,—N.E.2d—(1984)
51. 478 N.Y.S.2d 679 (July 12, 1988).
52. See A.B.A.J. (March 1, 1988) at 30 et seq.
53. 103 N.J. 591 (1986) at 603.
54. 217 N.J. Super. 313 (Ch. Div., 1987).
55. 455 U.S. 745 (1982) at 760—61.
56. 463 U.S. 248 (1983) at 260–61. See N.L.J. (October 26, 1987) at 19.
57. 40 N.Y.2d 543 (1976).
58. 69 N.Y.2d 602, 504 N.E.2d 395 (July 2, 1987); rev. 70 N.Y.2d 141, 511 N.E.2d 75 (1988).
59. 7 A.D.2d 507, 15 Misc. 2d 200 (1958).
60. 39 Misc. 2d 1083 (N.Y., 1963).
61. See *New York Times* (December 6, 1987) at 33.
62. Unreported—Cal. Rptr.—(Dkt. 134752, San Diego, 1987).
63. 727 P.2d 830 (Ariz., 1986).
64. See N.L.J. (November 30, 1987) at 3.
65. 525 A.2d 1095 (N.H., 1987).
66. 353 S.E.2d 704 (S.C., 1987).
67. S.N.E. v. R.L.B., 699 P.2d 875 (Alas., 1985).
68. D.H. v. J.H., 418 N.E.2d 286 (Ind., 1981).
69. Bezio v. Patenaude, 410 N.E.2d 1207 (Mass., 1980).
70. M.P. v. S.P., 404 A.2d 1256 (N.J., 1979).
71. S. v. S., 608 S.W.2d 64 (Ky., 1981).
72. J.L.P. v. D.J.P., 643 S.W.2d 865 (Mo., 1982).
73. Newsome v. Newsome, 256 S.E.2d 849 (N.C., 1979).
74. Jacobson v. Jacobson, 314 N.W.2d 78 (N.D., 1981).
75. M.J.P. v. J.G.P., 604 P.2d 966 (Okla., 1982).
76. Roe v. Roe, 324 S.E.2d 691 (Va., 1985).
77. See 59 S. Cal. L. Rev. 1079 (1986) at 1086.
78. See 240 Sci. Am. (June 1979) at 57 and 61; also Section 1.9.
79. See Brody v. Overlook Hospital, 332 A.2d 596 (N.J., 1975).
80. 266 N.E.2d 897 (Ill., 1970).
81. Infra note 77.
82. Infra note 78 at 61.
83. 335 S.E.2d 127 (Ga., 1987), cert. denied 106 S. Ct. 1464 (1987).
84. Id.
85. See 34 Cleve. St. L. Rev. 31 (1986).
86. See Logan v. Reaves, 354 S.W.2d 789 (Tenn., 1962).
87. See Ooms v. Ooms, 316 A.2d 783 (Conn., 1972).

88. See Johnson v. Myers, 277 N.E.2d 778 (Ill., 1972).
89. Note Bondurant v. Bondurant, 386 So.2d 705 (La., 1980).
90. See Cummings v. Jackson, 372 N.E.2d 1127 (Ill., 1978).
91. See Borst v. Borst, 251 P.2d 149 (Wash., 1952).
92. Sorensen v. Sorensen, 339 N.E.2d 907 (Mass., 1975).
93. Infra note 85. Note Kirschner v. Crystal, 474 N.E.2d 275 (Ohio, 1984).
94. 157 A.2d 497 (N.J., 1960).
95. Id. at 503.
96. 419 N.W.2d 576 (Iowa, February 17, 1988).
97. See *New York Times* (February 18, 1988) at B7.
98. In re CDM, 627 P.2d 607 (Alas., 1981).
99. In re PS, 452 N.E.2d 969 (Ind., 1983).
100. In re Moe, 432 N.E.2d 712 (Mass., 1982).
101. In re Grady, 426 A.2d 467 (N.J., 1981). See also Sherman, "Involuntary Sterilization Gains," N.L.Y. (March 7, 1988) at 3, 8.
102. 59 Cal. Rptr. 463 (1967).
103. 187 N.W.2d 511 (Mich., 1971).
104. See *For the Defense* (February 1989) at 2–4.
105. 516 So.2d 1311 (La App., 1987).
106. See Section 1.54 of Warren Freedman's *Richards on Insurance* (6th ed., 1990).
107. 340 S.E.2d 625 (Ga. App., 1986).
108. Note, 100 Harv. L. Rev. 1086 (1987).
109. See *New York Times Magazine* (December 13, 1987) at 44 et seq.
110. Id.
111. See *New York Times* (November 15, 1987) at 10.
112. Infra note 108 at 1104–05.
113. See *New York Times* (November 30, 1987) at A9: "The technique was also used this year in a large-scale experiment by the police in Leicestershire, a county in the English Midlands. Blood and saliva samples were taken from 2,000 men living near the area where two 15-year-old girls had been sexually assaulted and strangled. Though the case remains unsolved, the genetic tests proved that a 17-year-old hospital worker, initially charged with the murders, could not have been involved. Moreover, Douglas Hurd, Britain's Home Secretary, has announced that the Government's seven forensic science laboratories will soon be using the new genetic method of identification."
114. See Note, "Designer Genes That Don't Fit: A Tort Regime for Commercial Releases of Genetic Engineering Products," 100 Harv. L. Rev. 1086 (1987).
115. Id. at 1105.

5

Baby Selling and Surrogate Motherhood

5.1 INTRODUCTION

Baby selling and surrogate motherhood are interrelated issues that might be considered examples of today's "contested commodification of aspects of sexuality," along with the issue of prostitution.[1] Indeed, poor women (and also wealthy women) may wish to sell a baby on the black market as they may wish to sell sexual services, perhaps even for such altruistic motives as providing adequately for other children or other family members.[2] When the baby becomes a commodity for sale, all of its personal attributes—sex, skin color, eye color, predicted IQ, predicted height and weight, and the like—become "commodified" as well. Value is attached thereto, although the participants may value the baby in a nonmarket fashion, despite the receipt of monetary payment. Baby selling constitutes an inevitable and grave injury to personhood,[3] perhaps a form of slavery that would be banned by the Thirteenth Amendment to the U.S. Constitution.[4] There is a fear of relinquishment of children when the transaction or the adoption is accompanied by market rhetoric: "conceiving of any child in market rhetoric wrongs personhood."[5] Baby selling therefore fosters an inferior conception of human progress.

Surrogate motherhood, on the other hand, was not historically a baby-selling operation, although in modern times it has taken on many of the aspects of baby selling.[6] Yet surrogate motherhood is fundamentally different from baby selling in that the public policies that require prohibition of payment in connection with adoption do not similarly require a prohibition of payment in surrogate motherhood.[7] The surrogate mother is entitled to compensation for conceiving, carrying, and delivering the baby. Yet some courts have applied the "baby broker" acts to prohibit surrogate arrangements.[8] The surrogate mother is at most selling gestational services or "womb services"; the woman who is paid to relinquish a baby for adoption is in effect selling the baby.[9] In either event, it may be argued that poor or ignorant women are being oppressed or degraded by the practice of "selling"; but statistics reveal that the poorest are not involved in any great numbers.[10] The surrogate mother bears a baby only in response to the demand of would-be parents; and unless there is compensation, there is a danger that unwanted children might remain parentless. The surrogate mother cannot pay her expenses with altruism.[11] Indeed, in Surrogate Parenting Associations v. Kentucky ex rel. Armstrong, the Kentucky court allowed the surrogate mother to change her mind about surrendering the child to the would-be parents.[12] In effect, the court wished to make the birth mother's decision to keep the child not an absolute right but only a very strong presumption, such as would be used in a custody dispute over a newborn baby in a divorce. The Kentucky answer to baby selling was self-evident.

5.2 THE CONSTITUTIONAL BASIS FOR SURROGATE MOTHERHOOD

The right of a married couple to engage in collaborative reproductive techniques such as surrogate parentage is constitutionally protected.[13] The U.S. Supreme Court has repeatedly upheld the individual right to make personal decisions relating to procreation,[14] conception,[15] and the rearing of children[16]—free from governmental interference. This procreative liberty encompasses even the right of the surrogate mother to abort the child she is carrying for another.[17] Procreative liberty includes the right of married couples to reproduce through noncoital sexual intercourse.[18] In Skinner v. Oklahoma, the highest court recognized that procreation is "one of the basic civil rights" and that government cannot infringe thereupon, absent a most compelling interest.[19] It would appear that all persons participating in the collaborative reproduction are also constitutionally protected, especially where such parties are essential to the reproductive process.[20]

States may enter the picture by alleging that the surrogate practice is contrary to the law of the state with respect to termination of parental rights or contrary to the law of the state with respect to adoption. Where the surrogate mother repudiates the contract of surrogacy, the state may step in to protect the constitutional relationship between the "parent" and the child, unless the surrogate mother has knowingly and voluntarily waived that right.[21] In the adoption context, the state may sanction the decision of the "parent" to terminate parental rights where the surrender is made freely and voluntarily, unless the state prohibits private adoptions other than by stepparents or relatives.[22] The Fourteenth Amendment to the U.S. Constitution (due process of law and equal protection of the law) is a significant factor in the state attitude toward surrogate parenting.[23] A state may not deprive an individual of his or her right unless the state's interest is more compelling and outweighs the individual right. The U.S. Supreme Court in Carey v. Populations Services International[24] declared that "where a decision as fundamental as that whether to bear or beget a child is involved, [state] regulations imposing a burden on it may be justified only (a) by compelling State interests, and must be (b) narrowly drawn to express only those interests."[25] It is submitted that a state law against baby selling in the surrogate relationship would not be compelling unless the constitutional right of privacy was also involved, as illustrated by the Michigan Court of Appeals holding in Doe v. Kelley (or Attorney General of Michigan).[26] However, almost fifty years ago in Prince v. Massachusetts, the U.S. Supreme Court did hold that a state could regulate activities of the family if the state regulation furthered the best interests of the child; but outlawing surrogacy would frustrate and not further the best interests of the child.[27] Such a state regulation would not be "narrowly drawn to express only those interests." Equal protection of the law means that when the state prohibits the surrogate mother from receiving compensation for her services, the state is treating her unequally, especially if the male sperm donor is paid for his "product." (No state has prohibited payments to men for sperm donations.)[28]

A total ban on surrogate parenting, it is argued, is an unwise restraint on choices that childless couples and willing surrogates should be permitted to make.[29] It is an unreasonable interference with personal autonomy: "The prime purpose seems to be the protection of the sensibilities of people with no interest in either being surrogates or obtaining children through this method. Indeed, the willingness of some people to use public power against behavior in which they have no interest in engaging, and therefore pay no price to forego, always is suspect."[30] Indeed,

> Surrogacy only infinitesimally adds to existing motivations for behavior which will result in child-creation and relinquishment. More importantly, the circumstances surrounding surrogacy actually maximize the chances that a child will be associated with a family that both wants and is capable of caring for it. It is possible that damage may be imposed upon the families of surrogate mothers solely because their mother created and abandoned a child. But under current concepts of individual autonomy, women are free to have children out of wedlock and to have abortions, and parents are free to divorce.
>
> These practices, despite their adverse impact, are permitted in the name of personal autonomy. Moreover, there exist no limitations upon a woman's right to work. Surrogacy would seem to be another instance where women wish to make choices regarding the disposition of their bodies no more radical and no more damaging to others than these other actions.[31]

5.3 THE CONTRACT FOR SURROGATE PARENTING

The contract for surrogate parenting generally states that the surrogate mother, once the reproductive process has begun, will provide a uterus for the fetus for nine months, that she will relinquish all parental rights to the child after birth, that she will give the child to the specified couple at a birth, and that she will be compensated with a specified fee plus reimbursement for her medical, hospital, and legal expenses related to the conception of the child, pregnancy, and termination of her parental rights to the child.[32] Generally the contract will stipulate that the surrogate mother must have already given birth to a child of her own so as to ensure the adopting couple that she is physically capable of bearing a healthy child. The surrogate mother may be required to undergo psychological and medical testing to attest to her present state of health and to her inability to transmit any genetic defects to a fetus. The surrogate mother will be required not to smoke or drink alcoholic beverages or take any drugs without the consent of a designated physician. Both the surrogate and her husband agree to ''assume all risks including the risk of death which are incidental to conception, pregnancy, child birth and postpartum complications.''[33] A typical clause on abortion might read as follows: ''The surrogate agrees that she will not abort the child once conceived except, if in the opinion of the inseminating physician, such action is necessary for the physical health of the surrogate or the child has been determined by said physician to be physiologically abnormal. In the event of either of these two contingencies, the surrogate desires and agrees to have said abortion.''[34]

The contracts for surrogate parenting have been frequently the subject of extended litigation, as illustrated by In re Baby Girl, where the Kentucky circuit court denied the request of the husband of the surrogate mother to terminate parental rights and to transfer custody of the newly born child to the biological father.[35] The biological father, who had left Kentucky, was not, according to the court, the legal father, for a child born in wedlock is presumed to be the legitimate child of the surrogate mother and her husband. Furthermore, the biological father had not, in violation of statute, filed the proper application for permission to place or receive the child for adoption. The Michigan appellate court in Syrkowski v. Appleyard refused to resolve the dilemma posed by the surrogate mother contract.[36] Here both adopting parents filed, prior to the child's birth, a complaint requesting an order of filiation and the entry of their names as natural parents on the child's birth certificate. The Michigan court stated that the request relief was beyond the scope of the Michigan Paternity Act.

Surrogate mothers are prohibited in many states from receiving compensation for their services, although there were, prior to the 1980s, few specific state statutes on point; only Arkansas had enacted a specific statue on surrogate mothering.[37] State statutes relating to adoption practices have been utilized in the attempted regulation of surrogacy; for example, Florida allows the mother to receive actual medical, hospital, confinement, and living expenses[38] California prohibits payments in excess of medical expenses to the mother or adoption agency;[39] Indiana allows payment and receipt of attorneys' fees, medical expenses, reasonable charges by a licensed adoption agency, and other court-approved charges;[40] Ohio authorizes the mother to receive payment for medical and legal expenses;[41] and Utah allows receipt of actual, reasonable medical, hospital, and confinement expenses.[42] Surrogacy has been regulated by many states under statutes dealing primarily with fetal experimentation, particularly where the fertilization was in vitro as opposed to artificial insemination of the natural parent without surrogacy.[43] (Artificial insemination is not deemed to be experimental and is therefore outside the pale of fetal experimentation.) But general state policies could prohibit surrogacy under the guise of preventing baby selling, promoting the best interests of the child, and promoting the natural family unit.[44] The Nebraska Supreme Court in Gray v. Maxwell held an adoption agreement to be unenforceable because an agreement to pay a mother more than the ''legitimate expenses of confinement and birth'' was against public policy.[45] California,[46] Florida,[47] Minnesota,[48] Missouri,[49] Tennessee,[50] and Washington[51] have statutes that prohibit a parent from assigning or transferring the right to custody of a child, and therefore these states could bar the operation of surrogacy.

The most prominent state court decision in recent years was In re Baby M, decided in 1988 by the New Jersey Supreme Court, forbidding payments to surrogate mothers.[52] A detailed examination of this case is in order, for its effect has been nationwide. Briefly, a father Stern in February 1985 entered into a surrogate parenting contract with Mary Beth Whitehead, whereby she would be impregnated artificially with his sperm, carry the resulting child to term, and immediately after birth surrender the child to him. This contract contemplated that her parental rights would be terminated, thus allowing for adoption of the child by the contracting husband and his wife. A fee of $10,000 was to be paid to Whitehead upon her surrender of the child. When Whitehead gave birth to Baby M, she refused to surrender the child pursuant to contract. In May 1985 a trial court ordered the custody of Baby M to be given to the contracting husband and his wife. Thereupon, Whitehead and her then husband ''fled the jurisdiction with the child,'' but the court ordered was enforced in Florida, where Whitehead had fled. At the subsequent trial of thirty-two days, the court held the surrogacy contract valid and enforceable, terminating Whitehead's parental rights and awarding sole custody of Baby M to the contracting husband, in the child's best interests.[53]

On appeal, the New Jersey Supreme Court ruled that the surrogacy contract was invalid because

> it conflicts with the law and public policy of this State. While we recognize the depth of the yearning of infertile couples to have their own children, we find the payment of money to a ''surrogate'' mother illegal, perhaps criminal, and potentially degrading to women. Although in this case we grant custody to the natural father, the evidence having clearly proved such custody to be in the best interests of the infant, we void both the termination of the surrogate mother's parental rights and the adoption of the child by the wife/stepparent. We thus restore the ''surrogate'' as the mother of the child.
>
> We find no offense to our present laws where a woman voluntarily and without payment agrees to act as a ''surrogate'' mother, provided that she is not subject to a binding agreement to surrender her child. Moreover, our holding today does not preclude the Legislature from altering the current statutory scheme, within constitutional limits, so as

to permit surrogacy contracts. Under current law, however, the surrogacy agreement before us is illegal and invalid.

The highest New Jersey court explained its reasoning for the invalidity and unenforceability of the surrogacy contract:

One of the surrogacy contract's basic purposes, to achieve the adoption of a child through private placement, though permitted in New Jersey "is very much disfavored." *Sees v. Baber,* 74 N.J. 201, 217 (1977). Its use of money for this purpose—and we have no doubt whatsoever that the money is being paid to obtain an adoption and not, as the Sterns argue, for the personal services of Mary Beth Whitehead—is illegal and perhaps criminal. *N.J.S.A.* 9:3–54. In addition to the inducement of money, there is the coercion of contract: the natural mother's irrevocable agreement, prior to birth, even prior to conception, to surrender the child to the adoptive couple. Such an agreement is totally unenforceable in private placement adoption. *Sees,* 74 N.J. at 212–14. Even where the adoption is through an approved agency, the formal agreement to surrender occurs only *after* birth (as we read *N.J.S.A.* 9:2–16 and –17, and similar statutes), and then, by regulation, only after the birth mother has been counseled. *N.J.A.C.* 10:121A–5.2(a). Integral to these invalid provisions of the surrogacy contract is the related agreement, equally invalid, on the part of the natural mother to cooperate with, and not to contest, proceedings to terminate her parental rights, as well as her contractual concession, in aid of the adoption, that the child's best interests would be served by awarding custody to the natural father and his wife—all of this before she has even conceived, and, in some cases, before she has the slightest idea of what the natural father and adoptive mother are like.

The foregoing provisions not only directly conflict with New Jersey statutes, but also offend long-established State policies. These critical terms, which are at the heart of the contract, are invalid and unenforceable; the conclusion therefore follows, without more, that the entire contract is unenforceable.

On the constitutional issues, the New Jersey Supreme Court pointed out that both parties argued that the New Jersey and the U.S. Constitutions supported their claims:

The source of their constitutional arguments is essentially the same: the right of privacy, the right to procreate, the right to the companionship of one's child, those rights flowing either directly from the fourteenth amendment or by its incorporation of the Bill of Rights, or from the ninth amendment, or through the penumbra surrounding all of the Bill of Rights. They are the rights of personal intimacy, child's best interests, to her companionship, we need not decide that constitutional issue, and for reasons set forth below, we should not.

The right to procreate, as protected by the Constitution, has been ruled on directly only once by the United States Supreme Court. *See Skinner v. Oklahoma, supra,* 316 U.S. 535, 86 L. Ed. 1655 (forced sterilization of habitual criminals violates equal protection clause of fourteenth amendment). Although *Griswold v. Connecticut, supra,* 381 U.S. 479, 14 L. Ed. 2d 510, is obviously of a similar class, strictly speaking it involves the right *not* to procreate. The right to procreate very simply is the right to have natural children, whether through sexual intercourse or artificial insemination. It is no more than that. Mr. Stern has not been deprived of that right.[54]

The court's conclusion contained some advice for the New Jersey legislature:

This case affords some insight into a new reproductive arrangement: the artificial insemination of a surrogate mother. The unfortunate events that have unfolded illustrate that its unregulated use can bring suffering to all involved. Potential victims include the surrogate mother and her family, the natural father and his wife, and most importantly, the child. Although surrogacy has apparently provided positive results for some infertile couples, it can also, as this case demonstrates, cause suffering to participants, here essentially innocent and well-intended.

We have found that our present laws do not permit the surrogacy contract used in this case. Nowhere, however, do we find any legal prohibition against surrogacy when the surrogate mother volunteers, without any payment, to act as a surrogate and is given the right to change her mind and to assert her parental rights. Moreover, the Legislature remains free to deal with this most sensitive issue as it sees fit, subject only to constitutional constraints.

If the Legislature decides to address surrogacy, consideration of this case will highlight many of its potential harms. We do not underestimate the difficulties of legislating on this subject. In addition to the inevitable confrontation with the ethical and moral issues involved, there is the question of the wisdom and effectiveness of regulating a matter so private, yet of such public interest. Legislative consideration of surrogacy may also provide the opportunity to begin to focus on the overall implications of the new reproductive biotechnology—*in vitro* fertilization, preservation of sperm and eggs, embryo implantation and the like. The problem is how to enjoy the benefits of the technology—especially for infertile couples—while minimizing the risk of abuse. The problem can be addressed only when society decides what its values and objectives are in this troubling, yet promising, area.

It would appear that if other states followed the New Jersey decision, surrogacy contracts would be a thing of the past. The major stumbling block is not the receipt of payment by the surrogate mother but the fact that she cannot agree irrevocably before conception to terminate her maternal rights and surrender her baby at its birth.[55] However, the U.S. Supreme Court in Griswold v. Connecticut[56] and in Eisenstadt v. Baird[57] had, in effect, strongly stated that a state statute could not constitutionally prohibit a couple desiring to have a child from entering into a surrogate parenting arrangement.[58]

The Michigan Court of Appeals in Doe v. Kelly in 1981 had taken a similar view that payment should not be allowed because "the primary purpose of this money is to encourage women to volunteer to be surrogate mothers."[59] A Michigan statute, effective September 1, 1988, made surrogacy contracts illegal and also made the arranging of such contracts to be a felony with penalties up to five years in prison and a $50,000 fine.[60] The stress here is on the surrogate mother's giving up her baby; however, the contract would be permitted if the surrogate mother did not have to decide until after the birth whether she wanted custody of the baby or whether she wanted to waive custody and receive payment for giving birth.[61]

Nebraska has legislatively declared that surrogate motherhood contracts are void,[62] as have Indiana, Kentucky, and Louisiana.[63] Only Arkansas and Nevada appear to accept such contracts as valid subject to judicial review.[64]

Uniform surrogacy laws have been gaining acceptance; eight states have already passed the Uniform Parentage Act.[65] Nevada has made commercial surrogacy possible by exempting surrogate contracts from the state adoption laws that prohibit payment to natural parents for the adoption of their child. Court-monitored commercial surrogacy would entail the filing with the courts of all surrogacy agreements, the requirement that all parties to the agreement would have to receive counseling, including an evaluation of the participants' emotional ability to handle the process, and proof that the wife of the intended couple was infertile or that pregnancy poses a significant risk to her health.[66] The popularity of surrogate parenting continues, for reasons explained by Judge Richard A. Posner in his leading 1989 article, ''The Ethics and Economics of Enforcing Contracts of Surrogate Motherhood'':[67]

> The first is scientific advances in the field of reproduction, which make infertile couples less prone to resign themselves to their infertility. The second (and I think related) factor is the decline in conventional attitudes toward sex and the family. The third, and perhaps most important factor is the acute shortage of babies for adoption. (I mean of healthy, white infants—there is no shortage of black, or handicapped, or older children for adoption, but this is because there is, unfortunately, very little demand for such children.) The extent, character, and causes of the shortage of babies for adoption are the subject of my writings on the gray and black markets in adoption, in other words, on ''baby-selling,'' a practice that, contrary to the impression fostered by the media and others, I have not advocated but have merely tried to explain. . . . The irony is that those who attack surrogate motherhood out of a general hostility to free markets do not realize that surrogate motherhood is itself a product, in part, of the interference with a market—the market in adoption. Yet even if there were no shortage of babies for adoption, there would be a demand for surrogate motherhood. People (a biologist would say their genes) desire genetic continuity, and surrogacy enables the man (although not his wife) to satisfy this desire . . .

Once the contract for surrogate parenting is breached, the usual remedies of specific performance and compensatory damages come into play. Under Arkansas law, for example (the only state with a surrogate statute), a surrogate mother or the adoptive parents could require specific performance of the contract, provided that the surrogate mother was unmarried.[68] Under general contract law, specific performance would require that the object contracted for is unique and that no value has been placed on it, but personal service contracts are not readily given specific performance.[69] Compensatory damages for breach of the contract are more probable, and if the surrogate mother was the guilty party, most courts would require her to return all fees paid to her by the adopting couple. Emotional distress of the adoptive parents is not readily recognized in terms of damages.[70] The adoptive parents may not even receive the child where there is a breach of the contract by the adoptive parents, and the biological father may have a duty of child support.[71]

5.4 REMEDIES OUTSIDE THE CONTRACT FOR SURROGATE PARENTING

Where the contract for surrogate parenting is unenforceable, for any reason whatsoever, there are remedies available to the participants. The adoptive father involved in the artificial insemination or in vitro fertilization is readily identifiable as the biological father and therefore can be made to support the child.[72] The surrogate mother would receive this financial support if she keeps the child; she is also entitled to medical and confinement expenses from the biological father.[73] However, under the Uniform Parentage Act,[74] a married surrogate mother must first overcome the presumption that the child is her husband's child. The human leucocyte antigen (HLA) blood test is generally useful and even conclusive on the issue of paternity.[75] In order to obtain support for the child (as well as for medical and confinement expenses), the surrogate mother may also have to prove that the state statute declaring that a sperm donor has no duty to a child conceived through artificial conception does not apply to surrogate mothering.[76]

The biological father in the absence of an enforceable surrogacy contract might obtain custody of the child by proving that he is the biological father.[77] However, if he is unmarried, he must overcome the objections (based on maintaining family unity) delineated in many state statutes, although such statutes may be unconstitutional under the Fourteenth Amendment's prohibition against unequal treatment of the law.[78] Even then the biological father seeking custody of the child might have to overcome the presumption that child custody should remain with the surrogate mother. Under the Uniform Parentage Act,[79] he may have no right to custody since the act states that a sperm donor has no interest in a child conceived by artificial insemination, although the constitutionality of that provision is still unresolved.[80]

Whether the contract for surrogate parenting is enforceable or not, the participants might still be subject to criminal prosecution under state statutes like that in Louisiana, which states that "it shall be unlawful to sell or surrender a minor child to another person for money or anything of value, or to receive a minor child for such payment of money or anything of value."[81] California,[82] Michigan,[83] Ohio,[84] and Oklahoma,[85] for example, have similar criminal statutes against baby selling, although Louisiana, for example, has made an exception for the payment of medical expenses incurred by a natural mother who places her child up for adoption.[86] Perhaps half of the states have enacted adoption statutes (described as baby broker acts) targeted at the elimination of the reputed black market for baby selling.[87] However, it is arguable whether these statutes prohibit surrogacy.[88] In contrast is England, judging by the 1984 Warnock Report,[89] which recommended that surrogacy should be criminalized and that IVF and ET should be closely monitored.[90]

"Surrogate Parenting: Analysis and Recommendations for Public Policy," published in 1988 by the New York State Task Force on Life and the Law, provides a detailed report of this complex problem.[91] It first describes the incidence and causes of infertility and then delineates the techniques and incidence of in vitro fertilization, artificial insemination, and surrogacy. Next, it focuses on the New York law on adoption, presumptions of paternity, and the manner in which parental resources bear on custody determinations. Interestingly, there is documentation on why New York courts will not enforce any parental agreement concerning custody, visitation, or support if to do so would not be in the baby's best interests. It discusses briefly the constitutional issues raised by surrogacy, treats social and ethical dimensions of surrogate parenting, and surveys other governmental, religious, and professional society activities, both national and international. The report concludes that surrogacy should be discouraged since most surrogacy is commercial, not deserving of the same privileged status as procreation, that surrogacy puts children at risk because they are deliberately conceived into fractured family relationships, and that the surrogacy contract "embodies a deeply pessimistic vision of the potential for human relationships and intimacy in contemporary society. It promotes legal obligations as the touchstone for our most private relationships instead of fostering commitments forged by caring and trust."

Perhaps in keeping with New York's view on surrogacy contracts are England and Bulgaria, which have adopted legislation stating that the woman who gives birth is to be considered in law the mother of the child.[92]

5.5 INTERESTS OF THE PARTICIPANTS IN SURROGACY

In Matter of Baby Girl L. J., the New York Surrogate's Court of Nassau County, on July 31, 1986, sustained the validity of the surrogate parenting arrangement as necessary for "the best interests of the child."[93] Here a private placement adoption, in which the adoptive child was born to a surrogate mother who was artificially inseminated (the donor was the adopting father), resulted in a $10,000 payment to the surrogate mother for bearing the child. In granting adoption, the court found that

> the child should be raised as the child of her biological father and the latter's spouse since by court investigation it has been found that it would be in the best interests of the child to approve the adoption. No other alternative, such as denying the adoption for the purpose of discouraging such procedures, is appropriate here. This child needs a home, and under the circumstances the home must be that of the petitioners.

On the issue of compensation for the surrogate mother, the New York court concluded that "current legislation does not expressly foreclose the use of surrogate mothers or the paying of compensation to them under parenting agreements. Accordingly, the court finds that this is a matter for the Legislature to address rather than the judiciary to attempt to determine by the impermissible means of (judicial) legislation.''[94]

The best interests of the child was the motivating factor in Reimche v. First National Bank of Nevada, where the Ninth U.S. Court of Appeals upheld an agreement giving custody of a child born to an unmarried couple to the child's father in exchange for his promise to support the child and provide for the child's mother in his last will and testament.[95] The court explicitly opined that ''bartering and child selling'' were not present in the arrangement. In In re Estate of Shirk, a Kansas court ruled that the laws against baby selling did not apply to a situation in which a woman took custody of her daughter's child in exchange for a promise to leave the daughter one-third of her sizable estate.[96] It should be stressed that sperm donors are paid without any moral or legal objection; egg donors are in the same posture, as are surrogate mothers, and any prohibition against compensation for any of the participants might indeed run afoul of the Fourteenth Amendment provision on equal treatment of the law.[97] The Kentucky Supreme Court in 1986 expressly ruled that baby-selling laws do not prohibit paid surrogacy.[98]

The interests of the natural father, in addition to those of the natural mother, should be considered before a child is put up for adoption.[99] Financial arrangements cannot be overlooked, but such considerations should not dominate the process. The U.S. Supreme Court in Stanley v. Illinois made it clear that the biological mother's surrender was not sufficient to ensure the legality of the adoption.[100] Both natural parents must have time to consider fully all the ramifications of the adoption procedure.[101]

The adoptive parents also have interests that must be protected; the high or exorbitant cost of surrogacy is a factor that militates against fairness and equality for poor, adoptive parents.

The interests of society at large are not consonant with any procedure labeling human beings as property, subject to sale.[102] Protection of the family interest may be at odds with baby selling, which is said to encourage and promote the destruction of the family unit.[103] Societal interest is also measured by the intense religious antagonism to surrogate motherhood, as expressed in the brief filed in 1987 by New Jersey's Roman Catholic bishops with the New Jersey Supreme Court in the appeal of In the Matter of Baby M.[104] That brief speaks of ''traffic for profit in human lives'': ''In surrogacy, a child is conceived precisely in order to be abandoned to others or his or her best interests are the last factors to be considered. . . . There is a great potential for psychological injury to the child when he realizes that he was born, not of a loving relationship, but from a cold, usually financial, relationship.''[105] Not all religious groups agree with these conclusions.

The American Bar Association has promulgated the Model Surrogacy Act, which would make surrogacy contracts enforceable and override the common law presumption that a mother is the woman who bears the child.[106] Minimum and maximum limits on payments to contractual surrogate mothers are set at, respectively, $7,500 and $12,500, with a review of the limits to take place every two years. Another provision of the act requires only one court appearance within a year of the child's birth. The act requires all the parties to the surrogacy to receive legal, medical, and psychological counseling before entering into the agreement. The surrogate mother must also have a previous history of childbirth, and only licensed agencies can make arrangements between the parties.[107]

5.6 SURROGATE PARENTING UNDER JEWISH LAW

The Israeli jurist Moshe Silberg in 1973 opined that

> Jewish law does not establish a causal connection between the commission of an offense and the voiding of a civil contract. . . . The violation of the law or of morality is one thing, and the legal validity of the contract is another. . . . Precisely because Jewish law does not distinguish between law and morality, and that practically every performance of an obligation is at the same time a fulfillment of a religio-moral commandment—as "the commandment" of repaying a debt of monetary obligation—the non-fulfillment of a contract entered into through a violation of law will only turn out to be an additional offense to supplement the original one committed by the transgressor.[108]

In short, even a contract requiring the commission of an illegal act is deemed enforceable, and it is possible that each party to the surrogate parenting may be held liable for his or her respective obligations under the contract.[109] Jewish law requires that "the object to be acquired must be in existence at the time of the transaction, and if it is not in existence, even if it is expected to exist in the future, the acquisition is invalid."[110]

> Accordingly, if a surrogate agreement is to be construed as a form of "baby selling" (as opposed to a contract for services rendered), the contract would not be legally binding since the object of the transaction (*i.e.*, the baby) does not exist at the time of consummating the agreement. Consequently, if the surrogate breaches the contract by refusing to be artificially inseminated, there are no remedies available to the parties. Whereas, in American law a surrogate agreement may violate public policy, in Jewish law, its validity stems from the absence of one of the constituent elements of contract law.[111]

According to Jewish law, parentage is determined by genes; the father, donor of the sperm, and the surrogate mother, who is both genetically and gestationally related to the child, are considered to be the biological parents. Where the embryo is transplanted in the surrogate mother, the identity of the mother is unclear.[112]

This commentary is but a sampling of the problem of recognition under Jewish law of surrogate parenting. Much is left to present and future situations for interpretation.[113]

NOTES

1. See generally 100 Harv. L. Rev. 1849 (1987).
2. See N. Baker, *Babyselling: The Scandal of Black-Market Adoptions* (1978).
3. Infra note 1 at 1926.
4. See 12 L. Med. & Health Care 115 (1984). "Baby giving," or the release of a child for adoption, might also be a form of enslavement.
5. Infra note 1 at 1927.

See *Hartford Courant* (March 1, 1989) at 8A, where writer Peter B. Gemma, Jr., compares baby selling to prostitution, slavery, and indentured servitude, which he states are "social and legal taboos." He describes women "willing to rent their wombs" or "willing to sell the use of her entire reproduction system and all of its functions"; the baby "is conceived, nurtured for nine months, and sold simply as a commercial product." The governor of New York in 1989 was quoted as stating that "surrogate parenting for a fee is indistinguishable from the sale of children and ought to be prohibited," N.Y.L.J (February 2, 1989) at 1, 2. About the same time, the New York State Bar Association called for legislation to ban the activities of middlemen who arrange surrogate parenting for profit but would permit surrogate parenting arrangements between consenting adults: "The potential for abuse and exploitation of poor women for profit, and the risk of tragic unintended outcome in particular cases, far outweigh the social benefit, if any, in permitting private brokers to arrange surrogate parenting for profit as a solution to the infertility problem" N.Y.L.J. (January 20, 1989) at 1 et seq.

Baby selling has been a matter of public concern for many years. In 1955 U.S. Senator Estes Kefauver conducted the first major congressional investigation on interstate adoption practices. These hearings focused attention on the lack of protection for children in many states and demonstrated that infertile couples were willing to purchase children. Senate bills 1123 and 2281 introduced in the Eighty-fourth Congress endeavored to make unlawful certain commercial dealings in minor children, but the bills were not enacted into legislation. See Freed and Brandes, "Surrogate Parenting: Alternative Reproductive Techniques," N.Y.L.J. (March 30, 1989) at 3, 7. In 1984 the National Committee for Adoption adopted the following policy statement:

> Surrogate mothering describes a woman's conceiving a child by artificial insemination by donor, carrying it to term, and relinquishing it to the sperm donor after birth in accordance with a preconception agreement. Usually the sperm donor's wife will adopt the child after the surrogate mother relinquishes it. The National Committee for Adoption opposes surrogate mothering as a method of obtaining a child and is strongly of the opinion that the practice should be outlawed in those states where it is not already illegal.
>
> Licensed agencies should not participate in surrogate mothering with the following exception: If a potential surrogate mother and potential adoptive parents seek the assistance of an adoption agency, counseling services should be offered to them but the agency should not participate in the process if the adoptive parents and the potential surrogate mother persist in pursuing this course.

Currently at least twenty-four States have adopted laws prohibiting baby selling: Ala. Code §26–10–8 (1986); Ariz. Rev Stat. Ann. §8–126 (West Supp. 1987); Cal. Penal Code §273 (West 1970); Colo,. Rev, Stat. §19–4–115 (1986); Del. Code Ann. tit. 13 §928 (1981); Fla. Stat. Ann. §63.2 (West 1985); Ga. Code Ann. §19–8–19 (1982); Idaho Code §18–1511 (1987); Ill. Rev. Stat. ch. 40,§§ 1526, 1701, 1702 (Smith-Hurd 1980); Ind. Code Ann. §35–46–1–9 (Burns 1985); Iowa Code Ann. §600.9 (West 1981); Ky.

Rev. Stat. §199.590 (Supp. 1986); Md. Fam. Law Code Ann. §5–327(a) (1984); Mass. Gen. Laws Ann. ch. 210, §11A (West 1987); Nev. Rev. Stat. §127.290 (1985); N.J. Stat. Ann. §9:3–54 (West Supp. 1987); N.Y. Soc. Serv. Law §374 (McKinney 1983); N.C. Gen. Stat. §48–37 (1984); Ohio Rev. Code Ann. §3107.10 (Anderson Supp. 1987); S.D. Codified Laws Ann. §25–6–4.2 (1984); Tenn. Code Ann. §36–1–135 (1984); Utah Code Ann. §76–7–203 (1978); and Wis. Stat. Ann. §94 716 (West 1982).

Unfortunately, many of these statutes have been "applied to a situation not anticipated by the legislature at the time of enactment." 5 J. Hum. Rts. (1987) at 86.

6. See Section 3.4.

7. See 20 Colum. J.L. & Soc. Probs.1 (1986) at 2.

In *Hartford Courant* (March 1, 1989) at 8A the writer, Lynn Scarlett, pleads not to close the path to parenthood: "The push to outlaw surrogacy is ill-conceived. A ban would close off options of couples aspiring to become parents. It would drive underground those intent on trying surrogacy as perhaps their last path to parenthood. . . . The push to ban surrogacy rests largely on imagined evils and narrow concepts of morality. . . . New technologies that make possible the creation or extension of life always spawn ethical dilemmas. But resolving these dilemmas lies not in avoiding them by outlawing medical advances and closing off avenues of choice that can augment our quality of life."

8. See Doe v. Attorney General of Michigan, 307 N.W. 2d 438 (Mich., 1981), cert. denied 459 U.S. 1183 (1983).

9. See 18 Gonz. L. Rev. 539 (1983) at 549.

10. See *Los Angeles Times* (March 22, 1987), 6, col. 2.

11. Infra note 1 at 1932.

12. 707 S.W.2d 209 (Ky., 1986).

13. See N.L.J. (November 2, 1987) at 18.

14. See Skinner v. Oklahoma, 316 U.S. 535 (1942).

15. Note Carey v. Population Services International, 431 U.S. 678 (1977).

16. Eisenstadt v. Baird, 405 U.S. 438 (1972).

17. See N. Ill. U.L. Rev. (1986) at 2, citing Roe v. Wade, 410 U.S. 113 (1973).

18. See In re Baby M., 217 N.J. Super. 313 (Ch. Div., 1987).

19. Infra note 14.

20. Infra note 13.

21. See Miranda v. Arizona, 384 U.S. 436 (1966).

22. Note Conn. Gen. Stat. §45–63 (1981); Del Code Ann. tit. 13, §904 (1981); Ga. Code Ann. §19–8–3 (1982); Mass. Ann. Laws, ch. 210, §2(A) (1981); Mich. Comp. Laws Ann. §710.51 (1983–84), and Minn. Stat. Ann. §259.22. (1982). See 44 La. L. Rev. (1984) at 1656.

23. See 39 Vand. L. Rev. 597 (1986), a 250-page dissertation on "Legal Rights and Issues Surrounding Conception, Pregnancy and Birth."

24. Infra note 15.

25. Id. at 686.

26. Infra note 8.

27. 321 U.S. 158 (1944).

28. Infra note 23, at 656. Also see 300 New. Eng. J. Med. 585 (1979).

29. See Bard and Kuriantzick, "Total Ban on Surrogate Parenting, An Unwise Restraint on Choice," N.Y.L.J (April 10, 1989) at 1, 2, 5.

30. Id. See generally Field, *Surrogate Motherhood* (1988) at 75 et seq.

31. Id.

32. For a typical contract, see Brophy, "A Surrogate Mother Contract to Bear a Child," 20 J. Fam. L. 263 (1981–1982) at 266–84.
33. Infra note 17, at 4.
34. See sect. XX of the typical contract set forth in note 32.
35. 9 Fam. L. Rep. (BNA) 2348 (Ky. Cir. Ct., March 8, 1983).
36. 333 N.W.2d 90 (Mich. App., 1983).
37. See Ark. Stat. Ann. §34–720–21(B) (1985).
38. Fla. Stat. Ann. §63.212(1)(d) (1985).
39. Cal. Penal Code §273 (1970).
40. Ind. Code Ann. §35–46–1–9 (1985).
41. Ohio Rev. Code Ann. §3107.10 (1980).
42. Utah Code Ann. §76–7–203 (1979).
43. Infra note 23, at 643.
44. Id. at 644.
45. 293 N.W.2d 90 (Neb., 1980).
46. Cal. Penal Code §181 (1986).
47. Fla. Stat. Ann. §63.212(1)(e) (1985).
48. Minn. Stat. Ann. §257.02 (1982).
49. Mo. Ann. Stat. §453.110 (1977).
50. Tenn. Code Ann. §36–1–135(3) (1984).
51. Wash. Rev. Code Ann. §26.33.370(1) (1986).
52. 537 A.2d 1227 (N.J., 1988).
53. 217 N.J. Super. 313 (1987).
54. The court delineated the custody issue at great length, and concluded, "Independent of the trial court's identical conclusion, . . . Melissa's best interests call for custody in the Sterns." On the visitation issue, the court concluded: "In all of this, the trial court should recall the touchstones of visitation: that it is desirable for the child to have contact with both parents; that besides the child's interests, the parents' interests also must be considered; but that when all is said and done, the best interests of the child are paramount.

"We have decided that Mrs. Whitehead is entitled to visitation at some point, and that question is not open to the trial court on this remand. The trial court will determine what kind of visitation shall be granted to her, with or without conditions, and when and under what circumstances it should commence."

55. See *New York Times* (February 5, 1988) at B5.
56. 381 U.S 479 (1965).
57. 401 U.S. 934 (1971).
58. See N.Y.L.J. (May 5, 1988). at 1, 7
59. 307 N.W.2d 438 (Mich., 1981), cert. denied 459 U.S. 1139 (1983). Note the critical commentary by Anthony D'Amato of Northwestern University School of Law on the Baby M. case, as set forth in "Letters to the Times," *New York Times* (February 18, 1988).
60. See *New York Times* (September 20, 1988) at A15.
61. Id. The Michigan law was declared constitutional on September 19, 1988.
62. See *New York Times* (February 6, 1988) at 28.
63. See *New York Times* (May 29, 1988) at 30.
64. Id. For additional reading, note the following: *Sacred Bond: The Legacy of Baby M.* by Phyllis Chesler (New York: Times Books); *The Baby Makers* by Diana Frank and Marta Vogel (New York: Carroll and Graf); and *Birth Mother* by Elizabeth Kane (New

York: Hartcourt Brace Jovanovich); also, see A.B.A.J. (December 1, 1988) at 113 et seq.

65. See N.L.J. (April 3, 1989) at 14.

66. For an example of a convoluted case involving a surrogate contract, a failed marriage, and a child born of a donor and a surrogate mother, see *New York Times* (January 26, 1989) at A12. Also see *A Mother's Story: The Truth about the Baby M Case* by Mary Beth Whitehead with Loretta Schwartz-Nobel (New York St. Martin's Press); *Between Strangers: Surrogate Mothers, Expectant Fathers & Brave New Babies* by Lori Andrews (New York: Harper & Row); and *Recreating Motherhood: Ideology and Technology in a Patriarchal Society* by Barbara Katz Rothman (New York: Norton). For a book review of the first book, see *New York Times* (March 12, 1989) at 14, where the reviewer concluded: "In a civilized and modern society, surrogate parenting is as anachronistic and abhorrent as beheading and blood sacrifice. For in addition to all the obvious moral and ethical arguments against it, we now know too much is at risk in the biological lottery of human birth without an unassailable—and unsalable—code of fixed accountability and assignment. One out of every four children born bears a defect of some sort; in one out of eight births the defect is major. And no one, rich or powerful or deserving as they may be, should have a better shot at a perfect baby than the rest of the us."

67. See 5 J. Contemp. Health L. & Pol. 21 (1989).

68. Infra note 37. The Arkansas statute declares that a child born to an unmarried surrogate mother is the child of the intended parents.

69. See 11 Williston, *A Treatise on the Law of Contracts*, sec. 1418 (3d ed., 1968) at 644–46.

70. See Warren Freedman, *International Products Liability* (2 vols., 1986) at Section 1.08.

71. Infra note 23, at 659.

72. Infra note 23, at 660.

73. Note 6 Whittier L. Rev. 789 (1984) at 791.

74. 9A U.L.A. 579 (1985). Also see section 10.2.

75. Note N.J. Stat. Ann. §9:17–44(a) (1985), for example.

76. Infra note 23, at 662.

77. See generally 10 Am. J.L. & Med. 243 (1984) at 246.

78. See 1983 Med. Trial Tech. Q. 149 (1983) at 157.

79. Infra note 74.

80. The Fourteenth Amendment's equal treatment of law provision; males cannot be treated unequally in comparison to women. Califano v. Goldfarb, 430 U.S. 199 (1977).

81. La. R.S. §14:286A (1984).

82. Cal. Penal Code §273 (1970).

83. Mich. Comp. Laws Ann. §710.54 (1983–1984).

84. Ohio Rev. Code §3107.10 (1980).

85. Okla. Stat. Ann. tit. 21, §866 (1983).

86. La. R. S. §14:286B (1984).

87. See 20 Columbia J.L. & Soc. Probs. 1 (1986) at 8, listing the following state statutes:

Ala. Code §26–10–8 (1975) (unlawful to "hold out inducements to parents to part with their offspring or in any manner knowingly become a party to the separation of a child from its parent"); Ariz.

Rev. Stat. Ann. §8–126 (1974) (no person "shall request, receive or accept any compensation or thing of value directly or indirectly . . . for placing out of a child"); Cal. Penal Code §273 (West 1970) (misdemeanor "to pay money or anything of value, to a parent for the placement for adoption, for the consent to an adoption, or for cooperation in the completion of an adoption of his child"); Colo. Rev. Stat. §19–4–115 (1973) ("No person shall offer, give, charge, or receive any money or other consideration or thing of value in connection with the consent to adoption"); Del. Code Ann. tit. 13 §928 (1981) ("No natural parent of any child whose adoption is proposed shall receive any contribution, fee or emolument of any sort" in connection with the adoption); Fla. Stat. Ann. § 63.212 (West Supp. 1984) (it is "unlawful . . . to sell or surrender or to arrange for the sale or surrender of a child to another person for money"); Ga. Code Ann. §19–8–19 (1982) (unlawful "to hold out inducements to parents to part with their children"); Idaho Code §18–1511 (1979) (illegal to "sell or barter any child for adoption"); Ill. Rev. Stat. ch. 40 §§1526, 1701, 1702 (1981) ("No person . . . shall receive or accept, or pay or give any compensation or thing of value directly or indirectly, for placing out of a child" for adoption); Ind. Code Ann. §35–46–1–9 (Burns 1985) (illegal to "[transfer] or receive any property in connection with the waiver of parental rights, the termination of parental rights, the consent to adoption, or the petition for adoption"); Iowa Code Ann. §600.9 (West 1981) ("a natural parent shall not receive any thing of value as a result of the natural parent's child or former child being placed with and adopted by another person"); Ky. Rev. Stat. §199.590 (Supp. 1985) ("No person . . . may sell or purchase or procure for sale or purchase any child for the purpose of adoption or any other purpose, including termination of parental rights"); Md. Fam. Law Code Ann.§5–327 (1984) ("unlawful . . . to charge or receive from or on behalf of either the natural parent or parents of the person to be adopted . . . any compensation whatsoever for adoptive placement"); Mass. Ann. Laws ch. 210 §11A (Michie/Law. Coop. 1981) (punishment for accepting "payment in the form of money or other consideration in return for placing a child for adoption"); Mich. Comp. Laws §710.54 (West Supp. 1985) ("a person shall not offer, give, or receive any money or other consideration or thing of value in connection with . . . (a) the placing of a child for adoption . . . (c) a release (d) a consent"); Nev. Rev. Stat. §127.290 (1983) ("No person . . . may request or accept, directly or indirectly, any compensation or thing of value for placing, arranging the placement of, or assisting in placing or arranging the placement of, any child for adoption"); N.J. Stat. Ann. §9:3–54 (West Supp. 1985) ("No person . . . shall make, offer to make or assist or participate in any placement for adoption and in connection therewith (1) pay, give or agree to give any money or any valuable consideration . . . or (2) take, receive, accept or agree to accept any money or any valuable consideration"); N.Y. Soc. Serv. Law §374 (McKinney 1983) ("no person may or shall request, accept or receive any compensation or thing of value, directly or indirectly, in connection with the placing out or adoption of a child . . . and no person may or shall pay or give to any person . . . any compensation or thing of value in connection with the placing out or adoption of a child"); N.C. Gen. Stat. §48–37 (1984) ("No person . . . shall offer or give, charge or accept any fee, compensation, consideration or thing of value for receiving or placing . . . any child for adoption"); Ohio Rev. Code Ann. §3107.10 (Page 1983) (A petition for adoption "shall not make or agree to make any disbursements in connection with the placement or adoption of a minor" except for physicians' expenses, hospital expenses, attorneys' fees, and agency expenses); S.D. Codified Laws Ann. §25–6–4.2 (1984) (illegal to offer, give, or receive any money or other consideration "in connection with the placing of any child for adoption"); Tenn. Code Ann. §36–1–135 (1984) (private placements prohibited); Utah Code Ann. §76–7–203 (1978) (payment "for the purpose of inducing the mother, parent, or legal guardian to place the child for adoption, consent to the adoption, or cooperate in the completion of the adoption" unlawful); Wisc. Stat. Ann. §946.716 (1982) (illegal to place child for adoption, solicit, negotiate or arrange placement of a child for adoption, or receive a child for adoption where payments "exceeding the actual cost of the hospital and medical expense of the mother and the child" are incurred).

For an up-to-date examination of the problem, see *New York Times* (October 29, 1987) at B1 et seq., headlined, "Baby Brokering: Desperate Girl's Case Reveals Shadowy World."

88. See generally 18 J.L. Ref. 4 (Summer 1985) at 868 et seq.

89. Department of Health and Social Security Report of the Committee of Inquiry into Human Fertilisation & Embryology (H.M.S.O., 1984). Also see Section 8.3 hereinafter.

90. See sections 1.3 and 1.4.

91. See 10 J. Legal Med. (1989) at 251 et seq.

92. United Kingdom, Department of Health and Social Security, Legislation on Human Infertility Services and Embryo Research, *A Consultation Paper* (London: Her Majesty's Stationery Office, 1986), and C. Byk and S. Galpin-Jacquot, *Etat comparatif des regles et juridiques relatives à la procréation artificielle* (Comparative Law and Regulation of Artificial Reproduction) (Paris, France: Ministère de la Justice, Ministère de la Santé et de la Famille 1986).

93. 132 Misc. 2d 972 (1986).

94. Id. at 978.

95. 512 F.2d 187 (9th Cir., 1975).

96. 350 P.2d 1 (Kan., 1960). Note the Michigan cases of Syrkowski v. Appleyard, 362 N.Y.2d 211 (Mich., 1985), upholding the right of the semen donor participating in the surrogacy agreement to establish his parenting rights. Also, Doe v. Kelly, 307 N.W.2d 169 (Mich App., 1981), cert. denied 459 U.S. 1183 (1983).

97. See 59 S. Calif. L. Rev. 939 (1986) at 1109 et seq.

98. Surrogate Parenting Associates Inc. v. Kentucky, 704 S.W.2d 209 (Ky., 1986). For an examination of the issue of "mothering for pay," see *New York Times* (October 16, 1987) at B24, and *Hartford Courant* (October 16, 1987) at A8.

99. Infra note 87, at 14–15.

100. 405 U.S. 645 (1972).

101. The state of Kentucky in Ky. Rev. Stat. §199.601 provides that no petition for a termination of parental rights may be filed prior to five days after the child's birth.

102. See Calif. L. Rev. 611 (1978) at 613.

103. Infra note 87, at 18.

104. See *New York Times* (July 19, 1987) at 28.

105. Id.

106. See A.B.A.J. (March 1, 1988) at 137.

107. Id. at 138. See Malm, "Paid Surrogacy: Arguments and Responses," 3 Pub. Aff. Q. 57 (April 1989) where the author concludes:

> I have considered and rejected five arguments in favor of prohibiting contracted child-bearing arrangements. I would like to conclude by raising a concern about the more moderate view that while contracted child-bearing arrangements are morally permissible, they ought not to be legally enforceable.
>
> Presumably, the grounds in favor of this view are that it would allow persons to enter into contracted child-bearing arrangements while protecting women from the harm of being obliged to waive their custodial right to child with whom they have bonded. So far so good. Yet if we are to protect the women who do bond with the child during pregnancy, without risking harm to those who do not, then the arrangements will have to be cancellable only by the woman. For we would not protect the latter group of women (nor the women in general) were the customers allowed to say, midstream, "I'm sorry, I've changed my mind, you keep the child and I'll keep the money."
>
> Now the concern I have about this view is the picture it paints in which the only interest the man has at stake is his money. It suggests that if the woman cancels the arrangement, then the man keeps his money and everything is status quo. But, of course, everything may not be status quo. For if the woman carries the child to term then the man has in existence a child—a son or daughter—

which, given some courts' current presumption against joint custody, and de facto presumption in favor of awarding sole custody to the mother, is a child about whom he is not likely to have custody. This is quite different from never having a child at all. I do not mean to suggest that the interests of the father outweigh those of the mother, but only that when passing legislation we need to be aware that both parties have important non-monetary interests at stake.

The timely article sets forth the following bibliography: Sara Ketchum, ''The Moral Status of the Bodies of Persons,'' *Social Theory and Practice*, 10 (1984), pp. 25–38; Sara Ketchum, ''Selling Babies and Selling Bodies: Surrogate Motherhood and the Problem of Commodification'' (presented at the Pacific Division Meetings of the American Philosophical Association, Portland, Oregon, March 1987); Elizabeth Landes and Richard Posner, ''The Economics of the Baby Shortage,'' *Journal of Legal Studies* 7 (1978), pp. 83–178; Clifton Perry, ''Surrogate Contracts: Contractual and Constitutional Conundrums in the Baby 'M' Case,'' *Journal of Legal Medicine* 9 (1988), pp. 105–22; Margaret Radin, ''Market Inalienability,'' *Harvard Law Review* 100 (1988), pp. 1849–1937; and John Robertson, ''Surrogate Mothers Not So Novel After All,'' *Hastings Center Report*, 13 (1983), pp. 28–34.

The book reviewer of *Surrogate Motherhood* by Martha A. Field (Harvard University Press, 1988) in 102 Harv. L. Rev. 1074 (1989) concluded:

An outright ban on surrogacy, aside from its impracticality, fails to respect the right to make fundamental choices about procreation. The *Baby M* case, for example, to the extent that it suggested that family associations may be formed only in approved ways, failed to recognize varying conceptions of the good as it relates to bearing and raising children. Regulation of legalized surrogacy, however, provides protections against exploitation without imposing a vision of the good on the parties. Field's voidability rule—one form of regulation—refuses to interfere with surrogacy arrangements as long as both parties are content with the terms and ensures the security of the child's placement after the mother has relinquished custody. Yet if the mother changes her mind in the interim, Field's approach prevents a contract from trumping the mother's physical and psychological connection to the child in determining custody. Such a rule, if combined with a clear statement of the legality of surrogacy contracts, would leave the choice whether to enter into such arrangements to individuals. A woman's choice to bear a child for an infertile couple is neither inherently irrational nor fundamentally in conflict with personal or social integrity; as such, it should be a legal, though regulable, option.

108. See Silberg, *Talmudic Law and the Modern State* (1973).

109. Note the excellent article by Warburg, ''Surrogate Parenting—Legal Issues under Jewish Law,'' N.Y.L.J. (March 11, 1988) at 1 et seq.

110. Id.

111. Id.

112. See Note, 22 J. Religion and Health 139 (1983).

113. Infra note 88. Also see Note, 14 Israel L. Rev. 480 (1979).

6

Religion and Morality in the Creation of the New Family

6.1 THE JUDEO-CHRISTIAN RELIGIOUS HERITAGE

All religions have opinionated views about the creation of the new family through modern reproductive techniques. The Roman Catholic church has taken the lead in opposing the new family. According to the *New York Times* (October 8, 1987), "A Vatican official told a group of medical professionals yesterday that test-tube fertilization reduces human beings to objects and degrades their 'being, value, and dignity.' "[1] However, a challenge came from a leading gynecologist who argued that the method permits devoted childless couples to have children. The Vatican document, dated March 1987 and entitled "Instruction on Respect for Human Life in Its Origin and on the Dignity of Procreation," declares the church's vehemently moral opposition to virtually all forms of artificial fertilization that bypass sexual intercourse, which is "a communion between two people in an act of love." The Roman Catholic view states that artificial procreation excludes "the person as a person from the procreative process" because the parents can be replaced by donors of sperm or of eggs or by surrogate mothers; artificial fertilization envisions the body as something apart from the person. . . . If mankind wants to enter this project, he must reduce himself to an 'object.' " Implicit in this question of personhood is the question of when human life begins.[2] The Roman Catholic church and some other religious groups believe that human life begins at conception.[3] Accordingly, co-religionists would argue that the embryo must be protected because of its potential to become a person and also because of its independent moral status.[4] Indeed, it is this potential to become a human being that is at the core of the religious view.[5]

In the Jewish religion, the Mishnah states: "If a woman finds it extremely difficult to give birth to her child and her life is endangered, the child must be sacrificed, since the life of the mother has priority over the life of the child. But if the greater part of the child has already emerged from the womb, it may not be touched, since the claim of one life cannot override the claim of another life.'' The meaning is clear: it is not permitted to kill one person in order to save the life of another person. A child in the womb is not yet a person in Jewish law, and therefore to destroy a fetus is not to commit an act of murder. When the fetus is destroyed in order to save the mother's life, it is not comparable to murdering one person in order to save the life of another. Thus, where the life of the mother is at stake, abortion is not only permitted in Jewish law but must be performed. However, the act of abortion has serious consequences and must be undertaken only for the weightiest of reasons. Abortion is not permitted for economic reasons or where the child is simply not wanted.[6] Yet from time immemorial society has struggled with the problem of abortion. Abortion was considered a proper procedure in Egypt and in China thousands of years before Christianity. Plato and Aristotle favored abortion, although Hippocrates included the prohibition of abortion in his famous medical oath some four hundred years before Christianity. Indeed, some ancient countries like Assyria even punished abortion with death. But there was no worldwide ban on abortion up to the nineteenth century. In common law in England from the thirteenth century onward, abortion performed before quickening was not considered an offense, although many English abortions up to 1967 carried a life sentence for the abortionist and the pregnant woman. Even in the United States abortion was not restricted until about 1930.

In Jewish law, pregnancy is no reason for the delay of execution when the mother has been sentenced to death as long as the birth process has not actually started. The point is that the fetus is considered to be as much a part of a woman's body as, say, her thigh.[7] Thus, according to Jewish law, the fetus is not considered a human being and has no juridical personality until after its birth. For this reason, many Jews do not equate abortion with murder. Indeed, in certain circumstances, Jewish law views abortion not only as a permissible choice for a woman but also as her religious and moral duty.[8]

Beyond this general consensus among Jews, different branches of Judaism and different groups within each branch disagree about the legal and moral status of abortion and about the specific circumstances under which abortion is permitted or required. Within the different strands of Orthodox Judaism, debate persists about the permissibility of therapeutic abortions in situations deleterious to the health of the mother, but not life threatening and in situations where there is a grave risk to her mental health.[9] Most Orthodox Jewish groups have traditionally opposed abortion except in pressing situations, such as the endangerment of the mother's life.[10] Other Orthodox Jews emphasize the physical and mental health of the woman as the paramount concern. ''The woman's pain 'comes first' . . . considered ahead of the husband's interest in his future child *and* ahead of the potential life of the child itself.''[11] These groups believe that ''insanity constitutes a danger to life and accordingly permit an abortion when it is feared that the mother may otherwise become mentally deranged.''[12] Further, they counsel that an abnormal fetus may constitute "a grave necessity" in certain instances that would mandate an abortion (for example, if the possible abnormality of the fetus causes great mental anguish to the mother).[13] Finally, such Orthodox groups permit abortion when the pregnancy is the result of rape.[14]

The Conservative, Reform, and Reconstructionist branches of Judaism view abortion differently from many of their Orthodox counterparts and from each other. These branches sanction a woman's decision to terminate a pregnancy and endorse the holding of Roe v. Wade.[15] Rabbi Balfour Brickner, senior rabbi of the Stephen Wise Free Synagogue and former director of the New York Federation of Reform Synagogues, noted that Reform Jewish thought is in accord with Roe v. Wade's holding that "the Constitution does not define 'person' in so many words. The use of the word is such that it has application only postnatally."[16]

Similarly, the official Conservative Jewish position paper, recently issued, endorsed the Roe v. Wade guarantees: "Conservative Judaism continues to affirm its strong support for the the 1973 Supreme Court decision of *Roe v. Wade*. Any weakening, limitation, or withdrawal of the *Roe v. Wade* decision is sure to produce tragic consequences. In light of the recent Supreme Court decision, we must be diligent in our efforts to safeguard and preserve the full personal and religious freedom given to the American people."[17]

Even among these Jewish groups, however, there is disagreement on the rationale for upholding a woman's right to terminate a pregnancy. Under certain circumstances, such as when a pregnancy threatens a woman's life, as the Orthodox view counsels, or where necessary to preserve a woman's health, Jewish law may compel termination of a pregnancy. Others would protect a woman's right to choose an abortion as the exercise of her own religious and moral convictions.[18] Many Reform Jews base their support of a woman's right to have an abortion before a fetus is viable on the belief that a woman should have control over her body. Others stress a woman's physical, psychological, and emotional well-being in support of her right to choose an abortion. Finally, some view abortion as necessary to safeguard the right of a couple to produce only that number of children for whom they can properly provide.

Adoption in the Jewish religion has no origin in the Bible, although legal adoption was recognized in the Code of Hammurabi (about 1700 B.C.E). No provisions are made for legal adoption in rabbinic law.

6.2 MORAL AND ETHICAL POSITIONS

The moral and ethical positions or the ethical morality of in vitro fertilization are deep and complex matters[19] because the positions involve highly personal beliefs and emotions. A threshold issue is whether modern reproductive techniques are a "natural" means of human reproduction or whether such techniques separating sex from procreation means it is inherently wrong.[20] It is said that conception under laboratory conditions degrades parenthood, but such conception provides a solution to the tragic problem of infertility and promotes the maintenance of the family relationship.[21] There is ethical and moral concern about the possible harm to the unborn child from modern reproductive techniques, but it is submitted that the measure of possible harm is no greater than that from normal sexual intercourse for procreation.

Another problem relates to the time when the embryo has the potential for birth as a human being. If the blastocyst is not recognized as a person and is not entitled to "human rights," the issues of morality and ethics do not enter the picture. The destruction of fertilized eggs, for example, would, however, present a different issue, even though the destruction was of a source for necessary genetic research and experimentation. The resolution of this dilemma[22] might entail not inducing superovulation, which in turn would allow for the recovery of a number of eggs and their subsequent use in in vitro fertilization, but following the natural cycle of the woman, which results in the retrieval of but one egg at a time for the process of fertilization and the subsequent transfer of the embryo to the genetic mother.[23]

Frozen embryos present a slightly different problem although ethically and morally the determinants are still whether the fetus or an embryo is a "person" and when life begins.[24] The U.S. Supreme Court in Roe v. Wade[25] declared that fetuses are not persons within the meaning of the Fourteenth Amendment and thus are not entitled to its due process or equal protection guarantees. (If a fetus is not a person, an embryo is not a person.) However, it is argued that the preimplantation embryo has an independent moral status because of the potential effects of manipulations on future offspring. The person that the embryo could become has a recognized right not to be harmed by prenatal or even preconception activities.[26] Leon Kass argues that "there are more and less human ways of bringing a child into the world" and that "the laboratory production of human beings is no longer human procreation, that making babies in laboratories—even 'perfect' babies—means a degradation of parenthood."[27] Joseph Fletcher regards the new reproductive techniques as preferable to natural reproduction: "Should we leave the fruits of human reproduction to take shape at random, keeping our children dependent on the accidents of romance and genetic endowment, of the sexual lottery or what one physician calls the 'meiotic roulette of his parent's chromosomes'? Or should we be responsible about it, that is, exercise our rational and human choice, no longer submissively trusting to the blind worship of raw nature?"[28]

As examples of other moral and ethical issues are the following illustrations, set forth by the *New York Times* (September 2, 1988):

> The Supreme Court has ruled that a woman's right to get an abortion is not subject to a veto by her husband, a precedent that the anti-abortion movement is now trying to persuade the Justices to reconsider. In the last few months, men have gone to courts trying, unsuccessfully so far, to block the abortions of fetuses that they say they fathered.
>
> Another conflict is over the duty a pregnant woman owes to a fetus that she does not

intend to abort but that is placed at risk by her actions or condition. A woman who gave birth to a brain-damaged baby in San Diego two years ago was charged with child abuse for failing to follow her doctor's advice to stop using amphetamines. The charges were later dropped.[29]

On December 23, 1988, the New York Supreme Court, Nassau County, in Matter of Kaelin J.,[30] ruled that a fetus was entitled to protection after the county Department of Social Services had alleged that the respondent mother neglected her child by ingesting cocaine in the third trimester of her pregnancy. The court held that a child in utero is a child entitled to protection:

Respondent argues that any act of omission prior to Kaelin's birth is shielded from governmental scrutiny by her right to privacy, citing Roe v. Wade, supra Roe v. Wade decided, inter alia, that during the first trimester a woman's right to abortion was, for all true purposes, absolute; that in the second trimester the state could reasonably regulate abortions to protect the woman's health; and that from viability (23 weeks) the state's interest in potential life becomes ''compelling''. (Penal Law, section 125.05; Roe v. Wade, supra). Further, however, the Court stated unequivocally that there is a legitimate and important state interest in protecting the potentiality of human life. It has also been held by that Court that this interest exists ''throughout the course of the woman's pregnancy (Beal v. Doe, 432 U.S. 438, 446), but is compelling only in the final trimester.

Roe v. Wade is an abortion case; the respondent here, to her credit, never chose to abort her child. Roe is no shield. Indeed, Roe underscored the legitimate interest of the state in the unborn child, which here, appropriately, allows the protection of article 10 of the Family Court to every unborn child. The right to abort is not the right to inflict the delicate body of one's unborn child with cocaine or simply to ignore the growing potential life.

This Court finds that where the mother of an unborn child ingests cocaine prior to birth there are no imminent or potential danger considerations; the health and well-being of the child have been directly affected by this ingestion of a powerful illegal drug.

''Child care'' refers broadly to any temporary surrogate parenting situation and includes several different components that serve various needs of children and families. In recent years, the skyrocketing costs of child care have prompted federal legislation, and federal funding has raised issues of the First Amendment with respect to the separation of church and state since a substantial percentage of these services are performed by churches and synagogues. But in Witters v. Washington,[31] the U.S. Supreme Court rejected an establishment clause challenge to the use of state vocational rehabilitation funds by a blind student for religious education. The Court held that the link between the state funds and the religious school was a ''highly attenutated one'' and that the student's choice to use the funds for religious education did not constitute a direct subsidy to religion. Indeed, in order to be upheld under the First Amendment's establishment clause, the program must have a secular purpose, its primary effect must neither advance nor inhibit religion, and it must not foster excessive entanglement between religion and government.[32]

Still another aspect of religion and the creation of the new family is seen in state statutory restrictions on abortions, as illustrated in Turnock v. Ragsdale.[33] It is contended that by interfering with a woman's access to abortion, the government is essentially endorsing the religious view or position that life begins at conception. When a state imposes that religious dogma on women, it violates the First Amendment's establishment clause. Another argument is that the decision to terminate a pregnancy is often based on a woman's religious beliefs, and if the state prevents her from implementing that personal religious decision, it is interfering with her First Amendment right to exercise her religious belief. The U.S. Supreme Court decision in Roe v. Wade[34] recognized the religious nature of the abortion decision. Note that the dissent of Mr. Justice Stevens in Webster v. Reproductive Health Services,[35] upholding Missouri's restrictions on the use of public employees or public facilities for the performance or assistance of nontherapeutic abortions, as well as Missouri's viability testing requirement, argued that the majority decision upholding the abortion regulations was erroneous in that the Missouri statute violated the establishment clause of the First Amendment. In short, the establishment clause and the free exercise of religion of the First Amendment require government neutrality and reasonable accommodation in the face of competing religious claims. Those constitutional principles simply do not allow states to set conditions for the termination of a pregnancy that effectively burden a woman's freedom of choice in such a way as to require her to follow the religious doctrine of a particular sect or sects and conform her conduct accordingly, even though she holds no such religious beliefs. As stated in School District of Abington Township v. Schempp,[36] "In the relationship between man and religion, the State is firmly committed to a position of neutrality."

Permitting the state to communicate the religious message that abortion is morally reprehensible flouts the guarantees of the establishment clause of the First Amendment, which prohibits the fusion of government and religion that occurs when government endorses or supports the theological tenets of one religion or several religions over others.[37] And in the Schempp case[38] the Court had intoned: "The wholesome neutrality of which this Court's cases speak thus stems from a recognition of the teachings of history that powerful sects or groups might bring about a fusion of government and religious functions or a concert of dependency of one upon the other to the end that official support of the state or federal government would be behind the tenets of one or of all orthodoxies; this is what the Establishment Clause prohibits."

Nowhere is this principle of government neutrality more important than in the highly controversial and emotional issue of reproductive rights.[39] For many women, the decision whether to terminate a pregnancy is an issue of fundamental religious belief, and statutes regulating abortion affect those fundamental religious interests and burden the free exercise of religion. Above all, those state statutes do not serve any compelling state interests that would justify incursions in religious liberty.

NOTES

1. At B3.
2. See 59 S. Cal. L. Rev. 1079 (1986) at 1090.
3. See Rhoden, "The New Neonatal Dilemma: Live Births from Late Abortions," 72 Geo. L.J. 1451 (1984) at 1466.
4. Infra note 2.
5. See 82 Yale L.J. 920 (1973) at 925, and Langerak, *Ethical Issues in Modern Medicine* (1983) at 174–75.
6. See D. Feldman, *Birth Control in Jewish Law* (Schoken, 1968): "Therapeutic abortion . . . is mandated by the Mishnah" (p. 284).
7. Id.
8. See H. Donin, *To Be a Jew* (Basic Books, 1972): "All halakhic scholars agree that therapeutic abortions—namely, abortions performed in order to preserve the life of the mother—are not only permissible but mandatory" (p. 141).
9. Infra note 6, at 284–94.
10. Infra note 6, at 275–83.
11. Infra note 6, at 291.
12. See J. D. Bleich, *Contemporary Halakhic Problems* 363 (1977).
13. Infra note 6, at 367.
14. Infra note 6, at 287.
15. 410 U.S. 113 (1973).
16. *A Statement on Abortion* (issued by the Social Justice Committee of the Rabbinical Assembly) (July 1989). Hearings Before the Subcomm. on Civil and Constitutional Rights of the House Comm. on the Judiciary, 94th Cong., 2d sess. 335 (March 24, 1976) (Rabbi Brickner, statement on behalf of the Religious Coalition for Abortion Rights) (citing Roe v. Wade, 410 U.S. at 157).
17. See M. D. Bial, *Liberal Judaism at Home: The Practices of Modern Reform Judaism* 13 (1971).
18. Id.
19. See generally 21 Gonz. L. Rev. 395 (1985/86).
20. See 247 J.A.M.A. 3235 (June 1982).
21. See Fletcher, "New Beginnings in Life: A Theologian's Response," *The Genetics and the Future of Man* (1972) 78–87.
22. According to Taymor, "Current Status of in Vitro Fertilization and Reimplantation," *Genetics and the Law* II 345 (1980).
23. Infra note 19, at 401.
24. Infra note 2, at 1088.
25. 410 U.S. 113 (1973).
26. Infra note 2, at 1091. A distinctive legal right has been described in Curlender v. Bio-Science Laboratories, 106 Cal. App. 3d 811, 165 Cal. Rptr. 477 (1980).
27. Kass, "Making Babies—the New Biology and the Old Morality," 26 *Public Interest* 49 (1972).
28. J. Fletcher, *The Ethics of Genetic Control* (1974) at 36.
29. At B6, other situations are also set forth:

> In McNamara v. County of San Diego, the father is challenging a ruling by a California appellate court that cut off his rights to contact with his daughter. The court did not find Edward McNamara

to be unfit as a parent; in fact, a lower court had declared him "a good parent who can provide a good, loving home." But the appeals court ruled that his child's "best interests" would be served by not letting him into her life six years after she had been placed with an adoptive family . . . "

30. Unreported,—N.Y.S.2d—(Nassau County, December 23, 1988). Also note "Letter to Editor," N.Y.L.J. (December 19, 1988) at 2:

31. 106 S. Ct. 748 (1986).

32. See Lemon v. Kurtzman, 403 U.S. 602 (1971).

33. DK7 88–790, 57 U.S.L.W. 3859, October term 1989; for lower court decisions, see 625 F. Supp. 1212 (N.D. Ill., 1985), modified 841 F.2d 1358 (7th Cir., 1988).

34. 410 U.S. 113 (1973).

35. 109 S. Ct. 3040 (1989).

36. 374 U.S. 203 (1963) at 206.

37. See Grand Rapids School District v. Ball, 473 U.S. 373 (1985) at 389.

38. Infra note 35, at 222.

39. See Griswold v. Connecticut, 381 U.S. 479 (1965), and Eisenstadt v. Baird, 405 U.S. 438 (1972). Also, see McRae v. Califano, 491 F. Supp. 630 (E.D.N.Y., 1980) at 696, rev'd sub nom. Harris v. McRae, 448 U.S. 297 (1980).

7

Related Legal Liability Matters

7.1 INTRODUCTION

In the creation of the new family by artificial conception and in accord with modern genetics, there is ever present the issue of legal liability upon the various participants in the new reproductive process. The law of negligence, for example, has great flexibility in its "adaptability to the conditions and needs of changing times."[1] A remedy is afforded where one's interests have been violated by the negligent conduct of another.[2] The New York court in Woods v. Lancet in 1951 best expressed it in these words: "No right is more inherent, more sancrosanct, than that of an individual in his possession and enjoyment of his life, his limbs, and his body. The law is not static and inert, but is sufficiently elastic to meet changing conditions. It is presumed to keep pace with present day concepts."[3] And in Renslow v. Mennonite Hospital, the Illinois court opined that "the judicial process by nature is a scheme of evaluating the varying forces which make society."[4]

The legal creation of the "reasonable man" concept has given flexibility to the determination of tort liability.[5] The conduct of the "reasonable man" of ordinary prudence varies with the situation that confronts him or her, and takes into account every factor of any significance in evaluating the reasonableness of his or her conduct. All of the participants—from the donors of the sperm or eggs to the surrogate mother to the inseminating physician and to the adoptive parents, as well as to the biological parents and others—must toe the mark of the reasonably prudent person and have their conduct adjudged accordingly if legal liability shall or shall not result. The absence of a standard of conduct does not excuse any of the participants from conduct that injures another. Among the elements of such a standard of care are moral qualities and intelligence.[6] A surrogate mother, for example, whose sole responsibility is to exercise the most stringent care while carrying the child, cannot escape liability for the consequences of her imprudent or even immoral conduct. A suit by a child alleging that the surrogate mother breached her duty in nurturing a healthy fetus may result in an enforceable wrongful death claim.[7]

In this nuclear age with radiation hazards even in the workplace, genetic effects can involve damage to the chromosomes. An irradiated person prior to conceiving a child or serving as a sperm donor or indeed any other person involved in the reproductive process may be legally responsible for genetic abnormalities in the child. Such abnormalities may not become apparent for an extended period of time.[8] The ramifications of radiation and reproductive health simply cannot be defined.

The abolition of interspousal immunity is another factor that must be taken into consideration in viewing legal liability. In Price v. Price, the Texas Supreme Court in 1987 made it possible for spouses to sue each other in tort (supplanting the 101-year-old common law doctrine of interspousal immunity).[9] More than forty states[10] have done similarly: "It is difficult to fathom how denying a forum for the redress of any wrong could be said to encourage domestic tranquillity."[11] The net effect of the abrogation of interspousal immunity is to open the door to liability against the negligent spouse in the new family relationship.

Another interesting aspect of liability is seen in those cases dealing with the assertion of jurisdiction over the providers of human donor organs.[12] In State of Missouri ex rel. Wichita Falls General Hospital v. Adolf, the federal district court refused to allow a Missouri trial court to assert jurisdiction over a Texas hospital in a negligence action.[13] The Texas hospital had allegedly misstated the blood type of a transplanted heart as being type A, not type B; the recipient died in Missouri, and the wrongful death action commenced in Missouri. According to the court, public policy restricts the normal availability of some tort concepts in "humanitarian medical treatment situations where human life is at stake." The court stated that its decision did not preclude recovery in the Texas court, but assertion of jurisdiction here would deter the willingness of hospitals to make human organs available in the future.

Health insurance coverage for infertility procedures has been relatively little discussed, although in recent years several appellate courts have faced that issue.[14] The Iowa Supreme Court in Witcraft v. Sundstrand initially determined that an infertility condition was an "illness" within the meaning of the health insurance policy and then compensated the insured for the expenses of treatments that included semen analysis, sperm counts, ultrasound to determine the effectiveness of the insemination procedures, fertility drugs to produce ovulation, and washed intrauterine insemination, plus a more complicated procedure.[15] The employer's insurer contested the coverage and the payments on the ground that the medical services were not performed due to illness or injury; indeed, artificial insemination did not encourage healing or reverse the malfunctioning reproductive systems of the parties. On the other hand, an Oklahoma appellate court in

Kinzie v. Physicians' Liability Insurance Co.[16] ruled that a woman's expenses for the conception of her child by in vitro fertilization[17] were not for a ''medically necessary'' service within the meaning of her comprehensive medical insurance policy. The court affirmed the trial court's holding that as a matter of law, in vitro fertilization was not a medically necessary service because it was elective and not required to cure or preserve the insured woman's health. Obviously, the high cost and growth in popularity of infertility treatments are a cause of grave concern to the health insurance industry; specific policy exclusions or increased premiums are but a partial answer.[18]

7.2 PRENATAL INJURIES

Prenatal injuries have historically not received the attention of courts for a variety of reasons, including the complexity of that injury alleged to have occurred while the child was in the uterus. In 1884 in Dietrich v. Northampton, the mother of the deceased child, when the mother was approximately five months pregnant, slipped on a defect in the road surface of a highway, fell, and suffered a miscarriage.[19] The Massachusetts court, more than 100 years ago, held that there was no cause of action, for the injuries were sustained ''in utero''; the fetus was part of the mother, and the tortfeasor had no duty of care to one not yet in being. The fetus was not viable at the time of the mother's injury, and therefore the prenatal injuries were uncompensable. Sixteen years later in Allaire v. St. Luke's Hospital, the Illinois court declared that an infant cannot maintain a cause of action for injuries received before birth.[20] An elevator accident in the hospital where the mother was due to give birth caused the injuries to the child. Even a representative of a deceased child was not permitted to maintain a cause of action for the child's prenatal injuries in Alabama in 1926.[21] The Alabama court opined that the alleged injuries to the unborn child were too remote to be compensated. In short, the child was part of the mother (who fell while descending from a train) before birth and the child is severed from the mother only at birth, thus precluding recovery for such injuries while the child was in the womb.

It was not until 1939 in the California case of Scott v. McPheeters that prenatal injuries were first compensated.[22] Here the mother's physician negligently used metal clamps and forceps in the process of delivering the child, and the child was born with a permanent paralysis. Since the California court found that the infant was viable, or capable of living, at the time of injury, it naturally followed that the child should be compensated for injuries: ''The difficulty of obtaining proof of the wrong should prompt greater leniency in affording the remedy, rather than a denial of plain justice.''[23] Seven years later in Bonbrest v. Kotz, the District of Columbia Court of Appeals acknowledged a cause of action for prenatal injuries sustained by an unborn, viable child.[24] The court recognized that the child was not part of the mother: ''The absence of precedent should afford no refuge to those who by their wrongful act, if such be proved, have invaded the right of an individual.'' In 1953 in Kelly v. George, a New York court extended recovery to a nonviable, three-month fetus whose expectant mother was struck and knocked down by an automobile.[25] Thus, a child born alive is entitled to relief for prenatal injuries sustained any time after conception as the result of another's negligent conduct.[26]

Today it would appear that every state allows an injured child subsequently born alive to recover for prenatal injuries.[27] Where the injured child was born alive but died subsequently as a result of the original injury, the parents may recover for the wrongful death.[28] The Iowa Supreme Court in Craig v. IMT Insurance Co. permitted the parents of an unborn child to recover for loss their consortium under the uninsured motorist provision of their automobile liability insurance policy, even though that court had previously held that an unborn child is not a person for purposes of protection under the Iowa wrongful death act.[29]

Recognition of a preconception tort for negligent medical treatment of a non-pregnant woman was given by the Michigan Court of Appeals in Monusko v. Postle.[30] The court allowed a severely retarded rubella-syndrome child to pursue her claims against physicians and a hospital for failing to test and immunize her mother more than a year before she was conceived: ''It is readily foreseeable that someone not immunized may catch rubella, and, if pregnant, bear a child suffering from rubella syndrome.''

Medical proof of causation is obviously paramount if the action for recovery of damages for prenatal injuries is to succeed.[31] If the claim for prenatal injury is instituted against the surrogate mother, it is necessary to substantiate the materiality of her conduct, even though the health and well-being of the fetus is, for the most part, utterly dependent on the surrogate mother. Competent medical evidence is still essential to establish the causal relation and the damage to the child.[32] However, medical science has advanced greatly in recent years; some infants with serious congenital anomalies such as meningomyelitis (a condition in which the spinal cord is exposed) and hydrocephalous (a condition in which fluid accumulates in the brain) are today alive. Many infants are now able to survive even iatrogenic injury. The Indiana case of In re Baby Doe points up one of the basic ethical decisions necessitated when an infant suffers from Down's syndrome and from tracheoesophageal fistula, a blockage of the digestive tract.[33] With the concurrence of the physician, the parents refused to consent to surgery to correct the blockage; food and water were withheld, and the baby was sedated until it died six days later. The Indiana court refused to intervene, and shortly thereafter the U.S. Department of Health and Human Services published a ruling[34] that the withholding of food and necessary medical treatment from handicapped infants constituted discrimination and violation of law.[35] But in 1983 in a suit brought by the American Academy of Pediatrics and other medical groups, the federal court invalidated the regulation on the ground that the federal agency had not followed the requisite procedure for issuing the regulation.[36] The final ruling was issued by the federal agency in January 1984, and hospitals were encouraged to establish infant care review committees and to consult with the federal agency.[37] Later that year, the New York Court of Appeals in Weber v. Stony Brook Hospital affirmed the parents' right not to have surgery performed on their handicapped infant: "The most private and most precious responsibility vested in the parents for the care and nurture of their children" should not be disturbed by hospitals or by the courts.[38] It should be noted that the New York appellate court had declared that "these concerned and loving parents have made an informed, intelligent and reasonable determination based upon and supported by responsible medical authority." Thereupon the federal agency sought to hold the hospital liable for violation of section 504 of the Rehabilitation Act, but the federal district court in New York refused to go along with the federal agency, holding that the hospital's "failure to perform the surgical procedures cannot possibly be regarded as a violation of the Rehabilitation Act."[39] Finally, in American Hospital Association v. Heckler,[40] the U.S. Supreme Court declared these final regulations of the federal agency to be invalid: "A hospital's withholding of treatment when no parental consent has been given cannot violate Section 504, for without the consent of the parents or a surrogate decisionmaker the infant is neither 'otherwise qualified' for treatment nor has he been denied care 'solely by reason of his handicap.' "[41]

7.3 MEDICAL MALPRACTICE AND PRENATAL INJURIES

Medical malpractice frequently involves prenatal injuries, as illustrated by Pratt v. University of Minnesota Affiliated Hospitals & Clinics, where the Minnesota appellate court held that genetic counseling is medical treatment, and the parents' action against two doctors for failure to inform them of the increased risk that their future offspring would suffer the same type of tragic birth defects as their most recent child, was not dismissible.[42] In at least a dozen states, physicians and other persons who negligently harm the in vitro embryo can be sued for malpractice.[43] Negligent or intentional termination of the embryo against the wishes of the couple could serve as the basis for a malpractice suit, as in Del Zio v. Manhattan's Columbia Presbyterian Medical Center, where the physicians in 1973 attempted to fertilize a woman's egg with her husband's sperm, and the department chairman of the hospital, without consultation with the other physicians or with the couple, removed the culture from the incubator and destroyed it.[44] A jury awarded the couple $50,000 in damages for their emotional distress. A Pennsylvania court in the 1985 decision of Amadio v. Levin[45] opined that "a rule which permits a physician to escape liability to an unborn child by preventing that child from reaching birth is intolerable."[46]

Infertile couples can play an important role in disciplining physicians who fail to provide relevant information or who act negligently and not in accord with community medical standards.[47] Negligent handling of embryos, for example, which leads to avoidable prenatal injuries, must be diligently prosecuted even at the expense of medical progress.[48] Negligent selections of donors or donees by a physician should be similarly actionable. Prenatal injuries, such as congenital deafness in Turpin v. Sortini[49] and Down's syndrome in Procanik v. Cillo,[50] are equally actionable by the infant against the tortfeasor-physician, although the question can be raised as to whether such handicaps are severe enough to render the child's life not worth living.[51]

Prenatal testing,[52] fetal monitoring, [53] amniocentesis,[54] and other testing and monitoring methods are essential to the defense of medical malpractice.[55] While amniocentesis has been the standard method of testing fetuses for chromosomal and genetic abnormalities, in recent years the procedure has been joined by chorionic villus sampling (CVS), which involves removing material from the outside of the fetal sac near the placenta. The CVS method can be performed nine weeks into the pregnancy (as opposed to sixteen weeks with amniocentesis), but CVS has a higher risk of spontaneous abortion.[56] Both procedures are designed to give the woman the option of aborting a fetus diagnosed as having some a defective chromosome or gene. Fetal monitoring alerts the physician to the possibility of brain damage to the infant; a fetal heart monitor, for example, graphically records the uterine contractions of the mother and the heartbeat of the fetus, and brain damage, if any, would show up in the graphic record.

Medical malpractice can also relate to wrongful pregnancies and wrongful conceptions.[57] In essence, the causes of action here alleged that but for the physician's negligence the mother would not have conceived or given birth to an unplanned but healthy infant.[58] Wrongful pregnancy is distinguishable from such other prenatal torts as wrongful birth, wrongful life, and fetal wrongful death actions in that the plaintiff is not the infant or the fetus but the parents themselves.[59] Also, the infant or fetus is healthy and not defective; the gravamen of the wrongful pregnancy complaint is that the parents who had made the conscious decision not to conceive tried to prevent pregnancy by obtaining professional health care, yet pregnancy occurred due to professional malpractice.[60] Many wrongful pregnancy cases involve negligently performed sterilization operations, such as tubal ligation and vasectomies,[61] negligently performed abortions,[62] failures to insert properly contraceptive devices,[63] and countless other negligent acts, such as negligently filling birth control prescriptions.[64] Courts have experienced no difficulty in giving relief for wrongful pregnancies despite the public policy argument that recognition of the cause of action may spawn fraudulent claims and may promote inequitable and exorbitant damages.[65] A common problem in wrongful pregnancy cases is that the relevant statute of limitations may run before plaintiff discovers the alleged negligence, especially where conception does not occur until several years after a negligent sterilization operation, for example.[66] Discovery statutes for such medical malpractice are one solution,[67] as is a judicial finding of fraudulent concealment by the physician.[68] The damages awarded in the wrongful pregnancy case encompass physical and mental pain and suffering incurred during pregnancy and childbirth, medical expenses incurred during pregnancy and delivery, lost wages, and perhaps a refund of the costs of the surgery, both original and subsequent correcting surgery.[69] But the costs of rearing and educating the unwanted child are rejected by a majority of states that favor offsetting the rearing costs against the value of the emotional benefits the parents derived from the child.[70] California and Ohio are among those few states that favor full recovery for rearing costs of the child.[71]

7.4 POSTNATAL INJURIES AND WRONGFUL BIRTHS

Wrongful birth and postnatal injury are the causes of action where the breach of medical procedures proximately causes the birth of a defective child.[72] Generally the parents bring the action to recover the harm inflicted upon them, and the thrust of the action is a negative deprivation of choice: the defendant's negligence deprived the parents of the information necessary to conceive or to continue a pregnancy.[73] If such a choice were available to them, the parents contend that they would not have had the child (who was born defective).

The New York Court of Appeals in Becker v. Schwartz mislabeled the cause of action wrongful life when in reality it was a wrongful birth action.[74] The complaint, on behalf of the defective infant, alleged that the defendant physicians negligently failed to inform plaintiff parents accurately of the risks involved in a pregnancy. The court concluded that the pleading did not state a legally cognizable cause of action because (1) it did not appear that the infant suffered any legally cognizable injury as a child does not have a fundamental right to be born as a whole, functional human being, and (2) damages recoverable on behalf of an infant are not ascertainable, as damages are designed to place the injured parties in the position they would have occupied but for the negligence of the defendants; and by the allegations of the complaint but for the negligence of defendants, the infant would not be in existence. But the highest New York court, while not recognizing the parents' damages for psychic or emotional harm alleged to have occurred as a consequence of the birth of an infant in an impaired state since the calculation of such damages was too speculative, nevertheless recognized a cause of action for pecuniary damages suffered as a consequence of the birth because such damages are ascertainable and the complaint alleged the existence of a duty flowing from defendants to plaintiffs and that the breach of that duty was the proximate cause of those damages.[75]

The 1982 Virginia decision in Naccash v. Burger illustrates the typical wrongful birth action resulting from negligent genetic testing.[76] Here the expectant father had a blood test to ensure that he was not a carrier of Tay-Sachs disease (a degenerative disease of the nervous system), for the couple would not have a child subject to that disease. After defendant assured the parents that the husband did not carry this disease, the expectant mother decided to have the baby, and the baby was subsequently diagnosed as having Tay-Sachs disease. Apparently defendant had confused the husband's blood sample with the sample of a noncarrier. The Virginia court observed that the erroneous blood testing result deprived plaintiffs of the chance to decide whether to terminate the pregnancy. Similarly, in Schroeder v. Perkel, the New Jersey court permitted the parents of two children born with cystic fibrosis (a genetic disease that results in chronic respiratory problems and death) to recover from the physician who had treated the first child but had failed to diagnose the child's disease in time to permit the parents to avoid the birth of a second child.[77] The highest New York court, in Park v. Chessin, permitted recovery where the parents were told incorrectly that chances of having a second child with polycystic kidney disease were "practically nil."[78] Indeed, the attending physician owes the parents seeking information and a choice of alternatives the minimum duty of reasonable care. There is even a duty on the part of the physician to disclose affirmatively facts relevant to the parents' decision to avoid the birth.[79] The parents' constitutionally protected right to obtain an abortion, for example, is said to create the physician's duty based in part on medical science's increased ability to predict the occurrence of birth defects attributable to genetic disorders.[80]

The proximate cause issue in wrongful birth situations is not that the physician's conduct caused the birth defects or that no one could have prevented the birth defects but the deprivation of information by the physician that would have led the parents to have made the decision to terminate the pregnancy in view of the probability of birth defects in the child.[81] On damages for wrongful birth, most courts permit the parents to recover the extraordinary medical costs needed to raise the defective child.[82] Yet the North Carolina court in Berman v. Allen allowed recovery of damages for mental and emotional distress but rejected the parents' claim for medical expenses of the child born with Down's syndrome.[83] (Courts in Idaho, Virginia, and Washington have approved recovery for both medical expenses and for mental and emotional distress.)[84]

The Fourth U.S. Court of Appeals in Gallagher v. Duke University, applying North Carolina law, permitted the parents to sue their cytogeneticist for wrongful conception of their second child who was born with severe genetic deformities.[85] The parents had consulted the cytogeneticist at Duke University after their first child was born with genetic defects that caused the baby to die a week after birth. The cytogeneticist conducted various tests and informed the parents that their chances of having another deformed child were the same as the general population. Later, the cytogeneticist discovered that he had misread the prior tests showing the abnormality. The jury returned a verdict for the parents in the sum of $1.031 million. The federal appellate court pointed out that the case here was not a wrongful birth act but a suit for wrongful conception due to the cytogeneticist's negligence before the child was conceived, and thus the parents could recover the costs of the child's birth and the cost of raising the child, including emotional distress without offset, because there are no real benefits in raising a severely deformed child.[86]

New York still refuses to permit recovery of the costs of raising a healthy child since wrongful conception does not set forth a legally cognizable claim: "It is well settled that a cause of action which seeks to recovery the ordinary costs of raising a healthy child for 'wrongful conception' does not set forth a legally cognizable claim" (see, O'Toole v. Greenberg, 64 NY2d 427 [1985]).

In Jean-Charles v. Planned Parenthood Assn. of Mohawk Val. (99 AD2d 542 [2nd Dept. 1984]), the Appellate Division held that there may be no recovery for future lost wages resulting from the mother's inability to carry on a job by reason of her obligation to raise the child. The Court did, however, recognize "the legal sufficiency of those portions of the complaint that seek recovery for medical expenses, pain and suffering and mental distress, but only to the extent that the distress resulted 'from the actual or anticipated physical pain and suffering associated with the pregnancy and delivery.' "[87]

7.5 THE WRONGFUL LIFE

The impaired child has a claim for wrongful life due to a myriad of causes, including negligent testing and negligent counseling.[88] The gravamen of the wrongful life claim is that the plaintiff infant is damaged by reason of his or her very existence and would not have been born but for the negligence of the defendant or defendants.[89] But the infant plaintiff, to sustain the cause of action for wrongful life and recover damages, must exhibit some defect, physical affliction, or disability.[90] The reasoning behind the judicial determination that the cause of action for wrongful life should not be recognized includes the following: (1) allowing the cause of action implies that nonlife is preferable to life in an impaired state, an unacceptable disavowal of the sanctity and worth of human life (in Elliott v. Brown, the Alabama court declared that "a legal right not to be born is alien to the public policy of this State to protect and preserve human life)";[91] (2) courts cannot handle the immense administrative responsibilities associated with recognition of "wrongful life";[92] and (3) plaintiffs cannot establish the essential elements of the tort: duty, breach, and injury.[93]

In recent years, however, the highest courts of California, New Jersey, and Washington have recognized wrongful life claims, as illustrated by Turpin v. Sortini[94] Procanik v. Cillo,[95] and Harbeson v. Parke-Davis, Inc.[96] In the *Turpin* case, the deaf child's claim resulted from a hearing specialist's erroneous diagnosis, and the California court reasoned that but for the tortfeasor's negligence, the child would have been born healthy and with normal hearing. The court compared life in the impaired state with no life at all and predicated liability not on the severity of the birth defect but on the predictability of the birth defect. The New Jersey decision in 1984, overruling the long-standing 1967 decision in Gleitman v. Cosgrove, recognized the validity of the cause of action for wrongful life.[97] Here the pregnant mother was erroneously tested for rubella, and the child was born with multiple defects, including eye lesions, heart disease, and auditory defects. Defendant's error was said to deprive the parents of information necessary to make an informed choice about terminating the pregnancy. The court found the damages measurable by the cost of the extraordinary medical care. The Washington decision in 1983 related to the defendant physician's prescription for the mother of an anticonvulsant drug to control her epileptic seizures; the physician did not advise about the probabilities of birth defects in the child. The defendant's failure to alert the plaintiff's parents to the effect of the drug on pregnancy foreseeably endangered the plaintiff's health. In 1986 Colorado joined the group recognizing the action for wrongful life in Continental Casualty Co. v. Empire Casualty Co.[98]

But a majority of states still refuse to recognize the wrongful life claim brought by or on behalf of a child, as delineated at length in Siemieniec v. Lutheran General Hospital.[99] Here the Illinois Supreme Court in 1987 pointed out that most courts are reluctant to view the attainment of life as a legally remedial injury; second, damages must be calculated by comparing the difference between life in an imperfect form and nonexistence, an extremely difficult, if not impossible, task. The same conclusion was reached by the Michigan court in Proffitt v. Bartolo,[100] which added the observation that finding an injury depends on personal feelings and attitudes, resulting in different and unpredictable outcomes.[101] And in Pitre v. Opelousas General Hospital, the Louisiana court viewed the wrongful life issue as a public policy matter more appropriately altered at the highest state court level, if at all.[102]

In contrast to wrongful life actions are wrongful birth actions, which are generally brought by the parents of a child born as a result of some alleged negligence of the defendant. The parents seek to recover damages for costs of bringing up a healthy but unexpected child or for costs related to an unexpected defective child. In Jacobs v. Theimer, the action was brought by the parents of a child born defective, alleging that defendant's negligence in failing to diagnose rubella in the mother while the mother was one month pregnant caused the problem.[103] The Texas Supreme Court limited recovery to "expenses reasonably necessary for the care and treatment of their child's impairment"; the parents received nothing for any noneconomic damages such as pain and suffering. Yet wrongful birth actions appear to be more frequently filed than wrongful life actions.[104] The list of common disorders that give rise to wrongful birth causes of action would embrace every known disease, disability, or injury.[105]

7.6 THE UNWANTED OR UNPLANNED PREGNANCY

The widespread use of the oral contraceptive pill in the United States (along with other devices) has generally resulted in claims of unwanted or unplanned pregnancies. These phenomena have been uniformly shown to be due almost entirely to patient failure. (The avid plaintiff's lawyer obviously would argue "product failure.") The official package circulars accompanying oral contraceptives, as well as the oral representation to the patient by the prescribing physician, make no guarantees whatsoever with respect to the absolute efficacy of the product. Indeed, there is a disclaimer against unwanted or unplanned pregnancies implied in the literature accompanying the product. The accidental nature of the event is beyond question.

The unwanted or unplanned pregnancy falls into the category of products liability because the thrust of the complaint is generally against the oral contraceptive product. (It may also involve a malpractice action against the prescribing physician and/or a negligence action against the hospital or institution.) In products liability law, whether the action is based upon negligence, breach of warranty, or strict liability, there is equally an insistence that a "harm" or "injury" or "property damage" or "economic loss" result before liability can attach to or be predicated against the product manufacturer. The mere fact that monetary damages may ensue, in the sense that the plaintiff was out of pocket certain dollars, is no proof that a harm or injury or loss legally occurred. The legal maxim *damnum absque injuria*, (damages without injury) is clearly applicable here to the unwanted or unplanned pregnancy. Accordingly, it is essential to differentiate initially between the harm or injury or loss and the ensuing damages. In other words, the mere existence of damages does not entitle the plaintiff to compensation unless the damages were preceded by a recognized legal harm or injury or loss and were consequential thereto. Roscoe Pound in his "Outlines of Lectures on Jurisprudence" emphasized that "the law does not create interests . . . it devises means for securing them when recognized and within the determined limits."[106] And the elements of a legal wrong are missing in the instance of the unwanted or unplanned pregnancy; Professor Henry T. Terry in *Duties, Rights and Wrongs* delineated the elements of a legal wrong in these terms: "(1) There must be a breach of duty. A violation of a right, i.e., injury to person or thing or pecuniary loss, does *not* amount to a wrong if it happens otherwise than as a consequence of a breach of duty, *as usually when it is the result of mere accident*; and (2) There must be a violation of right. A mere breach of duty which does not cause damage is not a wrong."[107]

There have been relatively few court decisions dealing with the issue of unwanted or unplanned pregnancies. Perhaps this fact alone reflects an honest evaluation of "patient failure" as opposed to "product failure": the user simply forgot to take her pill one day or even for two days, or perhaps she commenced consumption of the pills contrary to instructions. The missing element in these cases is positive proof that the pregnancy resulted not from product failure but from patient failure. However, regardless of causation, there is implicit in these decisions the fact that the plaintiff experienced no legal harm, no legal injury, and no legal loss because the birth of a child is universally deemed to be a joyous event.

Analogous to the concept of birth as a joyous event are those few cases brought by a child seeking damages simply because he or she was born. One such case involving an infant's claim for birth defects (not associated with use of the oral contraceptive product) was Stewart v. Long Island College Hospital in which the New York Supreme Court, Kings County, ruled that the infant had no cause of action: "There is no remedy for having been born under a handicap, whether physical or psychological, when the alternative to being born in handicapped condition is not to have been born at all. To put it another way, a plaintiff has no remedy against a defendant whose offense is he failed to consign the plaintiff to oblivion. Such a cause of action is alien to our system of jurisprudence."[108]

Under the particular facts, the defendant hospital had declined to terminate the mother's pregnancy, although the mother was believed to have contracted german measles during the early stages of her pregnancy. Judge Beckinella found no proof that the infant's disabilities could have been prevented by the defendant hospital because the evidence was clear that the birth defects resulted from german measles contracted by her mother and not from any breach of duty or violation of right on the part of the hospital. The court, in dismissing the infant's cause of action, opined:

> The rationale of our law of torts is to compensate individuals who have suffered a diminution of their faculties, temporarily or permanently, as a result of a defendant's carelessness. The gravity of a defendant's wrong is measured by the extent to which his conduct has put the plaintiff in a handicapped condition. The ultimate wrong that can be committed is to cause another person's death. It would be the antithesis of these principles to require the defendant hospital to respond in damages to the infant plaintiff because it did not prevent the infant's birth.

The New York court in the *Stewart* case approvingly cited Gleitman v. Cosgrove in which the New Jersey Supreme Court had ruled that the complaint of the infant (born with defects due to its mother's german measles) "is not actionable because the conduct compained of, even if true, does not give rise to damages cognizable at law." [109] The highest New Jersey court explained:

> The normal measure of damages in tort actions is compensatory. Damages are measured by comparing the condition plaintiff would have been in, had the defendants not been negligent, with plaintiff's impaired condition as a result of the negligence. The infant plaintiff would have us measure the difference between his life with defects against the utter void of nonexistence, but it is impossible to make such a determination. This court cannot weigh the value of life with impairments against the nonexistence of life itself. By asserting that he should not have been born, the infant plaintiff makes it logically impossible for a court to measure his alleged damages because of the impossibility of making the comparison required by compensatory remedies.

The ruling here is consonant with public policy, whether the action was brought in negligence, breach of warranty, or even strict liability in tort.[110]

The earliest reported decision on unwanted or unplanned pregnancy was by the Minnesota Supreme Court in 1934 in Christiansen v. Thornby.[111] Here the husband, who had undergone a vasectomy because he had been told that pregnancy would be dangerous to the life of his wife, sought $5,000 damages from the physician-surgeon for his anxiety and his expense in his wife's subsequent normal pregnancy and successful delivery. The highest court in Minnesota affirmed the trial court's ruling, which had sustained defendant's demurrer:

> The purpose of the operation was to save the wife from the hazards to her life which were incident to childbirth. It was not the alleged purpose to save expense incident to

pregnancy and delivery. The wife has survived. Instead of losing his wife, the plaintiff has been blessed with the fatherhood of another child. The expenses alleged are incident to the bearing of a child, and their avoidance is remote from the avowed purpose of the operation.[112]

In Pennsylvania in 1957, a local court decided Shaheen v. Knight.[113] After a sterilization operation upon the husband and the unwanted pregnancy of his wife, suit was brought by the husband alleging damages for support, rearing, and education of the child. The court ruled that the claim was contrary to the public policy of the commonwealth of Pennsylvania:

Defendant argues, however, and pleads, that plaintiff has suffered no damage; we agree with defendant. The only damages asked are the expenses of rearing and educating the unwanted child. We are of the opinion that to allow damages of the normal birth of a child is foreign to the universal public sentiment of the people.

To allow damages in a suit such as this would mean that the physician would have to pay for the fun, joy and affection which plaintiff, Shaheen, will have in the future rearing and educating of this plaintiff's fifth child. Many people would be willing to support this child were they given the right of custody and adoption, but according to plaintiff's statement, plaintiff does not want such. He wants to have the child and wants the doctor to support it. In our opinion to allow such damages would be against public policy.

The legal maxim *damnum absque injuria* is thus inherently applicable to the situation of the unwanted or unplanned pregnancy. The loss, hurt, or harm is without injury in the legal sense; there is no such breach of duty or violation of right redressable by a legal action. Such a "loss," therefore, does not give rise to an action for damages, even against the person or product manufacturer allegedly causing it.

Unsuccessful sterilization operations that subsequently result in a normal child through normal delivery, without permanent harm to the mother, have been described as not involving injury, and furthermore "the granting of damages on such grounds would be against public policy."[114] This rule of law has been sanctioned "despite any finding of negligence, breach of contract (or warranty), or misrepresentation on the part of the physician or surgeon" in the unsuccessful performance of the surgical operation. In Ball v. Mudge, the Washington Supreme Court in 1964 held that the husband and wife were not entitled to directed verdicts against the physicians for breach of warranty and negligence in failing to sterilize the husband successfully.[115] The child was normal, though delivered by a cesarean section: "As reasonable persons, the jury may well have concluded that appellants suffered no damage in the birth of a normal healthy child, whom they dearly love, would not consider placing for adoption, and 'would not sell for $50,000', and that the cost incidental to such birth was far outweighed by the blessing of a cherished child, albeit an unwanted child at the time of conception and birth."

Possibly to the contrary is the unique decision in Custodio v. Bauer, where the California Appellate Court in 1967 permitted recovery for the unwanted birth of a normal child following an unsuccessful sterilization operation.[116] The compensation was not for the normal birth of a normal child but rather to compensate the family financially in order that the new arrival would not deprive the other nine members of the family of what was planned as their just share of the family income. The court nevertheless observed that the unwanted child would not be more emotionally upset than a child born into one of the many families where attempts at planned parenthood have been unsuccessful; nor would such an unwanted child be more emotionally upset if he arrived in an environment where each of the other members of the family must contribute to his support; and by the same token, he would not have a happier and a more well-adjusted life if he brought with him the wherewithal to make it possible. The court indeed limited its decision and held that, although on the present state of the record it could not be ascertained to what extent the plaintiffs (if they could establish a breach of duty by defendants) were entitled to damages, it was clear that if successful on the issue of liability, the plaintiffs might establish a right to more than nominal damages. Thus, this California decision simply begs the question: Is there liability for the normal birth of a normal child? The fact that this court was willing to recognize "damages" is no proof that there was a breach of a duty or a violation of a right upon which liability could be predicated.

Aside from these sterilization cases, there are other factual patterns in cases directly involving the oral contraceptive pill. The Iowa District Court of Linn County in January 1967 handed down a decision in Maley v. Armstrong.[117] In this case, the husband and wife sued two physicians when she became pregnant after taking birth control pills prescribed for her. The Iowa Court expressly found no compensable damages against the two physicians:

> Birth control is clearly not against public policy. However, it would appear that if a cause of action of this particular nature (wherein the health of the mother has not been impaired and the child is normal and loved by the parents) should be sanctioned, it should be by the duly elected Legislature after complete public debate. A decision of this nature involving conflicting mores and far flung social ramifications should not depend upon the personal, religious and social views of a particular judge or jury.
>
> There is an ancient maxim that you can't have a rose without the thorns. Mental depression of the wife and temporary loss of consortium by the husband if attributable to pregnancy are elements of childbirth that will not be considered as compensable items of damage in absence of direction by the Iowa Supreme Court or by a legislative act, or judicial fiat.

In March 1969 in Troppi v. Scarf, the Michigan Circuit Court for Wayne County considered plaintiff's allegations that the defendant pharmacist gave the plaintiff a mild tranquilizer instead of the prescribed oral contraceptives, with the result that the plaintiff experienced an unwanted pregnancy.[118] Plaintiff claimed damages for medical and hospital bills, cost of confinement, loss of earnings, support for the child until the age of 21, and emotional stress and strain incidental to the unwanted pregnancy. The Michigan court dismissed the case:

To allow damages in a suit such as this would mean that a physician or a druggist, as in this instance, would have to pay for the conjugal pleasure and affection which these plaintiffs have had, will have in the future in rearing and educating this plaintiff's eighth child. It might be quite clearly said many people, not so fortunate to have such a healthy child, would be willing to support this child were they given the right of custody. This child, however, is as I am told, loved and properly cared for by these parents, and to allow such damages would be patently against public policy.

As to a policy of planned parenthood, the Michigan court said:

Be that public policy as it may, I do not subscribe to the proposition, that there can be, even in the case of this public policy to respect the birth control and contraception, a moral or legal responsibility on the part of a physician or a druggist as in this case to assume the costs of the natural result of a natural act of the marital relationship. There are two separate and distinct public policies involved.

The court concluded:

''The costs of rearing the child, the emotional problems involved, or fears, the fright on the part of the woman, the fear and the apprehension on the part of the husband, none of these in my judgment are compensable. To deviate from this course in my opinion would expose the medical profession or druggist to great, grave and serious abuses or processes. One could conceivably create mythical causes of action on the part of the mother.

A decision on October 17, 1969, by the Wisconsin Circuit Court, Milwaukee County, in Szczerbiak v. Fair Drugs, Inc. was an action in which the husband and wife sought $250,000 damages for the alleged negligence of a pharmacist in filling a birth control prescription for the wife with common cold tablets.[119] The unwanted pregnancy resulted in the birth of a normal child. Upon the pleadings, the defendant moved for judgment, and the court, finding no issue of fact, granted the motion, dismissing the complaint. Judge Drechsler decided that ''the natural birth of a healthy child, with no injury to the mother, is universally considered as a joyous event.''

Mr. and Mrs. Szczerbiak had alleged that the wife obtained in June 1965 a prescription for birth control pills, and two months later she was advised by her doctor that she was pregnant. The pharmacist is alleged to have read to the doctor (who called him in August 1965) the wrong prescription twice; the pharmacist allegedly filled the prescription with common cold tablets. Accordingly, plaintiffs alleged as damages the fact that the wife was ''forced to deliver the child when she was at an age when she desired no more children.'' Plaintiffs admittedly incurred medical and hospital expenses and had sold their mobile home and moved into larger quarters, allegedly to accommodate the addition to their family. The wife had terminated her employment and remained at home to raise the child; furthermore, plaintiffs contended they would expend money for raising and educating the child until the child reached its majority. Defendant replied that the wife did not bring him a prescription for birth control pills; he had not mistakingly sold her cold tablets for birth control pills; and when she was informed that she was not taking birth control pills, she continued to have sexual relations with her husband, such "damages" therefore being due to "their carelessness, negligence, and lack of ordinary care."

Judge Drechsler observed that this was "a case of first impression in this state" and that the wife alleged no pain and suffering "other than she previously had in bearing and delivering the child." Further, he posed the question: "Whether or not the public policy of this state, as framed here by the pleadings, as the public policy now exists, permits our courts to award damages for the birth of a well-born child and the costs incident to and following that birth, notwithstanding that the pharmacist was negligent in giving her pills other than prescribed birth control pills; and that such negligence may have been a cause of the well-born female child." Judge Drechsler answered simply in the negative and further pointed out:

> The alleged cause of action contravenes the public policy of this state. The costs and expenses incurred and the other damages claimed by plaintiffs are those which are normally associated with, and incident to the birth of a child; and so, are not compensable. It goes without saying, that the human race will not survive unless children are born; and for, and with the birth of children go the problems for which plaintiffs claim as damages for in this action.

He pointed that society is interested in "birth, care, support, maintenance and education of children" and that the lawsuit contravened these established "interests of society." Judge Drechsler observed that the child was "well-born and healthy" and cited with approval cases from other jurisdictions, such as *Custodio* (California), *Troppi* (Michigan), *Shaheen* (Pennsylvania), *Moley* (Iowa), and *Christensen* (Minnesota). He concluded:

> All birth control is not against public policy; yet a cause of action, as here asserted, cannot be allowed by the courts, for the health of the mother has not been impaired, the child is normal, and loved by the plaintiffs. The expenditures which plaintiffs have gone through, and will, are all the natural results of a natural childbirth. They cannot be compensable items of damage. They are involved in all cases of childbirth. The natural birth of a healthy child, with no injury to the mother, is universally considered a joyous event. This child may rise to great heights some day.
>
> Allowance of damages claimed in this case would "contravene good morals," and the "established interest of society," and so would be against public policy.
>
> To allow damages such claimed here would be in contravention of public policy.
>
> This decision is not predicated upon any moral nor religious view, but upon the

proposition that, even though birth control is practiced, and is suggested or advised in many areas, the basic concept of responsibility of parenthood for the well-born child could be destroyed if the damages as claimed here were compensable.

Indeed, this established policy that no recovery can be had for a normal delivery of a normal child, or for the costs of rearing the normal child, is consonant with the *Restatement of Torts* (1939), section 920: ''Where the defendant's tortious conduct has caused harm to the plaintiff or to his property and in so doing has conferred upon the plaintiff a special benefit to the interest which was harmed, the value of the benefit conferred is considered in mitigation of damages, where this is equitable.'' Although the *Restatement* was designed to create and even expand upon existing legal rights, the mere acknowledgment of ''the value of the benefit conferred'' is a redeeming feature. In Maben v. Maben the California court in 1961 noted the applicability of the *Restatement* position with reference to one seeking to recover for detention and treatment as a mental patient.[120] This case (and other examples given in the *Restatement*) clearly contemplates a benefit to the interest to be protected that is not compensable.

The great majority of states do not allow the recovery of child-rearing expenses in any form to the parents of a normal, healthy baby who was allegedly born as a result of a negligently performed sterilization procedure.[121] The rule allowing the costs of child rearing to be offset by the benefits of the child is recognized only in Arizona,[122] Connecticut,[123] the District of Columbia,[124] Maryland,[125] Michigan,[126] and in Minnesota, where the Minnesota Supreme Court in Sherlock v. Stillwater Clinic had little trouble in recognizing a cause of action for wrongful pregnancy and in finding that the parents should be compensated for prenatal and postnatal medical expenditures plus pain and suffering incurred by the mother and plus the loss of consortium directly related to the pregnancy and childbirth.[127] As to child-rearing expenses, the court opined: ''Ethical and religious considerations aside, it must be recognized that such costs are a direct financial injury to the parents, no different in immediate effect than the medical expenses resulting from the wrongful conception and birth of the child. Although public sentiment may recognize that to the vast majority of parents the long-term and enduring benefits of parenthood outweigh the economic costs of rearing a healthy child, it would seem myopic to declare today that those benefits exceed the costs as a matter of law.'' Thus, parents should be allowed to recover the reasonably foreseeable costs of child rearing ''subject to an offset for the value of the benefits conferred to them by the child.''

The issue of proximate cause is particularly relevant to the question of liability, if any, for the unwanted or unplanned pregnancy. The ''event'' of pregnancy can and does, in point of fact, result without the oral contraceptive product. Fertilization of the female was not caused by the pill. There was no breach of duty and no violation of a right on the part of the product manufacturer because the intervening sexual relations between the parents proximately caused the blessed event. It is indeed difficult to contemplate how the pill could have caused the pregnancy.

Prosser on Torts (1941 edition) delineated "many immoral acts which do not amount to torts" and pointed out that "the law has not yet enacted a golden rule": "It is impossible to afford a lawsuit for every deed of unkindness or betrayal, and there is much evil in the world which must necessarily be left to other agencies of social control" (p. 21).

Of course, the unwanted or unplanned pregnancy is neither an "immoral act" nor a "deed of unkindness or betrayal," nor is it an actionable wrong, tort, or breach of warranty. Society, in fact, has demanded that mythical causes of action must not be created; it does not intend to compensate for a healthy baby born normally to its parent or parents. In Gambill v. White plaintiff sued in negligence a hospital and her doctor for permitting her to give birth to a child when she was unattended.[128] The Supreme Court of Missouri affirmed the dismissal of the action, holding that she suffered no injury in delivering a normal child. Such a mythical cause of action may delight the esoterics but could hardly satisfy the demands of society, which accepts the normal birth of a normal child as a blessing.

7.7 ABORTION AND THE CHANGING LAW

In 1973 the U.S. Supreme Court in the landmark case of Roe v. Wade ruled that a woman has a constitutionally protected right to decide, free from governmental intrusion, whether to terminate her pregnancy.[129] This fundamental right is not unqualified. During the first trimester, the abortion decision belongs to the pregnant woman and her physician.[130] At the end of the first trimester, the state has a compelling interest in protecting the health of the mother and "may, if it chooses, regulate the abortion procedure in ways that are reasonably related to maternal health."[131] At the end of the second trimester, the state's compelling interest is in the potential life of the fetus, and the state "may, if it chooses, regulate, and even proscribe, abortion except where it is necessary, in appropriate medical judgment, for the preservation of life or health of the mother."[132] Mr. Justice Blackmun observed that

> the detriment that the State would impose upon the pregnant woman by denying this choice altogether is apparent. Specific and direct harm medically diagnosable even in early pregnancy may be involved. Maternity, or additional offspring may force upon the woman a distressful life and future. Psychological harm may be imminent. Mental and physical health may be taxed by child care. There is also the distress, for all concerned, associated with the unwanted child, and there is the problem of bringing a child into a family already unable, psychologically and otherwise to care for it.[133]

In his concurring opinion, Mr. Justice Douglas reminded his audience that "elaborate argument is hardly necessary to demonstrate that childbirth may deprive a woman of her preferred lifestyle and force upon her a radically different and undesired future."[134] (It should be noted that the challengers of the abortion statutes were gestational or surrogate mothers, not natural mothers.)

Immediately following this 1973 decision, antiabortion forces began their fight to restrict that right to abortion by every means possible.[135] A series of cases prompted the U.S. Supreme Court to hold that neither the Constitution nor federal legislation required states to provide funding of nontherapeutic abortions for indigent women.[136] In the 1980 case of Harris v. McRae,[137] the Court rejected the constitutional attacks on versions of the Hyde amendment that limited public funding for most medically necessary abortions.[138] It seems clear that the Court was primarily concerned with protecting the bodily integrity of the female—that is, the gestational aspect of pregnancy and its effect upon the female's health. In 1976 in Planned Parenthood of Central Missouri v. Danforth, the Court declared that this right to abortion cannot be vetoed by anyone in the surrogate arrangement.[139] The state cannot require the spouse's consent to the abortion: the state "cannot delegate to a spouse the veto power which the State itself is absolutely and totally prohibited from exercising during the first trimester of pregnancy."[140]

The abortion law of Pennsylvania, among the most restrictive legislation ever enacted by a state, was the subject of Thornburgh v. American College of Obstetricians and Gynecologists, decided in 1986 by the U.S. Supreme Court.[141] Did the Abortion Control Act of 1982 violate the constitutionally protected liberty of women to seek an abortion? By a 5–4 vote, the Court answered "yes," affirming the principles set down in Roe v. Wade[142] and in Akron Center for Reproductive Health v. Akron.[143] In short, the state may not require doctors to read a specified list of statements about abortion to all patients, nor may the state require doctors in all cases to employ the abortion method most likely to lead to a live birth in any case in which the fetus may be viable.[144] The majority opinion struck down the state act because it impermissibly attempted to "deter a woman from making a decision that, with her physician, is hers to make." More specifically, the Pennsylvania physician was required

> to give every woman seeking an abortion an identical litany of information at least twenty-four hours before she gave her "voluntary and informed consent." This information included a warning of the medical risks associated with the procedure used, an estimate of the gestational age of the fetus, assurances that medical benefits might be available for prenatal care and childbirth, and assurances that the father would be liable for financial assistance. Doctors were also required to furnish printed material stating that agencies were available to help a prospective mother "carry [the] child to term," and giving a description of what the fetus would probably look like at two-week gestational increments. . . . Physicians were required under the Act to sign reports prepared by the abortion clinic or hospital giving detailed information about the patient, such as her state, political subdivision, age, race, marital status, and the method of payment. Although the identity of both the reporting person and the patient ostensibly would remain confidential, each report nevertheless would be available for public inspection and copying within fifteen

days of receipt. . . . Physicians were required to file official reports with the state explaining the basis for their determinations that fetuses were not viable after the first trimester. . . . If the fetus was potentially viable, the Act required that a second physician be consulted . . . and that physicians use the same degree of care for a fetus that they would use to "preserve the life and health of any unborn child intended to be born and not aborted." . . . The physicians were required to employ the technique "which would provide the best opportunity for the unborn child to be aborted alive unless . . . [it] would present a significantly greater medical risk to the life or health of the pregnant woman." . . . The American College of Obstetricians and Gynecologists, individual physicians who perform abortions, and other interested parties . . . challenged the constitutionality of several provisions of the Pennsylvania Act, seeking declaratory and injunctive relief.[145]

The highest court also struck down the reporting provisions of the act, concluding that the public availability of the reports, as well as some of the data required in them, went well beyond the state's legitimate interest in maternal health and failed to respect the patient's "confidentiality and privacy." The court invalidated the provisions of the act relating to the degree of care and choice of procedure for postviability abortions and the provision requiring that a second physician be consulted before abortion of a viable fetus. The second-physician requirement was invalid because it did not provide an exception for situations in which the delay necessary to find a second physician would endanger the health of the woman. The court reaffirmed the unconstitutionality of state statutes that mandate a trade-off between the mother's health and the survival of her fetus rather than placing the primary emphasis on protecting the woman.[146] Thus, the court extended the protection that Roe v. Wade accorded a woman's freedom of choice to invalidate state regulations that would have minimal, if any, impact on the woman's decision making.[147]

On November 14, 1989, some four months after the monumental decision in Webster v. Reproductive Health Service,[148] Pennsylvania enacted a most restrictive law banning most abortions in public hospitals and banning all abortions after twenty-four weeks.[149] The only exception on the ban allows an abortion necessary to save the woman's life or to prevent "substantial and irreversible impairment of her major bodily functions."

Within ten days, Turnock v. Ragsdale, an Illinois case pending before the U.S. Supreme Court, was settled out of court.[150] The case involved Illinois regulations requiring abortion clinics to be equipped and staffed like hospital operating rooms. The settlement obligated the state to drop regulations that abortion rights supporters viewed as medically unnecessary and burdensome to abortion clinics.[151] However, the state retains the authority to inspect abortion clinics and enforce rules it deems necessary to protect the health and safety of patients. If the Illinois regulations had been upheld by the Court, most abortion clinics would have been forced to close or to raise their fees, effectively putting abortions beyond the reach of most poor women.[152]

On July 3, 1989, the U.S. Supreme Court by a 5–4 vote issued the long-awaited decision in Webster v. Reproductive Health Service, upholding the constitutionality of several provisions of the Missouri statute restricting access to abortions.[153] The Missouri statute[154] had stated in its preamble that life begins at conception and that unborn children have a protectable interest in life and health; that it shall be unlawful for any public employee to perform or assist or any public facility to be used for an abortion not necessary to save the life of the mother; that the use of public funds for counseling a woman to have an abortion not necessary to save her life was prohibited; that before a physician performs an abortion on a woman believed to be twenty or more weeks pregnant, the physician shall determine if the unborn child is viable by exercising care, skill, and proficiency; and in determining viability, the physician "shall perform . . . such . . . tests as are necessary to make a finding of the gestational age, weight and lung maturity of the unborn child." The plaintiffs, licensed health professionals and public facilities offering abortion services as well as pregnant women seeking abortions, contended that the Missouri statute infringed upon their constitutional rights of privacy and equal protection of the law. Both the federal district court and the Eighth U.S. Court of Appeals found the Missouri statute to be unconstitutional, but the Supreme Court reversed, thus giving the states the right to implement restrictive abortion laws.[155]

The Court did not overrule Roe v. Wade but substantially narrowed the holding in the 1973 case; the preamble was viewed as simply expressing Missouri's "value judgment favoring childbirth over abortion."[156] The five-justice majority of the Court upheld the restrictions on the use of public employees or public facilities for the performance or assistance of nontherapeutic abortions. Chief Justice Rehnquist compared the provision to previously supported welfare regulations that provided payments for medical expenses relating to childbirth, but not for nontherapeutic abortions:

> The [welfare] regulation places no obstacles—absolute or otherwise—in the pregnant woman's path to an abortion. The State may have made childbirth a more attractive alternative, thereby influencing the woman's decision, but it has imposed no restriction on access to abortions that was not already there. The indigency that may make it difficult—and in some cases, perhaps, impossible—for some women to have abortions is neither created nor in any way affected by the [state's] regulation. Slip op. at 10, *quoting Maher v. Roe*, 432 U.S. 464, 474 (1977).

The chief justice opined that "nothing in the Constitution requires States to enter or remain in the business of performing abortions. Nor, as the plaintiffs suggest, do private physicians and their patients have some kind of constitutional right of access to public facilities for the performance of abortions."

On the issue of medical tests for viability, the majority opinion observed that the Missouri statute created a presumption of viability at twenty weeks, which must be rebutted by medical tests before an abortion may be performed. Indeed, the state has a compelling interest in "potential human life," and it has chosen "viability as the point at which its interest in potential human life must be safeguarded.'' Yet the chief justice and the majority opinion could not see ''why the State's interest in protecting potential human life should come into existence only at the point of viability, and that there should therefore be a rigid line allowing State regulation after viability but prohibiting it before viability.'' In concluding, the chief justice commented on Roe v. Wade:

> The experience of the Court in applying Roe v. Wade in later cases . . . suggests to us that there is wisdom in not unnecessarily attempting to elaborate the abstract differences between a ''fundamental right'' to abortion, as the Court described it in *Akron*, a ''limited fundamental constitutional right,'' which Justice Blackmun's dissent today treats *Roe* as having established, or a liberty interest protected by the Due Process Clause, which we believe it to be. The Missouri testing requirement here is reasonably designed to ensure that abortions are not performed where the fetus is viable—an end which all concede is legitimate—and that is sufficient to sustain its constitutionality. . . . The facts of the present case, however, differ from those at issue in *Roe* . . . [and *Webster*] therefore affords us no occasion to revisit the holding of *Roe*. To the extent indicated in our opinion, we would modify and narrow *Roe* and succeeding cases. Slip op. at 22–23.

The dissenting opinions of Justices Blackmun, Brennan, Marshall, and Stevens criticized the majority opinion because the majority would ''return to the States virtually unfettered authority to control the quintessentially intimate, personal, and life-directing decision whether to carry a fetus to term.'' The separate dissent of Mr. Justice Stevens bitterly opposed the Missouri preamble that life begins at conception and that conception occurs at fertilization as ''an unequivocal endorsement of a religious tenet of some but by no means all Christian faiths that serves no identifiable secular purpose'' and therefore violates the First Amendment's establishment clause. Furthermore, ''a woman's constitutionally protected liberty encompasses the right to act on her own belief that—to paraphrase St. Thomas Aquinas—until a seed has acquired the powers of sensation and movement, the life of a human being has not yet begun.'' Indeed, the bodily integrity of the pregnant female may take precedence over the father's desire for children: ''The obvious fact is that when the wife and husband disagree on this decision, the view of only one of the two marriage partners can prevail. Inasmuch as it is the woman who physically bears the child and who is more directly and immediately affected by the pregnancy, as between the two, the balance weighs in her favor.''[157]

Note that the husband has no right to halt an abortion, as is illustrated in the New York case of Steinhoff v. Steinhoff.[158] The court held that under Roe v. Wade and its progeny, the state is clearly barred from interfering with a woman's right to choose abortion, regardless of whether her husband consented to the abortion and what her reason for the abortion was.[159] As the court explained,

> Beginning with Roe v. Wade (410 US 113), the Supreme Court of the United States erected a qualified bar to state intervention in a woman's right to choose between abortion and childbirth. Interference with this right may only occur if supported by a compelling

state interest (Roe v. Wade, 410 US 113 at 163). A state interest in the survival of the unborn child does not arise until the point of medically determined viability. (Colautti v. Franklin, 439 US 379 at 388). Spousal consent has been specifically ruled to be interference with the right to choose. (Planned Parenthood of Central Missouri v. Danforth, 428 US 52 at 67). The state and the husband cannot interfere with the right afforded the defendant wife by Roe v. Wade until viability. It necessarily follows that I cannot.

In so ruling, I have fulfilled the requirements of my oath of office. That oath requires, as a minimum, that I adjudicate without regard to my personal beliefs, without regard to fear of favor. I also recognize that whatever my personal views, the subject of abortion is a matter of serious controversy. That said, I cannot help but express my feeling that the abortion of a potential life for purely cosmetic reasons is simply intolerable in a society which claims any pretense to civilization.

In Ostreicher v. Ostreicher, the plaintiff husband claimed that he had a right to know about his wife's abortion and therefore filed suit against her for having an abortion without his knowledge or consent, as part of his overall suit for divorce.[160] But the New York court gave no comfort to the husband, for, as set forth in the 1976 U.S. Supreme Court holding in Planned Parenthood of Central Missouri v. Danforth,[161] "Inasmuch as it is the woman who physically bears the child and who is the more directly and immediately affected by the pregnancy, as between the two, the balance weighs in her favor."[162]

Interference with the woman's right brought a lawsuit in Oregon against an antiabortion group that had interfered with a mother's decision to terminate the life of a baby born with a severe cerebral defect that doctors said was terminal. The antiabortion group had obtained a court order requiring the hospital to provide life support for the baby and then had the state file suit accusing the couple of failing to provide medical treatment for the child, and the baby was removed from the custody of the couple. The baby died seven days later, and the couple were billed for $10,000 in medical expenses. The case was eventually settled for a payment of $217,500 to the couple by the antiabortion group.[163]

The absolute right of a pregnant woman to an abortion during the first trimester[164] was an issue in the 1987 New York case of Martinez v. Long Island Jewish Hillside Medical Center, although the case centered on the woman's antiabortion beliefs.[165] She had been negligently advised by the defendants that certain medicine she had taken would result in her baby's being born with certain specific and major birth defects. Based upon that negligent medical advice, she had an abortion and subsequently sued defendants, pointing out that abortion was a sin to her unless it was under exceptional circumstances, which were not present here: "Mrs. Martinez suffered mental anguish and depression from her awareness that, as a result of defendants' negligence, she had needlessly committed an act in violation of her deep-seated convictions." The New York Court of Appeals agreed: "The emotional distress for which she seeks recovery does not derive from what happened to the fetus; it derives from the psychological injury directly caused by her agreeing to an act which, as the jury found, was contrary to her firmly held beliefs. Defendants' breach of duty was the precipitating and proximate cause of her injury.'' The point here is simply that abortion and no abortion are both protected rights and cannot be infringed upon by those persons or hospitals charged with a duty not to interfere therewith.

Antiabortion statutes first reared their legislative heads in the United States between 1821 and 1841, and by the Civil War era almost every state proscribed abortion at every state of fetal development.[166] By the year 1900 many states had prohibited even the advertising, distribution, or publication of birth control information.[167] Antiabortionists in recent years have pressured state legislatures into enacting statutes abolishing tort actions brought by parents who alleged that a health care professional negligently or intentionally interfered with their right to decide whether to have an abortion.

Today Idaho, Minnesota, Missouri, South Dakota, and Utah have enacted legislation prohibiting wrongful birth actions.[168] The constitutionality of the Minnesota statute was upheld by the Minnesota Supreme Court in the 1986 case of Hickman v. Group Health, Plan, Inc.,[169] despite the obvious fact that the statute significantly interfered with a woman's right to decide to terminate pregnancy.[170] These wrongful birth statutes are a ''studied effort to restrict the flow of medical information necessary to the exercise of a constitutionally protected right to decide without interference from the State whether to terminate pregnancy. Such statutes license doctors to disregard patients' rights and values and to inject their own moral convictions into patient decisionmaking. In so doing, wrongful birth statutes violate the due process and equal protection clauses of the fourteenth amendment.''[171] It should be recalled that the U.S. Supreme Court in 1986 had proclaimed that ''the States are not free, under the guise of protecting maternal health or potential life, to intimidate women into continuing pregnancies.''[172] Three years earlier, the highest court had invalidated a Missouri statute that required abortions after twelve weeks to be performed in hospitals and with the attending physician to be present.[173] On September 8, 1987, a federal district court in Georgia struck down a Georgia statute that required minors under 17 years of age to notify their parents before having an abortion; clinics or hospitals performing abortions without proof of parental notification would be guilty of a misdemeanor.[174] The requirement that an adult accompany the juvenile to the clinic or hospital is unconstitutional, according to the court, because it ''unduly burdens the minor's rights. . . . No matter how thoroughly discussed and well considered the decision to terminate the pregnancy may be, a family acting on good faith compliance with the statute may not be able to implement that decision without unnecessary, costly and medically dangerous delay and expense.''[175]

The U.S. Supreme Court in Hartigan v. Zbaraz in 1987 by a 4–4 vote let stand a ruling of the Seventh U.S. Court of Appeals against an Illinois law that could have limited the right of some teenage girls to have abortions.[176] The Illinois statute, according to the federal appellate court, had improperly required women under the age of 18 to wait twenty-four hours before having an abortion so that their parents could be notified.[177] It should be noted that twenty-one other states have similar laws requiring parents to be notified or for parents to give their consent before minor unmarried daughters could have an abortion. The Illinois statute, the Parental Notice Abortion Act, enacted in 1983, was challenged constitutionally by several individuals representing two classes: licensed physicians performing or wishing to perform abortions for unemancipated minors and disabled persons and unemancipated minors capable of giving informed consent to an abortion or whose best interests would not be served by parental notice. The federal district court had found the twenty-four-hour waiting period unconstitutional because it unduly burdened the minor's right to have an abortion in the absence of compelling state interest. The judicial procedure for waiver of notice to the parents was also unconstitutional. The Seventh U.S. Court of Appeals affirmed with respect to the waiting period but did not find the waiver provisions unconstitutional.[178]

It is interesting to review briefly the various circumstances that serve as grounds for abortion: therapeutic, eugenic, extramarital pregnancy, pregnancy of a minor, late pregnancy, pregnancy due to criminally prohibited relations, incestuous relations, and socioeconomic grounds.[179] Therapeutic grounds—preservation of the woman's life—has almost universally been accepted as suitable grounds for an abortion. To avoid serious physical or mental injury to the woman, or to preclude aggravation of an existing physical ailment untreatable by regular medical procedures are additional grounds for the therapeutic abortion.[180] Eugenic grounds are raised to prevent transfer of hereditary disease or the birth of a defective child, due for example, to an intrauterine injury, maternal disease, or exposure to radiation. Extramarital pregnancy is not readily acceptable as a ground for abortion, although the social stigma attaching thereto can disrupt or even terminate the marital and family relationship. A minor's pregnancy may entail far greater physical risks of childbirth than those of abortion, and courts are more willing to approve such abortions, especially in view of the likelihood that the child will be physically or mentally defective.[181] Justification for terminating a minor's pregnancy, particularly when the minor is unmarried, appears to be socially acceptable. Late pregnancy may be eugenically eligible for abortion; in Israel, regulations provide that a pregnant woman over the age of 37 years is entitled to a diagnostic test of the amniotic fluid after the sixteenth week of pregnancy; if fetal abnormality is found, abortion is authorized.[182] Pregnancy due to criminally prohibited relations such as rape are additional grounds for abortion. Incestuous relations justify abortion, although incest is not necessarily immoral or criminal; in Israel, the crime of incest refers only to intercourse with "an unmarried girl above the age of 17 and under the age of 21 years who is the man's descendant."[183] There are also socioeconomic grounds for abortion, as illustrated by section 316(a) (5) of the Israel Penal Law, which provided prior to 1979 that abortion could be approved where "continuance of the pregnancy is likely to cause grave harm to the woman or her children owing to the difficult family or social circumstances of the woman and her environment."

The physician's role in the abortion process has attained a certain constitutional status,[184] as illustrated by City of Akron v. Akron Center for Reproductive

Health,[185] where the highest court struck down mandatory abortion information disclosure by the attending physician, and by Colautti v. Franklin,[186] where the Court invalidated the Pennsylvania abortion statute that regulated physicians. In Doe v. Bolton, the U.S. Supreme Court had ruled unconstitutional a Georgia criminal abortion statute requiring that a hospital abortion committee approve each abortion procedure and that two other physicians confirm the attending physician's determination.[187] The Court held that these restrictions severely burdened the woman's privacy right and unduly interfered with the judgment of the attending physician. It is the attending physician who must make the medical determination of maternal health in the light of all the factors relevant to the patient's well-being.[188] Note that in 1979 the court had in Bellotti v. Baird[189] found a Massachusetts statute requiring parental consent to abortion for pregnant minors under 18 years of age deficient in that the procedure permitted judicial approval to be withheld from a mature and competent minor and because it required parental consultation or notification in each and every instance.[189] But the next year in H.L. v. Matheson, the court upheld the Utah parental notification statute when a 15-year-old pregnant girl challenged the statute that required the physician to notify the parents or guardian of a minor upon whom an abortion was to be performed.[190] The burdens imposed were sufficiently tailored to the state's compelling interest in the welfare of the minor. But abortions on teenagers are not curbed by parental interference resulting from state-imposed notification requirements, which can only cause minors to delay their abortion decisions until after the first trimester.[191]

In August 1987, federal health officials reported a decrease in the number of abortions in the United States for the first time since record keeping began in 1969.[192] According to the Federal Centers for Disease Control in Atlanta, Georgia, about 1,268,987 legal abortions were performed in 1987, a 2 percent decrease over the previous year. The greatest number of abortions occurred in California (about 210,000) and the lowest number in Wyoming (about 711). On the international front, Great Britain is said to lead the developed world in making birth control available to its people, and the United States ranks seventh, according to the Population Crisis Committee.[193] Serious shortages in family planning services existed in eighty-two nations in 1987; Laos, Libya, and Cambodia, for example, have no family planning services. Taiwan was the top ranked of the developing nations, followed by Singapore and South Korea.[194]

Antiabortionists have in recent years taken to the streets to picket abortion clinics and even physicians who perform abortions. In Pursley v. City of Fayettesville, the Eighth U.S. Court of Appeals refused to bar picketing outside a physician's home and invalidated a city ordinance that prohibited demonstrations around private homes.[195] The First Amendment was said to protect antiabortion activists in their picketing; although the city has a legitimate interest in protecting the peace and privacy of the home, the city ordinance was too broad because its effect was to "completely ban picketing anywhere a home is located." Every public street, according to the court, is a public forum.

Medical use of fetal tissue is generally deemed to contribute to recent advances in the use of tissue transplants to treat Parkinson's disease, Alzheimer's disease, Huntington's chorea, spinal cord injuries, diabetes, leukemia, aplastic anemia, and even radiation sickness, but antiabortionists bitterly oppose such uses.[196] They fear that new medical uses for fetal tissue may help to legitimize abortion. Fetal tissue is particularly valuable in implant treatments because it grows faster than adult tissue, is more adaptable, and causes less immunological rejection.

7.8 RECOVERY FOR EMOTIONAL DISTRESS AND FOR INVASION OF PRIVACY

A lesbian love triangle prompted the Supreme Judicial Court of Maine in Rowe v. Bennett to hold that an action for emotional distress can be maintained without evidence of corresponding physical injury.[197] Here plaintiff had been treated by defendant therapist (employed by the Diocesan Human Relations Services Incorporated) for five months for her difficulties with her female lover. After the therapist and plaintiff became emotionally involved, plaintiff and her former female lover split up, and the former lover moved in with the therapist. Plaintiff thereupon suffered what her psychiatrist diagnosed as "acute reactive depression"; she allegedly felt abandoned and humiliated and suffered intense emotional turmoil manifested by sleeplessness, loss of weight, poor concentration, crying spells, and impulses to commit suicide. The court held that "because of the unique nature of the psychotherapist-patient relationship, a patient may recover damages for serious mental distress resulting from the therapist's negligence despite the absence of an underlying tort."[198] According to the court, emotional distress resulting from a nontactile tort may be compensable when the requisite elements of the tort of intentional infliction of emotional distress are fulfilled: "(1) the conduct be intentional or reckless; (2) the tortfeasor's conduct be extreme or outrageous; (3) the wrongful conduct and emotional distress be causally connected; and (4) the emotional distress be severe."[199] The court concluded: "Absent tactile contact, a person's mental tranquility is also protected in the limited situation where a person intentionally or recklessly places another in fear of imminent harmful or offensive contact, thus fulfilling the requirements of the intentional tort of assault."[200]

An Illinois appellate court in Horak v. Biris in 1985 awarded the plaintiff damages for emotional distress when his male social worker had sexual intercourse with plaintiff's wife during the course of their marital counseling: "The very nature of the therapist-patient relationship . . . gives rise to a clear duty on the therapist's part to . . . refrain from any activity or conduct which carries with it a foreseeable and unreasonable risk of mental or emotional harm to the patient."[201] Three years earlier another Illinois appellate court, in Martino v. Family Service Agency of Adams County, had refused to recognize the tort of a social worker malpractice under similar facts.[202]

In 1978 in Del Zio v. Columbia Presbyterian Medical Center, the federal district court for the Southern District of New York approved a jury award of $50,000 against the hospital when the chief physician had wilfully destroyed plaintiff's fertilized egg prior to implantation.[203] The New York Court of Appeals in June 1987 in Martinez v. Long Island Jewish Hospital created a new cause of action in New York that allows recovery of tortious damages for emotional distress derived from one's own subjective feelings of guilt in following the negligently given advice of a physician.[204] Here the distressed female underwent an abortion based upon erroneous advice and apparently suffered serious emotional distress and required professional counseling. It should be noted that two earlier New York decisions, Tebbutt v. Virostek[205] and Vaccaro v. Squib,[206] had rejected recovery for emotional distress. In *Tebbutt*, the same court had held that a mother on whom amniocentesis had been negligently performed could not recover for the emotional distress caused when the fetus was delivered stillborn. In *Vaccaro*, the same court had ruled that there was no duty to the plaintiff mother on the part of the drug product manufacturer whose drug product allegedly caused the birth of plaintiff's child with severe birth defects. In 1984 in Bovsun v. Sanperi, the same New York Court of Appeals had held that emotional distress was not compensable unless such emotional distress was "tied, as a matter of proximate causation to the observations of the serious injury or death of the family member and such injury or death must have been caused by the conduct of the defendant."[207]

The landmark California decision of Dillon v. Legg, followed by perhaps a dozen or more states, had recognized emotional distress recovery by a person or persons outside the so-called zone of danger if physical injury was suffered by a close family relative and if such emotional distress was reasonably foreseeable.[208] Section 436(3), Comment f, of *Restatement (Second) of Torts*, while recognizing recovery for emotional distress, emphasized the necessity to utilize a "reasonably objective standard." The 1987 decision of the New York Court of Appeals in the *Martinez* case did not adhere to this objective standard; the opinion stressed the fact that her emotional distress was caused not by the abortion but by the attack upon her "firmly held beliefs" against abortion.[209]

Recovery for breach of the right of privacy[210] is perhaps one aspect of emotional distress recovery, although the right of privacy has been accorded constitutional protection, as shown in Roe v. Wade[211] and in Griswold v. Connecticut,[212] the latter case finding the Connecticut statute prohibiting the use of contraceptives to married persons to be unconstitutional since the married couple's right to use contraceptives was within a protected zone of privacy: "We deal with a right of privacy older than the Bill of Rights—older than our political parties, older than our school system," according to Mr. Justice Douglas.[213]

But subsequently in numerous federal appellate decisions, that right of privacy has been limited and restricted, as illustrated by the Fourth U.S. Court of Appeals opinion in Lovisi v. Slayton.[214] Here a married woman was convicted under a Virginia sodomy statute for acts of fellatio she performed on both her husband and a third party. These consensual actions of fellatio were performed in the couple's bedroom, and photographs were taken of the sexual acts. The court rejected any right of privacy in a family situation, especially where a third party is accepted as a viewer and as a participant in the marital bedroom.[215] The married couple was said to have waived their right of privacy under the Fourteenth Amendment.[216] It is arguable as to whether the right of privacy is waived when a married couple takes the reproductive process outside the marital chamber to the laboratory or to the surrogate motherhood situation. The U.S. Supreme Court in Eisenstadt v. Baird had remarked in 1972 that "if the right of privacy means anything, it is the right of the individual, married or single, to be free from unwarranted governmental intrusion into matters so fundamentally affecting a person as the decision whether to bear or beget a child."[217]

Privacy rights may also be jeopardized by child custody rulings, sometimes in the name of "the best interests and welfare of a child."[218] Recently in the New York case of Burgel v. Burgel, for example, the court ordered a spouse to submit to hair analysis for the purpose of determining her continued use of cocaine.[219] The information sought was clearly relevant to the mother's fitness for custody of the child. The dissenting opinion stressed that courts cannot compel litigants to become unwilling participants in a wholly experimental exercise. But the best interests of the child mandate that a court have adequate information before it. However, the U.S. Supreme Court in Schmerber v. California did rule that an involuntary blood test constituted a search and seizure within the Fourth Amendment scope requiring probable cause.[220] And in Winston v. Lee,[221] the Court ruled that since bodily intrusion may additionally endanger the health of persons sought to be tested, compelling need must be shown.[222]

7.9 THE COMMON LAW MARRIAGE

The common law marriage has been recognized in numerous states such as Georgia by statute: "Prerequisites to valid marriage—To constitute a valid marriage in this state there must be parties able to contract, an actual contract, and consummation according to law."[223] Georgia courts have held that proof of an express agreement to be husband and wife is not necessary, it being sufficient if, from circumstantial evidence, such a conclusion may be inferred, and that proof of marital cohabitation and the holding out by the parties as husband and wife is sufficient.[224] South Carolina by statute provides that "nothing contained in this article shall render illegal any marriage contracted without issuance of a license."[225] By court decision in South Carolina, the only requirement necessary to conclude a common law marriage is that "the facts and circumstances show an intention on the part of both parties to enter into a marriage contract usually evidenced by a public and unequivocal declaration of the parties."[226] On the other hand, New York in 1933 abolished common law marriages,[227] although it does recognize common law marriages that are legal in other states.[228] Most recently in Kellard v. Kellard, a New York court in July 1987 ruled that three days' cohabitation in South Carolina and in Georgia in 1978 constituted a valid marriage in New York.[229] The parties had lived together since 1958 and had held themselves out as husband and wife. The New York court, in upholding the valid marriage, explained that to hold otherwise "the financial security of the parties is jeopardized and the offspring declared illegitimate."

In Ranger Insurance Co. v. General Accident Fire and Life Assurance Corp., Ltd., G had settled an injury claim with the county, for which an individual who hit his van had been employed.[230] G's female roommate then filed a petition in the state court for a declaration that she was entitled to some of the insurance proceeds as G's common law wife. Her petition was dismissed, and later the county's insurer filed suit in a federal district court for a declaration that G's insurer should be the primary insurer, central to the success of which declaration was whether she and G had a common law marriage. The Third U.S. Court of Appeals ruled that dismissal by the state court of the petition for a declaration that the couple had a common law marriage did not collaterally estop an insurer from litigating in the federal district court the same issue of a common law marriage.

The U.S. Supreme Court in Stanley v. Illinois[231] had opined that "the law has [not] refused to recognize those family relationships unlegitimized by a marriage ceremony. The Court had declared unconstitutional a state statute denying natural, but illegitimate children a wrongful death action for the death of their mother, emphasizing that such children cannot be denied the right of other children because familial bonds in such cases were often as warm, enduring and important as those arising within a more formally organized family unit."[232] The point is abundantly clear, as the highest court "has frequently emphasized the importance of the family. . . . The integrity of the family unit has found protection in the Due Process Clause of the Fourteenth Amendment."[233] Thus, the presence of a common law marriage should not be a stumbling block in according full respect and legal recognition to the conduct of members of the family unit.

In Stanley v. Illinois, the petitioner had lived for eighteen years with his common law wife, and upon her death the custody of the children went to the state of Illinois under a statute making the children of unwed fathers the wards of the state.[234] The U.S. Supreme Court in 1972 could not accept this discriminatory situation against the common law marriage and ruled that the petitioning parent under the due process clause of the Fourteenth Amendment was entitled to a hearing on his fitness as a parent before his children were taken from him; the fact that he can apply for adoption or for custody and control of his children did not bar his attack on the dependency proceeding, and the state of Illinois cannot, consistent with due process requirements, merely presume that unmarried fathers in general and petitioner in particular are unsuitable and neglectful parents. (Parental unfitness must be established on the basis of individual proof.)[235]

Recently in California there has been a rush toward "confidential marriages," permitted under a nineteenth-century California statute meant to give couples in the remote frontier a discreet way to legitimize their children with only a pastor's knowing the wedding date. Registrations of those unions were kept secret in church records, away from public records and prying townfolk.[236] In 1972 the California legislature updated the law to record such marriages with the state, thus giving birth to the "commercial wedding chapel" business for quick and unpublicized marriages. In sharp contrast is Jackette v. Jackette, where a New York court refused to recognize a marriage because the ceremony had been performed by a minister of the Universal Life church, which is not authorized to perform marriage ceremonies in the state.[237] But:

> The State of New York will honor a common-law marriage, if it was validly contracted in another state (see, Matter of Pecoreno's Estate 64 Ad2d 711 [2d Dept. 1978] motion for leave to appeal denied). The law to be applied in determining the validity of an out-of-state marriage is the law of the state in which the marriage allegedly occurred (see, Mott v. Duncan Petroleum Trans., 51 NY2d 289, 292 [1980]).
>
> The State of Pennsylvania recognizes common-law marriages (see, In re Manfredi's Estate, 399 Pa. 285, 159 A.2d 697, 700 [Pa. 1960]). Pennsylvania requires three elements to prove a common-law marriage: (1) constant cohabitation; (2) general reputation that the parties are married; and (3) an express agreement of the parties evidenced by words in the present tense. The party who claims the existence of a common law marriage is under a heavy burden to prove it (see, In re Manfredi's Estate, 159 AD2d 697, 700–701, supra).
>
> In Cross v. Cross, (112 AD2d 62 [1st Dept. 1985]), the Appellate Division held that under the circumstances of an alleged common-law marriage, pedente lite relief would not be appropriate until the bona fides of the marriage in New York was proved. The Court stayed all financial discovery until the alleged common law marriage was judicially established.
>
> Based on the foregoing, the Court is of the opinion that the parties were not validly married in the State of New York and that plaintiff has not yet established, if at all she can, that the parties were married by common-law in the State of Pennsylvania.

In modern times lesbians and homosexuals have sought legal recognition of their respective "marriages." According to the *New York Times* (January 30, 1989), "thousands of lesbians around the country are having children. Most are living in lesbian relationships. Some have lived together for more than a decade, wanting children but often blocked as adoptive or foster parents. Now more and more of these women are choosing to have their own babies, most often by artificial insemination. . . . Lawyers are formulating custody agreements to try to insure legal rights for lesbian mothers, their female partners, and the fathers of their children."[238] One of the prime problems is recognition of the "marriage," followed by the fact that many state laws recognize only the biological mother as a parent and do not allow her lesbian partner to adopt the baby and thereby form the family.

Gay couples also seek recognition.[239] On July 6, 1989, the New York Court of Appeals found that gay as well as unmarried heterosexual and other nontraditional, couples can be viewed as the legal equivalent of a family in rent-controlled matters.[240] In at least six cities (Madison, Wisconsin; Takoma Park,

Maryland; Berkeley, California; Santa Cruz, California; West Hollywood, California, and San Francisco) there are domestic partner ordinances allowing persons of the same sex to register as couples living together in a financially and emotionally interdependent relationship.[241]

7.10 DEFENSE OF PATERNITY

The defense of paternity generally presents itself in a proceeding by the mother against the putative or reputed father for the support of the child.[242] When the putative father denies paternity, the question of paternity is decided before the court can commence support proceedings. Once paternity is established, the putative father who defaults in his obligation to support the child can be imprisoned.[243] The U.S. Supreme Court in Rivera v. Minnich in 1987 ruled that paternity need not be proved by clear and convincing evidence; preponderance of the evidence is sufficient to protect the putative father's due process rights.[244]

Surrogate parenthood is generally regulated by statutes on paternity and determinations of paternity.[245] There is a presumption in favor of the paternity of the natural mother's husband, a presumption that may or may not be rebuttable.[246] Under the Uniform Parentage Act (UPA),[247] for example, the husband of the married woman is presumed to be her child's father if the child is born during the marriage or within 300 days of a divorce or separation.[248] As long as the wife receives artificial insemination through a licensed physician and her husband has consented to the procedure, the husband is treated under section 5(a) of the UPA as the child's natural father. While the UPA allows any ''interested party'' (section 6(b)) to bring an action to determine paternity, only the child, the natural mother, or the man presumed to be the natural father may under the UPA qualify to bring an action to declare or deny the existence of a parent-child relationship.[249] It would appear that the UPA deprives the natural father of standing to establish his paternity if the surrogate mother is married when she conceives the natural father's child.

But the issues are not clear, as illustrated by the 1979 decision of the New Jersey court in C.M. v. C.C.[250] Here an unmarried woman wishing to have a child artificially inseminated herself with the sperm of a male friend, and she conceived a child. The male donor then successfully obtained visitation rights (and presumably support obligations): ''If a woman conceives a child by intercourse, the donor who is not married to the mother is no less a father than the man who is married to the mother. Likewise, if an unmarried woman conceives a child through artificial insemination from semen from a known man, that man cannot be considered to be less a father because he is not married to the woman.''[251] If the woman who conceived had been married, the presumption is that her husband would be the natural father of the child.

The Michigan Supreme Court in Syrkowski v. Appleyard had found that the state's paternity act did not bar the alleged father from having his paternity and his child support obligation established, despite the statutory presumptions that treat the child born after the artificial insemination procedure of the mother as the legal child of the mother and her husband.[252] According to the court, neither presumption will operate to estop the alleged biological father from establishing his paternity if the mother's husband simply withholds his consent to his wife's artificial insemination procedure.

In a New York case, Anonymous v. Anonymous, a husband who had acknowledged his paternity of a child may not subsequently renounce his fatherhood in a divorce action by claiming that he did not comply with the legal requirement that he consent in writing to his wife's artificial insemination.[253] The court stated that it "will not countenance such a result in this case when the plaintiff many times has, in writing, announced his paternity. . . . The plaintiff's position that the child is his if the defendant and he live in California, but not if they live in New York is not consonant with a challenge to paternity. Whatever promises defendant may have made to him and broken should not inure to the detriment of the child who is innocent of wrongdoing and in any case, not barred by agreements the plaintiff and defendant made between themselves." And in Michael M. v. Gerald D., a California court ruled that the state may block a man from trying to prove he fathered the child of a woman married to someone else by employing a conclusive presumption that the husband is the father.[254] In dismissing the suit, the court said that the conclusive presumption of a husband's fatherhood is based on "a determination by the Legislature as a matter of overriding social policy . . . that the husband is to be held responsible for the child and integrity of the family unit should not be impugned." In Josephine B. v. Nathan S. the New York court ruled that a woman who waited until her son was almost 21 years of age to seek to have a man other than her husband legally declared his father is not estopped by the passage of time from proceeding with the paternity action.[255] The court reviewed

> a line of decisions which found the presumption of legitimacy rebutted, and explicitly or impliedly rejected the estoppel argument. . . . These cases are notable for having in common with this case the presence of one or more of the following elements: 1) child was conceived prior to the marriage; 2) the husband and wife never lived together; 3) the husband and wife did not have sexual intercourse at anytime crucial to the conception of the child; 4) the non-existence of a relationship between the husband and the child; 5) no holding out by the wife of the husband as the child's father; and 6) the paternity proceeding was not a vehicle to advance the mother's custody rights. . . . The presumption of legitimacy comes into play in any case where it is claimed that the child of a married woman was fathered by a person other than her husband. However, Matter of Findlay, 253 N.Y. 1, while acknowledging that it was "potent, and one of the strongest and most persuasive known to the law, it was subject to sway of reason, and in historical times its rank was higher." 253 N.Y. at 7.
>
> Although there was a time when the presumption was viewed as conclusive, sub. non. "rule of the four seas," Judge Cardozo noted that as early as 1732 decisional law held that the presumption could be overcome. The profound deference accorded the pre-

sumption of legitimacy must be viewed from the prospective of the historical context in which the doctrine evolved.

The sacrament of marriage was intended to be for a lifetime. Dissolution could be accomplished only with the greatest of difficulties, and indeed was the province of the ecclesiastical courts. After annulment ceased to be the near exclusive means of sundering a marriage, the grounds for divorce sounded in adultery, which was a capital offense.

The consequences of annulment were horrendous, with the child of the marriage rendered illegitimate, filius nullius, nobody's child and unable to inherit from either mother or father. In contrast, today's customs and law are more relaxed. No societal opprobrium attaches to divorce, and only slightly to being a non-marital child. Indeed the presumption of legitimacy which for centuries had been absolute, and then difficult to rebut, is far more susceptible to being controverted by legally competent scientific evidence than was previously the case. . . .

While it is true that these cases stand for the proposition that estoppel will apply to preclude the illegitimizing of a child born during the course of a marriage, the facts of this case militate against the application of that doctrine for two reasons. In the first, a person seeking the invocation of an equitable remedy must themselves come to equity with clean hands. In the circumstances of this case, respondent cannot meet that burden. Simply put he is estopped from asserting estoppel. Secondly, and more important, the policy considerations that underlie the holdings which foreclose a parent from challenging the paternity of a child arise in factual contexts which are diametrically the opposite of those found in this matter. Accordingly the motion to dismiss is denied.

In Patrick v. Lisa and William, the New York Suffolk County Family Court granted the motion to dismiss where the petitioner who brought a paternity suit alleged that he was the biological father of the two infants.[256] Respondents moved to dismiss on the ground of equitable estoppel 186.5, contending that petitioner's delay and the fact that the children were from an intact family should bar the suit. The court in dismissing pointed out that the petitioner failed to establish that his claim as a father would be in the best interest of the infants. The court concluded that "it would be anomalous to allow respondent to interpose the doctrine of estoppel because 1) petitioner waited almost 21 years to bring suit, 2) the child's birth certificate and 3) petitioner's judgment of divorce listed her former husband as the father when petitioner a) had lived with and supported the child, b) arranged to have the child's last name changed to his own, and c) named him his beloved son and sole beneficiary in a 1978 will."

The U.S. Supreme Court in 1973 in Gomez v. Perez[257] condemned state regulations that denied illegitimate children the right to support from their fathers when the state otherwise accorded that right to other children.[258] Nine years later in Mills v. Habluetzel, the Court reaffirmed that view by outlawing a Texas statute that required paternity suits initiated to obtain child support to be filed before the child becomes a year old.[259]

Paternity may be rebutted by blood tests, which, at most, are able to predict the probability or likelihood of paternity to an exceptionally high degree.[260] Blood tests work on the theory that every person's blood has distinctive characteristics that pass to the offspring. Today the human leucocyte alloantigen

(HLA) test and the electrophoresis test are the most popular in excluding paternity.[261] In Matter of Ettore I. v. Angela D., the New York Appellate Division, Second Department, in 1987 examined paternity proceedings instituted by petitioner to establish his fatherhood of a 3-year-old child, allegedly conceived during an adulterous affair with the child's mother.[262] Blood tests indicated that the petitioner could have been the father; the results of his HLA test, which were submitted to the court and later introduced into evidence, disclosed "a plausibility of paternity score of 99.82%, which was characterized by the laboratory as paternity 'practically proved.' " Both the mother and her husband opposed the paternity claim, although the husband, while supporting the child, was separated from the wife. The New York court ruled that the petitioner is estopped from claiming paternity because of the delay in bringing the proceeding, even though he argued that he had waited patiently for the separation between the mother and her husband so as not to interfere with the marital relationship:

> "The excuse profferred by the petitioner, in an attempt to justify his delay, is patently insufficient to defeat the defense of estoppel. . . . Acceptance of such a self-serving excuse would be fundamentally inconsistent with the purpose of estoppel, which is to protect innocent children from an irreparable loss of legal rights and status and to protect the rights of unsuspecting persons who have developed strong bonds with the child during the period of inaction.

Chapter 815y of General Statutes of Connecticut, entitled "Paternity Matters," is an interesting document that delineates in great detail the filing of a paternity petition by the mother or expectant mother, the procedure in the action brought by the expectant mother, the action by state or town, the issue of stillbirth or other premature termination of pregnancy, the testimony of the mother and the putative father, the nature of blood tests, disclosure of name of putative father, acknowledgment of paternity, and agreement to support; in addition, there are provisions setting forth the claim for paternity by the putative father, as well as a procedure for evaluating foreign paternity judgments and the like.[263]

DNA testing has been accepted in judging paternity, according to the New York court in Matter of Baby Girl S.[264] DNA testing is a three-year-old technique that can isolate unique genetic characteristics from blood, hair, body fluids, or tissues. Such evidence made it "totally clear, convincing, satisfactory, and basically uncontroverted" that a man identified as Gustavo R. was indeed the father of the three-year-old girl. To establish paternity scientifically, the court here ordered the standard HLA blood test, as well as the new genetic marker tests based on analysis of DNA. The New York court concluded:

> Although DNA testing is a relatively new scientific achievement, its potential application in many areas, including the law, is striking. For the purpose of this paternity case, since it is undisputed that the DNA probe is a blood genetic marker test, it was admitted into evidence under the clear language. . . . The combined results of the standard HLA and related blood tests produced a 99.99 percent probability that Gustavo was the father of

the baby. The tests' combined paternity index was 56,481 to 1. The probability that Gustavo was the father was also 99.99 percent under the DNA test, but the combined paternity index was "a staggering 8,077,911 to 1."

The Ohio Supreme Court in 1989 in Hulett v. Hulett approved genetic testing to challenge the presumption that a man is the natural father of a child who is born while he is married to the child's mother.[265] The mother of the child successfully introduced evidence of genetic tests to overcome the presumption that her husband was the child's father. In Matter of Nancy M. G. (Anonymous) v. James M. (Anonymous), the New York Appellate Division, Second Department, in March 1989, observed that the plaintiff had introduced the results of an HLA test, which combined with testing for other genetic markers indicated a 98.72 percent likelihood of the defendant's paternity: "Although the HLA test has not yet been recognized as conclusive evidence of paternity . . . we place great reliance upon such test results as being highly accurate and carrying a high degree of probative value on the issue of paternity."[266] The dissenting opinion argued: "While it is true that the results of the HLA test are highly probative, they are not conclusive. Such test results are only one item of evidence among many which the trier of facts has at its disposal to aid in its determination, and the results need only be given such weight as the trier of fact deems appropriate." Another New York court, in Matter of A.T. (M.K.), ruled that a DNA test with a 99.993 percent positive probability was not sufficient on its own to establish paternity.[267] The petitioner had not established the claim by "clear and convincing evidence, evidence which is completely satisfactory and which created a genuine belief that the respondent is the father of the child." The court, in addition to "high probability blood tests," found it necessary to consider other evidence, such as the approximate time of conception, testimony as to whether the mother and respondent had a sexual relationship during the period of conception, "lack of evidence" on whether another man had sexual access to the mother during the conception period, and the witness's credibility. The case arose when the respondent, the putative father, and his wife sued the petitioner in another New York court for slander, alleging that the plaintiff and mother of the child made a statement that the respondent was the father of her child. That slander case was dismissed after a DNA test showed a probability of paternity and HLA tests excluded A.T.'s husband as the biological father and revealed the probability of M.K.'s being the father at 99.98 percent. In her family court suit, A.T. claimed the doctrine of collateral estoppel prevented M.K. from contesting paternity, but the family court disagreed.[268] The slander suit of King v. Tanner[269] resulted in dismissal of the $1 million claim based on paternity allegations later proved by genetic analysis:[270] "The petitioner has failed to establish that his belated entry into Kristyn's life, as her biological father, would in any way be in Kristyn's best interests. Given that the court is duty bound to

zealously safeguard the welfare, stability and best interests of the child (Ettore 1, 127 AD2d at 13), the court is constrained to dismiss the instant petition, in the interests of

Kristyn and in furtherance of her obvious need for legitimacy and stability. Clearly, on this record, the petitioner cannot be permitted to disrupt the child's life and to disturb her intact family, with its attendant security, structure and parental identifications. No purpose will be served in suddenly illegitimizing Kristyn, in breaking the legal relationship she has with her sibling, in disrupting the bond with her presumed father, and in subjecting Kristyn to the stark reality that she is the product of an illicit relationship had between her mother and a man who was, at one time, a neighbor. Given the obvious trend in recent years towards the protection of the child in paternity proceedings and away from traditional policy or fiscal considerations, and in view of the broad language of Ettore 1, it is difficult to create a factual scenario wherein the estoppel doctrine would not be applied in a case of this nature. Indeed, the court cannot help but wonder if there can *ever* be a viable paternity proceeding by a putative father regarding a child who lives and thrives in an intact, traditional family unit.

For a detailed statistical analysis of such testing, see Martin, "Probability of Paternity,"[271] citing such recent New York cases as Menaldino ex rel. Aletha "TT" v. Mark "UU,"[272] Tamara B. v. Pete F.,[273] Shirley R. v. Ricardo B.,[274] and the Oregon case of Pelem v. Walter.[275] Martin concluded that "the almost reflexive recitation of the 'probability of paternity' by New York courts indicates that the parties using, or facing, such evidence should be extremely careful that they understand exactly what the numbers do—and do not—express."

7.11 MATERNAL RIGHTS VERSUS FETAL RIGHTS

The eternal conflict between maternal rights and fetal rights has never been resolved, although it appears that courts generally favor fetal over maternal rights.[276] Moral, ethical, and religious opinions intermeddle, and frequently the fetus is protected at the expense of the mother.[277] Undoubtedly a pregnant woman's medical decisions will affect her own life, as well as the life of the fetus she is carrying; her right to her bodily integrity may have to succumb to the state's compelling interest in the child after the first trimester of her pregnancy. On the other hand, the mother does have a legal right to refuse medical treatment pursuant to the informed consent doctrine,[278] provided that the fetus is not viable.[279] The mother's rights are enhanced by the U.S. Supreme Court's recognition of the right to parental autonomy,[280] although courts will intervene when a child's life is at stake.[281] Indeed, the right to refuse medical treatment for a minor child may be overridden where the minor child's life is at stake.[282]

Fetal rights probably commence with viability—the time when a fetus can exist independent of its mother. In Roe v. Wade, the highest court in 1973 refused to assign personhood to the fetus until it was viable, at which time the state's compelling interest might take over.[283] Yet in Bennett v. Hymers in 1958, the New Hampshire Supreme Court had adopted the view that a fetus becomes a separate organism from the time of conception for purposes of recovery for prenatal injury.[284] The New Jersey Supreme Court in 1960 in Smith v. Brennan had proclaimed that a child has a legal right to begin life with a sound mind and a sound body.[285] Some state child neglect statutes actually label a fetus as a "child." In Hoerner v. Bertinato, a New Jersey court ruled that the parents had statutorily neglected their unborn child by refusing to consent to a blood transfusion.[286] The same result occurred three years later in Raleigh Fitkin–Paul Morgan Memorial Hospital v. Anderson, holding that "the unborn child is entitled to the law's protection."[287] And in In re Baby X, the Michigan appellate court specifically found that the pregnant woman's prenatal conduct—extensive narcotic ingestion—constituted statutory child neglect.[288] By such circumlocutionary interpretation, fetal rights can override maternal rights.

Where maternal rights clash with fetus rights, the states have on occasion entered the fray, and courts have protected the mother's right to refuse intervention, as illustrated in Taft v. Taft.[289] Here the highest Massachusetts court upheld the mother's refusal to submit to a suturing procedure, designed to prevent the miscarriage of her not-yet-viable fetus. The court recognized the mother's right to her religious beliefs against such surgery and her previous bad experiences with such surgery. But the state's compelling interest in the well-being of unborn children was not infringed upon, nor was it challenged in a similar view by the Maryland appellate court in Mercy Hospital v. Jackson, where the mother refused blood transfusions during a consensual cesarean section because of her religious convictions.[290]

The Michigan appellate court in Grodin v. Grodin faced an unusual claim by a child whose teeth at birth were discolored because of her mother's ingestion of tetracycline.[291] Since child-parent liability immunity was not involved, the court concluded that the mother should bear the same degree of liability for negligently injuring her child as would any other third person. The thrust of this pernicious opinion is to expose parents to multitudes of suits for alleged prenatal injuries suffered by their own offspring. California by statute has somewhat limited a woman's increased liability for prenatal injuries of her own child; the statute provides that no cause of action arises against a parent on a claim that the parent's child should not have been conceived or, if conceived, should not have been born.[292]

In the workplace where women are increasingly present, the conflict persists between maternal rights and fetal rights. Courts have generally upheld the employers' policies that are designed to protect the fetus, as illustrated in Wright v. Olin Corp.[293] Here the Fourth U.S. Court of Appeals opined that the safety of workers' unborn children should be no less a legitimate business concern than the safety of the traditional business licensee or invitee. Thus, employers may impose otherwise impermissible restrictions on women's employment opportunities if those restrictions are reasonably necessary to protect the health of the unborn child of female employees against the hazards of the workplace.

The question has been raised whether "fetal abuse" should be recognized as a crime.[294] Advocates of criminalization argue that fetal abuse can be controlled through the "use of post-birth sanctions in egregious cases" after education and treatment have failed. Those opposed contend that criminalization of fetal abuse is untenable, an unconstitutional invasion of privacy; improved social services for pregnant women are preferred. The Illinois Supreme Court in Stallman v. Youngquist declined to recognize a tort action for maternal prenatal negligence.[295]

7.12 HOMICIDE AND THE FETUS

After injuring a pregnant woman while driving drunk, the defendant was indicted for manslaughter for causing the death of the woman's seven-month fetus in People v. Vercelletto.[296] Here the New York court had occasion to review the U.S. Supreme Court 1973 decision in Roe v. Wade that a fetus, after the first trimester of pregnancy, is conclusively presumed to be viable and capable of meaningful life outside the mother's womb.[297] In this case the fetus was well beyond the first trimester but was not yet a "person" under section 125.12 of the New York Penal Law, which provides that "a person, when referring to a victim, means a human being who has been born and is alive." Accordingly, the court dismissed the charge of manslaughter for causing the death of the seven-month fetus.[298]

However, courts have generally expanded fetal rights by considering the fetus as the "victim" under a criminal statute, as illustrated by Commonwealth of Massachusetts v. Cass.[299] Here the Massachusetts court defined as homicide the infliction of prenatal injuries that result in the death of a viable fetus before or after its birth. The court was mindful of a 1975 decision that a viable fetus was a "person" for the purpose of the Massachusetts wrongful death statute.[300] The dissenting opinion in *Cass* argued that it was dangerous to rely on a civil wrongful death case to interpret a criminal statute.

7.13 ADOPTION AND LEGAL LIABILITY

Adoption practices are, for the most part, set forth in state statutes, as illustrated by Chapter 778 of the General Statutes of Connecticut, which defines adoption as "the establishment by court order of the legal relationship of parent and child."[301] The Connecticut statute delineates the nature of and the hearing on the petition to terminate parental rights, the appointment and duties of the statutory parent, who may give a child in adoption and when a child is free for adoption, the procedure on application for adoption, the effects of the final decree of adoption, the availability and confidentiality of adoption records, and the establishment of an adoption review board.

The confidentiality of adoption records is part and parcel of the entire adoption procedure, but many states, like Virginia, allow adoption records to be open to the adopted child who is 18 years of age or older.[302] Other jurisdictions limit availability of adoption records to judicial orders. The availability of adoption records to the adopted child might open Pandora's box and interfere with the adoption by the natural parents or other participants in the procedure.[303] Confidentiality of adoption records is perhaps best preserved by agency placements, which are generally fully regulated by state law.

The adoption of children born to surrogate mothers has prompted a great deal of litigation, as witnessed recently in Kentucky, Louisiana, Michigan, Ohio, and the District of Columbia. In 1981 the Kentucky attorney general issued an advisory opinion declaring that contracts by which artificially inseminated surrogate mothers bear children in Kentucky on behalf of childless couples were illegal and unenforceable in Kentucky.[304] The thrust of the advisory opinion was that Kentucky statutes prohibited any person or agency from accepting remuneration for procuring any child for adoption purposes.[305] In the 1983 case of In re Baby Girl, a Kentucky circuit court ruled that a surrogate mother was not permitted to terminate her rights to a child conceived through artificial insemination under a contract to transfer custody to the sperm donor.[306] The mother and her husband sought to have the alleged biological father declared the natural father, with authority to adopt the child after first having his name placed on the child's birth certificate. In denying the petition, the Kentucky court reasoned that a child born in wedlock is presumed to be the legitimate child of the husband and surrogate mother: "The mere affidavit as to artificial insemination without other positive proof of nonaccess and blood grouping is not sufficient for this court to assume and adjudge the donor to be the natural and biological father of the child."[307] The court pointed out that even if the presumption of the husband's paternity could be overcome, a petition to terminate parental rights would still not be the appropriate procedure in Kentucky because the child was not being put up for adoption in a licensed child-placing agency. However, another Kentucky circuit court the same year, in Kentucky v. Surrogate Parenting Association (concerning a challenge of the right of defendant to do business in Kentucky), resulted in a judicial declaration that surrogate arrangements are not governed by the Kentucky adoption statutes disallowing payment: "How can a natural father be characterized as either adopting or buying his own baby? . . . He does not (and cannot) buy the right to adopt a child with which he already has a legal and natural relationship. . . . [Since] the natural father is not paying to gain rights to the child because he already has a legal, as well as natural relationship" to the child, there can be no violation of the adoption statutes.[308] Thus, it would be beyond the power of the Kentucky court to apply the policy of the adoption statutes to the termination of parentage statutes because such an application would be tantamount to enacting a new statute.[309] The Kentucky attorney general, however, had the last word because the Kentucky Court of Appeals in 1985 reversed and declared that surrogate motherhood was a violation of both the letter and the policy of the Kentucky statute, prohibiting payment in connection with adoption. The highest Kentucky court explained that adoption is an integral part of the surrogate motherhood arrangement, and termination of parental rights by the surrogate mother and her husband is but a necessary prerequisite to a subsequent adoption by the infertile wife and her husband.

In Louisiana, the attorney general in 1983 stated that where the adoptive parents pay a surrogate mother a fee above and beyond the actual medical and living expenses associated with birth, the Louisiana statute against the sale of minor children would be violated by any subsequent adoption.[310] In Michigan in Doe v. Attorney General, plaintiff had brought suit seeking a declaratory judgment that the Michigan statutes prohibiting payment in connection with adoption were unconstitutional.[311] But the court rejected the argument that the right to adopt a child based upon payment was a fundamental personal right: "A contract to use the statutory authority of the Probate Court to effect the adoption of a child wherein such contract provides for valuable compensation, is not deserving of, nor is it, within the constitutional protection of the right of privacy as defined by the many cases of the United States Supreme Court."

The Ohio adoption statutes are apparently not violated by a privately arranged surrogate mother contract negotiated directly between the surrogate mother and the adopting parents.[312]

In In re R.K.S. the District of Columbia Superior Court acknowledged that it could streamline the adoption procedure to accommodate parties to a surrogate relationship where the petitioner is "a spouse of the natural parent of the prospective adoptee and the natural parent consents to the adoption."[313]

In Pennsylvania under statute, the surrogate mother has a right to revoke the adoption consent any time before the court enters an adoption decree or a parental rights termination decree.[314] This possibility places the adopting couple in Pennsylvania in an awkward position: the contract has been performed, but the statute might deny them the full benefit of their contractual agreement. The adopting couple's remedy is an action against the surrogate mother for involuntary termination of parental rights.[315] The Pennsylvania court is mandated to give primary consideration to the needs and welfare of the child.[316] In In re Adoption of Michael, the Pennsylvania Superior Court emphasized that view in its decision: "Whether a parent has demonstrated a continued inability to conduct his or her life in a fashion that would provide a safe environment for the child, whether that child is living with the parents or not, and the behavior of the parent is irremediable as supported by clear and competent evidence" are the prime questions before the court.[317] Other Pennsylvania statutes have rebutted the presumption that a mother should always receive custody of an infant child or that a natural parent should raise the child or that custody should be given always to two-parent families.[318]

It has been pointed out that the cost of pursuing a private adoption today is exorbitant.[319] The sum of $20,000 or more is a realistic figure. However, private, independent adoptions appear to be illegal in Delaware, Massachusetts, Michigan, Minnesota, and North Dakota; other states, including Connecticut, impose various requirements that discourage private adoptions.[320]

In New York religious placement is an important factor in adoptions, but in Matter of Baby Girl Z, a natural mother's challenge to the private adoption of her child because she was not told the adoptive father's religion was dismissed by the New York Appellate Division, Second Department.[321] At issue was the desire of the natural mother, a 25-year-old graduate student, to have her daughter, born out of wedlock, placed with a Christian family and to have the infant raised religiously. The court found that the adoptive parents, the adoptive mother's sister, the couple's attorney, and the natural mother's attorney had all withheld the fact that the adoptive father was Jewish, despite the natural mother's repeatedly expressed concern that her child be raised as a Christian. The court initially pointed out that the material issue was "the religion in which the child was to be raised and not the religious heritage of the adoptive father. . . . It is uncontroverted that the birth mother declined an opportunity to meet with the prospective adoptive parents to further evaluate their suitability, the child has been baptized in the Catholic faith (of the adoptive mother) and there has been no recanting of the commitment to raise the child as a Christian."

7.14 THE RAPE SUIT

A Maryland court in Cobey v. State of Maryland ordered a new trial for a man convicted of rape because the trial court had rejected genetic evidence that linked him to the victim's aborted fetus.[322] In effect, the court attacked the reliability of the so-called chromosome variant analysis, which studies and compares chromosome samples, and had apparently concluded that the man on trial was likely to have impregnated the rape victim. The court ruled that the test had not been "generally accepted in the relevant scientific community . . . as a reliable test . . . to establish paternity."[323]

Sexual exploitation of patients is another aspect of the problem of rape, meriting close attention.[324] Emotionally weakened yet hopeful for a cure through treatment, patients of mental health practitioners are often vulnerable to sexual exploitation by therapists from whom they seek help. The sanctity of the therapeutic relationship, as well as professional codes of ethics and standards of care protecting patients, should be examined.

7.15 THE INTENTIONAL TORT

The intentional tort is seen in action in countless situations already delineated. Here we focus on several important examples. Tort liability for sexually transmitted diseases[325] is illustrated by Long v. Adams, which involved an intimate sexual relationship between two unmarried persons, the male claiming that his female partner intentionally infected him with genital herpes.[326] The Georgia appellate court opined, finding negligence but not necessarily an intentional act:

> First, what legal duty, if any, is owed by one sexually active person to another? The duty owed is the same one that every individual in this state owes another: the duty to exercise ordinary care not to injure others. Having established that standard of care to which appellee was required to conform, we move to the second element—failure to conform to the standard. Appellant alleged that appellee intentionally and negligently

had sexual intercourse with him at times when she knew she was infected with genital herpes, a contagious venereal disease, and that he was not informed of her condition at the time the acts occurred. Since the record before us does not contain any sworn testimony to refute the allegations (although the existence of a deposition is alluded to), the trial court was required to regard the allegations in the light most favorable to the appellant, with all doubts resolved in his favor, on the appellee's motion to dismiss. *Harper v. DeFreitas*, 117 Ga. App. 236, 160 SE 2d (1968). Examining the complaint in that light, it can be said that appellee may not have conformed to the required standard of care. What amounts to the exercise of ordinary care under the circumstances is a jury question. *Hand v. Harrison*, 99 Ga. App. 429 (3), 108 SE 2d 814 (1959). There being no evidence that absolutely resolved the issue, we conclude that the second element of an actionable negligence claim exists.

The penultimate element, a close causal connection between appellee's conduct and appellant's injury, is established. It is commonly known that herpes is a contagious and incurable disease, transmitted primarily by intimate sexual contact . . . appellee argues otherwise. Nowhere in the record does appellee assert that she did not have genital herpes during the period of her relationship with appellant. Rather, she argues that she was not obligated to disclose her condition to him. Since it it undisputed that appellee had the disease during the time in question, engaged in sexual intercourse with appellant, did not disclose her condition to him, and that he later contracted the disease, we can conclude that a causal connection existed between her conduct and his injury. We can also dispose of the last element, recognizing that appellant has suffered damage by being afflicted with an incurable disease.

In light of the foregoing analysis, we conclude that appellant stated a cause of action based on negligence.

In Barbara A. v. John G. the California court imposed liability upon "one sexual partner who by intentionally tortious conduct causes physical injury to the other."[327] According to the court,

Respondent's representation about his procreative inability was false, and he knew it was false. It was made with the intent to induce appellant to engage in sexual intercourse, protected or not. Appellant, relying on respondent's assurance of his sterility, consented to and did engage in sexual intercourse with respondent. . . . As a result of sexual intercourse with respondent, appellant became pregnant. The pregnancy was determined to be tubal, and, as a consequence, appellant was forced to undergo surgery to save her life. Her Fallopian tube was removed and she was rendered sterile by the surgery. She suffered physical, emotional and financial injuries as a result of the pregnancy.

In B.N. v. K.K., the Maryland court recognized intentional infliction of emotional distress upon a nurse for sexual transmission of genital herpes from a doctor. He had a duty to disclose the contagious disease even though there was no traditional or conventional confidential relationship between the nurse and the doctor.[328] The court found that the doctor's conduct "easily crosses the extreme and outrageous" threshold of the intentional tort. According to the court, "one who has genital herpes may be deprived of most normal sexual activity, marriage may be virtually out of the question, and childbearing may be practically ruled out (Herpes is lethal to up to 60% of infected newborns and for surviving babies, there is a 50% risk of blindness or brain damage)."[329] It concluded: "One who knowingly engages in conduct that is highly likely to infect another with an incurable disease of this nature, and who also is aware of the nature of the disease, not only engages in intentional or reckless conduct . . . he or she has committed extreme and outrageous conduct."

Another intentional tort is seen in those situations where life support systems are withdrawn, although most courts bar the removal of life supports.[330] In In re Jobes the New Jersey Supreme Court held that there was sufficient evidence to show that Mrs. Jobes was in an irreversible vegetative state and that a surrogate decision maker who declines life-sustaining equipment must secure statements from at least two doctors showing that there is no possibility the patient will recover.[331]

7.16 DAMAGES GENERALLY

The cases are legion, but a few selected cases can illustrate the measure of damages in these circumstances. In Hicks v. Storlazzi, a Massachusetts court recognized a mother's claim for loss of filial consortium of a newborn caused by obstetrical negligence.[332] In the Texas case of St. Elizabeth's Hospital v. Garrard, proof of physical injury, illness, or impairment was not required for recovery where negligent infliction of mental suffering was claimed.[333]

> After admission to St. Elizabeth Hospital, Mrs. Garrard gave birth to twins. A male was born alive and healthy. A female was stillborn. Although the attending physician and Mr. Garrard agreed to have the stillborn infant autopsied, no autopsy was ever performed. Instead, the infant's body was delivered to a mortuary and disposed of in an unmarked, common grave without the knowledge or consent of either parent. After alleging specific acts of negligence by the hospital and the pathologist, the Garrards' petition alleged that each of them had suffered and would continue to suffer "mental anguish" as a proximate consequence of defendant's negligence because they would (1) never know the cause of their baby's death and would worry about future pregnancies, (2) never know where their baby was buried and therefore be unable to follow traditional memorializations, such as placing flowers on a grave or visiting a grave site, and (3) lose the opportunity to conduct a funeral and experience that normal and usual time of grief and its sublimation necessary to the continuation of life as usual after a death.

Bottom line: Plaintiffs sought damages only for their mental suffering.[334] In Craig v. IMT Insurance Co., an unborn child in Iowa was a "person" for the consortium claim brought by the parents.[335] But damages for emotional distress for a homosexual relationship were not recognized in Coon v. Joseph, where the plaintiff witnessed an assault upon his intimate male friend.[336]

A usual aspect of damages can be found in the recognition of a master's degree as marital property, seen in McGowan v. McGowan, where the New York court observed, "It is now settled that where, during a marriage, one spouse begins and completes a medical education, the professional license which is conferred in recognition of the completion of that medical education, qualifies as marital property which is subject to equitable distribution."[337] But here the court found that the teaching certification earned by the plaintiff wife was not marital property. It observed:

> The consideration of a license or degree as marital property represents but one of several methods by which the courts throughout the United States have sought to remedy a single social injustice, i.e., the injustice that results when one spouse, to the detriment of his or her own fulfillment, labors in order to support the other spouse through an educational program, only to be divorced before the economic rewards of that program are realized. Virtually every appellate decision which has been written on issues such as those presented here recognizes that the so-called " 'student-spouse, working-spouse' syndrome" is the basic underlying problem to which a just solution is sought (see, *O'Brien v. O'Brien*, 106 AD2d 223, 231, *mod* 66 NY2d 576, *supra*; *Conner v. Conner*, 97 AD2d 88, 106–107 [Bracken and Brown, J.J., concurring]). The debate concerns itself only with the issue of whether the cure for this "syndrome" may be worse than the syndrome itself. It has been unanimously decided by the Court of Appeals that with respect to professional licenses such a cure is not. It would certainly amount to a gross injustice, however, to consider a license or degree to be property, where the symptoms of the "student-spouse working-spouse syndrome" are completely absent.

In a later New York case, Kalnins v. Kalnins, the M.B.A. degree was recognized as divisible property in a matrimonial case.[338] The academic degree from Harvard University School of Business was deemed to be marital property to be valued and divided under equitable distribution in a divorce action. The court valued the enhanced earning capacity of the Harvard M.B.A. of the defendant husband, who made more than $100,000 in salary and bonuses at a bank, at $70,000 and the wife's lump-sum present-value share at $15,000. The court cited the 1985 New York Court of Appeals decision in O'Brien v. O'Brien, which dealt with apportioning the value of a medical license, and the court pointed out that "advanced educational degrees" constitute marital property also.[339] The plaintiff in this divorce action was a 43-year-old woman with permanent brain damage sustained in an automobile accident prior to her marriage. Fourteen years later, she sought divorce on the grounds of abandonment. The parties stipulated that her handicap "will more than likely make it impossible for her to earn a living in the future and that permanent maintenance is appropriate. . . . In addition to maintenance, plaintiff seeks equitable distribution of the marital property."

The New York court, in citing the *O'Brien* case,[340] specifically noted that the New York Court of Appeals had "neither overruled nor reaffirmed" Conner v. Conner,[341] which is directly on point with the case at bar:[342]

> There, the Court held that a Harvard M.B.A. does not constitute marital property. In that case, the court may have been influenced by the fact "that during the entire time

[the degree-earning spouse] was enrolled in the Harvard . . . program, [he] was the sole financial support of the household. Id. at 90, 468 N.Y.S.2d at 485. Since the O'Brien decision, at least one trial court has applied the reasoning of Conner to a Bachelor's degree, thus maintaining a dubious distinction between a license and a degree. See Cronin v. Cronin, 131 Misc.2d 879, 502 N.Y.S. 2d 368 (Sup. Ct., Nassau Cty. 1986). It should be noted, however, that the court in Cronin did apply the reasoning in O'Brien to the wife's law degree acquired during the marriage. Cronin, supra, at 881, 502 N.Y.S. 2d at 370. The degree not considered marital property was the husband's Bachelors of Science in Marketing. Id. 882–83, 502 N.Y.S. 2d at 371. While the Cronin Court was unwilling to extend the holding of O'Brien to a B.S., this ruling is seemingly bottomed on the understandable distinction between graduate and undergraduate degrees. There is a difference in the earning potential of a professional who has an undergraduate degree only and a professional who holds an advanced degree.

A number of post-O'Brien cases have extended the reasoning of O'Brien to an advanced educational degree. In McGowin v. McGowin, 142 A.D. 2d 355, 535 N.Y.S. 2d 990 (2d Dep't 1988), the Second Department held, contrary to its own holding in Conner, that a Masters degree which entitled plaintiff to a higher salary as a teacher constituted marital property. See McGowin, supra, at 358, 535 N.Y.S. 2d at 992. The trial court in McGowin had noted that the arguments once raised in Conner seemed very close to those raised unsuccessfully in O'Brien; and concluded that while a license does confer a privilege whereas a degree does not, "certain degrees may, as a practical matter, enhance the earning capacity of the holder." McGowin v. McGowin, 136 Misc. 2d 225, 229, 518 N.Y.S. 2d 346 (Sup. Ct. Suffolk Cty. 1987) modified, 142 A.D. 2d 355, 535 N.Y.S. 2d 990 (2d Dep't 1988). This Court agrees. Post O'Brien decisions suggest that an advanced degree constitutes marital property, at least for the purposes of classification under the equitable distribution law. See McAlpine v. McAlpine, 143 Misc. 2d 30, 539 N.Y.S. 2d 680 (Sup Ct., Suffolk Cty. 1989) (fellowship in the Society of Actuaries); Golub v. Golub, 139 Misc. 2d 440, 527 N.Y.S. 2d 946 (Sup. Ct. N.Y. Cty. 1988) (celebrity status gained during marriage). See also Freyer v. Freyer, 138 Misc. 2d 158, 524 N.Y.S. 2d 147 (Sup. Ct., Suffolk Cty. 1987) (research scientist's Ph. D).

7.17 TORT LIABILITY FOR SEXUAL TRANSMISSION OF AIDS

Sexual transmission of AIDS (acquired immunodeficiency syndrome) is an accepted fact. However, it is not clear who is legally responsible for causing exposure to the AIDS virus, especially in the face of the numerous defenses that one sexual partner can raise in a given situation.[343] Equally important is the fact that the medical community is constantly revising its theories about who is at risk and the modes of transmission of AIDS. Still another aspect of the problem is that the sexual activity itself may constitute the crime of adultery or sodomy.

The causes of action here may be negligence,[344] battery,[345] negligent misrepresentation,[346] deceit,[347] and intentional infliction of emotional distress.[348] Potential defenses include illegality of the sexual activity,[349] assumption of the risk,[350] contributory negligence,[351] breach of right of privacy,[352] statute of limitations,[353] and interspousal immunity.[354]

All persons who test positive for the presence of AIDS antibodies are considered to be at risk for spreading the disease and therefore should take precautions to avoid exposing others to the disease. The U.S. Public Health Service[355] has recommended that infected persons do not donate blood, sperm, or organs; that they do not share drug needles; that they avoid exchanging body fluids during sexual activity; and that they avoid oral-genital contact and intimate kissing.[356]

As to the negligence cause of action,[357] it is well established that a person who negligently exposes another person to a contagious disease is liable for resultant damages.[358] Lack of knowledge as to the existence of the disease is not an excuse or defense, according to the New York court in Alice D. v. William M., where the defendant honestly believed that he was sterile, and in reliance on his representation of his sterility, the plaintiff female consented to sexual intercourse; she became pregnant, and the court held him negligently liable.[359]

Battery, an action for direct physical contact, was the cause of action in State of Delaware v. Lankford, where the defendant, knowing that he had syphilis, continued to have sexual intercourse with his wife without informing her of his affliction.[360] After she sustained the disease, the court held that defendant's conduct also constituted criminal battery. Section 892B of *Restatement (Second) of Torts* states that where X consents to sexual intercourse with Y, who knows that X is ignorant of the fact that Y has a venereal disease, Y is subject to liability to X for battery. In Kathleen K. v. Robert B., the California court found for the plaintiff after the defendant male had infected her with genital herpes during sexual intercourse.[361] And in Barbara A. v. John G.,[362] the California court held that a cause of action for battery is maintained where there is an unwarranted invasion of plaintiff's interest in freedom from intentional, unlawful, and harmful or offensive contact with the person of the plaintiff.[363]

Negligent misrepresentation is delineated in section 311 of *Restatement (Second) of Torts*, holding X liable for physical harm to Y as a result of X's misrepresentation if X intends or should reasonably know that his statement will cause Y to act in reliance thereon for its honesty and accuracy, and X either knows the statement is false or has failed to ascertain whether the statement is or is not true.[364] As stated in Alice D. v. William M., the defendant had in fact made a false claim that he was sterile prior to engaging in sexual intercourse with plaintiff, and the New York court found that the facts supported a cause of action for negligent misrepresentation.[365] Indeed, the defendant male owed a duty to the female plaintiff to give accurate information concerning his sterility.

Deceit or fraudulent misrepresentation[366] is illustrated in Barbara A. v. John G., where plaintiff claimed that the defendant—her attorney and lover—fraudulently misrepresented his sterility, with the result that she suffered an abnormal pregnancy.[367] The California court held that she had established the cause of action for deceit based on defendant's affirmative misrepresentation that he could not get anyone pregnant.

The cause of action for intentional infliction of emotional distress will ordinarily be brought in advance of the disease since the fear of the disease gives rise to the cause of action. But the conduct of the actor must be intentional and outrageous, as illustrated in Kathleen K. v. Robert B., where it was found that the defendant knew or should have known that his conduct would cause actual injury and/or emotional distress to the plaintiff.[368]

Defenses to the various causes of action for liability for sexual transmission of AIDS generally begin with the defense of illegality of the sexual conduct in which both parties have engaged.[369] The defendant argues that plaintiff is barred from bringing a civil suit for injuries resulting from a criminal act. However, the Texas court in DeVall v. Strunk[370] refused to accept the defense of illegality, declaring that the illegality defense applies only where the parties are of equal guilt.[371]

The defense of consent is shown where the defendant pleads that plaintiff consented to the very act or acts producing her injuries. In short, the sexual intercourse resulting in the plaintiff's sustaining AIDS was consensual. However, while the female plaintiff may have consented to sexual intercourse, she did not consent to experiencing AIDS. Of course, consent obtained by deceit or fraud is vitiated,[372] as would consent to an unlawful act or conduct.[373]

Assumption of the risk may not be a valid defense, especially where it is almost common knowledge that males and females are carriers of the AIDS virus, and therefore "forewarned is forearmed." But before this defense can be utilized, the defendant must show that the plaintiff was aware of the risk and appreciated its unreasonable character, unless, for some inexplicable reason, the plaintiff expressly agreed to accept the risk. [374] Of course, if the plaintiff asked the defendant whether he had AIDS and defendant answered incorrectly or dishonestly, then the defense will not hold up.[375]

Contributory negligence defense is similar to the defense of assumption of the risk. But in Stephen K. v. Roni L., the defendant contended that the plaintiff's false and intentional misrepresentation that the defendant was using birth control should free him from financial responsibility for the child.[376] The California court responded, "Stephen cannot claim he was duped into fathering a child by Roni's misrepresentation because he was in a position to take precautionary measures as well."

The right to privacy defense simply refers to the argument that courts should not be involved in AIDS lawsuits because of the extreme privacy interests therein. On the other hand, plaintiffs can argue that privacy interests must be protected against defendant's charges of illegality.[377] In Barbara A. v. John G., the California court, in favoring plaintiffs, opined that "the right to privacy does not insulate a person from all judicial inquiry into his/her sexual relations, especially where one sexual partner, who by intentionally tortious conduct, causes physical injury to the other."[378] On the other hand, in Matter of Pamela, the New York court held that in the case centering about false representations about the use of birth control, "this kind of inquiry into 'procreative choice' is an impermissible invasion of the zone of privacy created by several fundamental guarantees.''[379] The U.S. Supreme Court in Eisenstadt v. Baird in 1972 had proclaimed that if the right of privacy means anything, it is the right of the individual to be free from unwarranted governmental intrusion into matters so fundamentally affecting a person as the decision to bear or beget a child.[380]

The statute of limitations is a well-recognized defense in all situations, but the peculiarities of the AIDS virus present special problems. For example, the incubation period cannot be accurately predicted nor can the time of transmission, but in general there may be a lengthy delay between initial exposure to the disease and the realization that one has actually contracted AIDS. The statute of limitations may commence from the time of the original wrong,[381] from the date of last exposure,[382] or from the date that the plaintiff discovered or should have discovered the wrong.[383]

The defense of interspousal immunity, while of ancient origin, is not of much weight in modern society.[384] In Lusby v. Lusby, the Maryland court allowed the wife to bring a tort action against her husband, despite claims of interspousal immunity, because of the outrageous character of his intentional tort: at gunpoint the husband forced his wife off the road and raped her.[385]

The AIDS problem has also found its way into the workplace where employment discrimination[386] of workers with AIDS has resulted in a large volume of litigation.[387] The *New York Times* recently reported that there is ''false security'' in believing that there is ''safe sex.''[388] A 1989 study among Belgian women found that over a three-year-period, a dozen women had caught the AIDS virus from the same civil engineer. The *New England Journal of Medicine*, which had sponsored the study, concluded that ''women who do not consider themselves at risk because they do not engage in what they perceive as high-risk practices may have a false sense of security. . . . Emphasizing only sexual relations with multiple partners as a risk factor for women may be irrelevant and even counterproductive since it implies that the absence of multiple partners makes women safe.''

NOTES

1. See Simon v. Mullin, 380 A.2d 1353 (Conn., 1977), recognizing that a child has a cause of action for prenatal injuries sustained any time after conception. See generally 34 Cleve. St. L. Rev. 311 (1986).
2. See 3 Blackstone, *Commentaries* 123.
3. 278 A.D. 913, 105 N.Y.S.2d 417 (1951).
4. 67 Ill. 2d 348, 367 N.E. 2d 1250 (1977).
5. See 34 Cleve. St. L. Rev. 311 (1986) at 343.
6. Id. at 344.
7. See Turpin v. Sortini, 643 P.2d 954 (Cal., 1982), and Harbeson v. Parke-Davis, Inc., 656 P.2d 483 (Wash., 1983).
8. See 13 Ecol. L.Q. 879 (1987) at 887.
9. 718 S.W.2d 65 (Texas, June 24, 1987), rev'd. 732 S.W.2d 316 (Tex., 1987).

10. See Flagg v. Loy, 734 P.2d 1183 (Kan., 1987), and Tader v. Tader, 737 P.2d 1065 (Wyo., 1987), two of the most recent court decisions abrogating the interspousal tort immunity.

11. Infra note 9.

12. See Baron, ''Human Donor Organs: Asserting Jurisdiction over Providers,'' *Trial* (December 1987) at 83–85.

13. 728 S.W. 2d 604 (Mo. App., 1987).

14. See Goldstein, ''Health Insurance Coverage for Infertility Procedures,'' *For the Defense* (February 1989) at 2–4.

15. 420 N.W.2d 785 (Iowa, 1988).

16. 750 P.2d 1140 (Okla. App., 1987).

17. See Section 1.3.

18. Infra note 14 at 4.

19. 138 Mass. 14 (1884).

20. 56 N.E. 638 (Ill., 1900), overruled fifty-three years later by Amann v. Faidy, 114 N.E.2d 412 (Ill., 1953).

21. See Stanford v. St. Louis-San Francisco Railway Co., 108 So. 566 (Ala., 1926).

22. 92 P.2d 678 (Cal., 1939), aff'd 93 P.2d 562 (Cal., 1939).

23. Id.

24. 65 F. Supp. 138 (D.C., 1946).

25. 282 A.D. 542, 125 N.Y.S.2d 696 (1953).

26. Infra note 5, at 319.

27. Infra note 1. See also 63 Mich. L. Rev. 579 (1965) and 110 U. Pa. L. Rev. 554 (1962).

28. See Porter v. Lassiter, 87 S.E.2d 100 (Ga., 1955), and note 33 S.C.L. Rev. 797 (1982).

29. 407 N.W.2d 584 (Iowa, 1987).

30. Unreported—N.W.2d—(Dkt.95314, Mich. App., February 23, 1989).

31. Infra note 5, at 341–42. Also see Sinkler v. Kneale, 164 A.2d 93 (Pa., 1960).

32. See, for example, Woods v. Lancet 303 N.Y. 349, 102 N.E.2d 691 (1951).

33. Unreported—N.E.2d—(Ind. App., 1982), cert. denied 104 S. Ct. 394 (1983).

34. See 47 Fed. Reg. 26,027 (1982).

35. Section 504 of Rehabilitation Act of 1973, 29 U.S.C. 794 (1982).

36. American Academy of Pediatrics v. Heckler, 561 F. Supp. 395 (D.C., 1983).

37. 48 Fed. Reg. 30,846 (1983) and 49 Fed. Reg. 1621 (1984).

38. 60 N.Y.2d 208, 456 N.E.2d 1186 (1983).

39. See United States v. University Hospital, 575 F. Supp. 607 (E.D.N.Y., 1983).

40. 476 U.S. 610 (1986); for a lower court opinion, see 585 F. Supp. 541 (S.D.N.Y., 1984), aff'd 794 F.2d 676 (2d Cir., 1984).

41. Id.

42. 403 N.W.2d 865 (Minn., 1987).

43. See Delgado v. Yandell, 468 S.W.2d 475 (Tex. Civ. App., 1971) (child injured in third month of gestation); Wolfe v. Isbell, 280 So.2d (Ala., 1973) (injury occurred in third month of gestation): Simon v. Mullin, 34 Conn. Supp. 139, 380 A.2d 1353 (1977) (fourth month of gestation); Day v. Nationwide Mut. Ins. Co., 328 So. 2d 560 (Fla. Dist. Ct. App. 1976) (sixth week of gestation); Hornbuckle v. Plantation Pipe Line Co., 212 Ga. 504, 93 S.E.2d 727 (1956) (sixth week); Daley v. Meier, 33 Ill. App. 2d 218, 178 N.E.2d 691 (1961) (one-month gestation); Womack v. Buchhorn, 384 Mich. 718,

187 N.W.2d 218 (1971) (fourth month of gestation); Bennett v. Hymers, 101 N.H. 483, 147 A.2d 108 (1958) (no gestational date given); Smith v. Brennan, 31 N.J. 353, 157 A.2d 497 (1960) (no gestational age given; child born two and one half months after injury); Kelly v. Gregory, 282 App. Div. 542, 125 N.Y.S.2d 696 (1953) (third month of gestation); Sinkler v. Kneale, 401 Pa. 267, 164, A.2d 93 (1960) (one-month gestation); Sylvia v. Gobeille, 101 R.I. 76, 220 A.2d 222 (1966) (no gestational age given); Labree v. Major, 111 R.I. 657, 306 A.2d 808 (1973).

44. Unreported (Dkt 74–3558),—F.Supp.—(S.D.N.Y., 1978).

45. 501 A.2d 1085 (Pa., 1985).

46. Id. at 1100.

47. See 59 S. Cal. L. Rev. 939 (1986) at 1036.

48. Id.; for a contrary view, see 2 In Vitro Fertilization & Embryo Transfer 65, 80–81 (1985) and also 4 Am. J.L. & Med. 319 (1978).

49. 643 P.2d 954 (Cal., 1982).

50. 478 A.2d 755 (N.J., 1984).

Yet the eventual degree of mental retardation in the infant with Down's syndrome is unpredictable, as is the case with an infant suffering respiratory distress syndrome (in which the infant is placed on a mechanical ventilator due to immature lung development). It is not possible to predict the degree of mental impairment resulting from an occurrence of intraventricular bleeding, the possibility of blindness from an overdose of oxygen, or the possibility of long-term and permanent dependence on the respirator. See Hodgman, "Chronic Lung Disorders" in *Neonatology: Pathophysiology and Management of the Newborn* (G. Avery, 2d ed., 1981), at 398–400; and Stahlman, "Acute Respiratory Disorders in the Newborn" in the same publication at 371 and 384.

There is indeed a challenge for society with respect to the imperiled infant. Society must learn to live with and protect imperiled newborns and handicapped infants, but at the same time society must learn to allow selective nontreatment in those instances in which life would not be a benefit to the newborn or infant. See Reich, "Quality of Life and Defective Newborn Children: An Ethical Analysis," in *Decision Making and the Defective Newborn: Proceedings of a Conference on Spina Bifida and Ethics* 489 (Swinyard ed., 1978), and Rachels, "Active and Passive Euthanasia," 292 New Eng. J. Med. 78 (1975).

51. Infra note 38, at 989.

52. See *Insight* (November 9, 1987) at 51 et seq.

53. See Williams and Hawes, "Caesarean Section, Fetal Monitoring and Perinatal Mortality in California," 69 Am. J. Pub. Health 864 (1979).

54. See Williams, *Obstetrics* 335–37 (17th ed., 1985).

55. The recent discovery is that women who take over-the-counter multivitamin pills early in pregnancy sharply reduce the risk of having a baby with a type of serious neurological defect, according to a study by the Boston University Center for Human Genetics, as reported in the *New York Times* (November 24, 1989) at 1, A28. This correlation between vitamins and absence of birth defects means that medical malpractice will embrace the failure of the prescribing physician to advise the pregnant patient of the importance of multivitamin pills early in pregnancy. The neural tube defects in babies cause death or paralysis in about 4,000 babies a year, or 1 or 2 in 1,000 babies. About 23,000 women participated in the study:

> Neural tube defects include anencephaly, in which nearly all of the brain is missing, and spina bifida, in which a piece of the spinal cord protrudes from the spinal column. People with spina bifida have

paralysis of all or part of the lower body. They may also have hydrocephaly, an improper drainage of fluid in the brain, a condition that can cause mental retardation.

The defects occur at about six weeks of pregnancy, or two weeks after the first missed menstrual period. This means that if vitamins prevent the defects, women would have to start taking vitamins as soon as they have the slightest hint that they are pregnant or, preferably, start taking vitamins while they are trying to conceive and continue until they are six weeks pregnant.

The idea that vitamin deficiencies might have something to do with neural tube defects originated after the World War II, . . . when women in England, Holland and Germany who had been malnourished gave birth to unexpectedly large numbers of babies with neural tube defects. Since then, researchers have been trying to see if vitamin supplements can prevent the birth defects.

The new study follows several smaller studies, most of which also indicated that women who took vitamins before conception and early in pregnancy were less likely to have a baby with a neural tube defect.

56. Infra note 52, at 51.

57. See 39 Vand. L. Rev. 597 (1986) at 724 et seq.

58. See 22 J. Fam. L. 677 (1984) at 690–91.

59. See University of Arizona Health Sciences Center v. Superior Court, 667 P.2d 1294 (Ariz., 1983).

60. Note, 7 Am. J. Trial. Advoc. 385 (1984) at 385–86.

61. See Wilbur v. Kerr, 628 S.W.2d 568 (Ark., 1982); Mason v. Western Pennsylvania Hospital, 453 A.2d 974 (Pa., 1982); and Cockrum v. Baumgartner, 447 N.E.2d 385 (Ill., 1983), cert. denied 464 U.S. 846 (1983).

62. See Jean-Charles v. Planned Parenthood, 471 N.Y.S.2d 622 (A.D., 1984).

63. See Jackson v. Baumgardner, 321 S.E.2d 541 (N.C., 1984).

64. See Troppi v. Scarf, 187 N.W.2d 511 (Mich. App., 1971).

65. See In Re Fulton-deKalb Hospital Authority, 314 S.E.2d 653 (Ga., 1984).

66. Note Harrison v. Schrader, 569 S.W.2d 822 (Tenn., 1978), and Spoljaric v. Pangan, 466 N.E.2d 37 (Ind. App., 1984).

67. Prosser and Keeton, *On the Law of Torts*, sec. 30, at 166–67.

68. See Sanders v. Nouri, 688 S.W.2d 24 (Mo. App., 1985).

69. Infra notes 62, 64, 65.

70. Infra note 57, at 733–39. See Section 7.6.

71. Note Custodio v. Bauer, 59 Cal. Rptr. 463 (1967), and Bowman v. Davis, 356 N.E.2d 496 (Ohio App., 1976).

72. Infra note 57, at 471 et seq.

73. See DiNatale v. Lieberman, 409 So. 2d 512 (Fla., 1982).

74. 46 N.Y.2d 401, 386 N.E.2d (1978).

75. According to the court,

While courts have struggled with the concepts of ''wrongful conception'' or ''wrongful diagnosis'' as cognizable causes of action, they have had little difficulty in rejecting a cause of action which may be distinguished by use of the term ''wrongful birth''. In the latter cause of action an illegitimate, but otherwise healthy child, seeks recovery in his or her own behalf for the injury suffered as a consequence of his or her birth into this world as a stigmatized child. To this point, courts have refused to sustain this cause of action. (See *Williams v. State of New York*, 18 NY2d 481 [action against state which had custody of mother]; *Stills v. Gratton*, 55 Cal App 3d 698 [action against physician for alleged negligent performance of an abortion]; *Zepeda v. Zepeda*, 41 Ill App 2d 240, cert den 379 US 945 [action against father]; *Slawek v. Stroh*, 62 Wis 2d 295 [action against father].)

Standing distinctly apart from claims based upon a wrongful conception, a failure to diagnose a pregnancy, or an illegitimate birth, in which the essence of the wrong for which compensation is sought is the birth of a healthy and normal—albeit, unplanned—child, plaintiffs' claims are premised upon the birth of a fully intended but abnormal child for whom extraordinary care and treatment is required. It is not contended that the defendant physicians' treatment of Dolores Becker and Hetty Clark caused the abnormalities in their infants (see *Renslow v. Mennonite Hosp.*, 67 Ill 2d 348 [sustaining cause of action based upon blood transfusion given to mother]; *Sylvia v. Gobeille*, 101 RI 76 [sustaining cause of action based upon failure to prescribe drug during pregnancy]; cf. *Jorgensen v. Mead Johnson Labs.*, 483 F2d 237 [sustaining cause of action based upon injurious oral contraceptive]), but only that had plaintiffs been properly advised by defendants of the risks of abnormality, their infants would never have been born.

Irrespective of the label coined, plaintiffs' complaints sound essentially in negligence or medical malpractice. As in any cause of action founded upon negligence, a successful plaintiff must demonstrate the existence of a duty, the breach of which may be considered the proximate cause of the damages suffered by the injured party. (See Restatement, Torts 2d,§281; Prosser, Torts [4th ed],§30.)

An examination of plaintiffs' complaints leads to the conclusion that, insofar as plaintiffs allege claims on behalf of their infants, whether denominated as claims for wrongful life or otherwise, they have failed to state legally cognizable causes of action. If it be assumed that under the facts at bar defendants, as physicians, owed a duty to the infants *in utero* as well as to their parents (cf. *Woods v. Lancet*, 303 NY 349), defendants' breach of that duty may be viewed as the proximate cause for the infants' birth. Had Hetty and Steven Park been accurately advised by their physicians of the chances that a future child of theirs would suffer from polycystic kidney disease, they allege that they would not have chosen to conceive a second child. Similarly, had Dolores and Arnold Becker been accurately advised of the chances that their already conceived child would be born afflicted with Down's Syndrome, and of the availability of an amniocentesis test, they allege that they would have undergone that test, and had it indicated the presence of Down's Syndrome in their child, that they would have terminated the pregnancy within the permissible time period. (See *Roe v. Wade*, 410 US 113; Penal Law, §125.05.)

. . . Of course, this is not to say that plaintiffs may recover for psychic or emotional harm alleged to have occurred as a consequence of the birth of their infants in an impaired state. The recovery of damages for such injuries must of necessity be circumscribed. Controlling on this point is *Howard v. Lecher* (42 NY2d 109, *supra*), in which parents of a child born afflicted with Tay-Sachs disease sought recovery for the trauma they endured witnessing their child succumb to this degenerative disorder. Similar to the present cases, the plaintiffs in *Howard* alleged that their physician failed to inform them of the risk involved in their pregnancy and of the availability of tests to determine whether their child would be born afflicted with Tay-Sachs disease. Had they been so advised, the plaintiffs maintained, they would have undergone the available tests, the results of which, if indicative of the presence of Tay-Sachs disease in their unborn child, would have precipitated a decision on their part to terminate the pregnancy.

While sympathetic to the plight of these parents, this court declined for policy reasons to sanction the recovery of damages for their psychic or emotional harm occasioned by the birth and gradual death of their child. To have permitted recovery in *Howard*, we observed, would have "inevitably led to the drawing of artificial and arbitrary boundaries." (42 NY2d, at p. 113, *supra*.)

Contrary to the contention of the dissent, to permit plaintiffs to recover for pecuniary loss while precluding recovery for alleged emotional injuries suffered as a result of their infants' birth does not run counter to this court's decision in *Johnson v. State of New York* (37 NY2d 378). In *Johnson*, we sustained a cause of action for emotional harm predicated upon the plaintiff's receipt of a notice informing her of the death of her mother when, in fact, she was very much alive. In so holding, we recognized the existence of a duty on the part of the defendant flowing to the plaintiff daughter to refrain from issuing such notices in a negligent manner. The breach of that duty, we held, entitled the plaintiff to recover damages for "the proven harmful consequences proximately caused by the breach." (37 NY2d, at p. 383, *supra*.) Recovery was, therefore, permitted not only for the plaintiff's pecuniary loss, but also for emotional harm caused by the tortious act.

Seizing upon the broad principle stated in *Johnson*, the dissent posits that recognition of a duty flowing directly from defendants to plaintiffs would require recognition of plaintiffs' right to recover damages for emotional harm, as well as for pecuniary loss occasioned by the birth of their infants. To do so, maintains the dissent, would eviscerate our holding in *Howard v. Lecher* (42 NY2d 109, *supra*). However, nothing in *Johnson* mandates this result.

76. 290 S.E.2d 825 (Va., 1982).

77. 432 A.2d 834 (N.J., 1981).

78. 46 N.Y.2d 401, 386 N.E.2d 807 (1978).

79. Infra note 57, at 745.

80. See Roe v. Wade, 410 U.S. 113 (1973) and also Blake v. Cruz, 698 P.2d 315 (Idaho, 1984) and Harbeson v. Parke-Davis, Inc., 656 P.2d 483 (Wash., 1983).

81. See Eisbrenner v. Stanley, 308 N.W.2d 209 (Mich. App., 1981).

82. Note *Harbeson* case, infra note 80.

83. 322 S.E.2d 567 (N.C., 1984).

84. Infra notes 76 and 80.

85. 852 F.2d 773 (4th Cir., 1988).

86. See Johnson v. Ruark Obstetrics and Gynecology Associates, 465 S.E.2d 909 (N.C., 1988).

87. Jenkins v. Sleepy Hollow Medical Group, Unreported,—N.Y.S.2d—(Westchester County, January 4, 1988).

88. Infra note 57, at 750 et seq.

89. Probably the earliest "wrongful life" cause of action was voiced in Zepeda v. Zepeda, 190 N.E.2d 849 (Ill App., 1963), cert. denied 379 U.S. 945 (1964). Here the plaintiff child sued his father on the theory that since plaintiff was born an adulterine bastard, he should be allowed damages for having been born to such a status. But the court disallowed the claim on grounds of public policy. Cf. Gildener v. Thomas Jefferson University Hospital, 451 F. Supp. 692 (E.D. Pa., 1978), where Tay-Sachs disease went undetected during pregnancy; and Karlsons v. Guerinot, 394 N.Y.S.2d 933 (1977), where the child was born with Down's syndrome, which had a high probability. See generally Note, "Wrongful Life: The Right Not to Be Born," 54 Tulane L. Rev. 480 (1980). Also see Dumer v. St. Michael's Hospital, 233 N.W.2d 372 (Wis., 1975).

90. See Elliott v. Brown, 361 So.2d 546 (Ala., 1978); Speck v. Finegold, 439 A.2d 110 (Pa., 1981); James G. v. Caserta, 332 S.E.2d 872 (W.Va., 1985); and Bruggeman v. Schimke, 718 P.2d 635 (Kan., 1986), for examples.

91. Infra note 90.

92. Infra note 89.

93. Infra note 57, at 753; also note Nelson v. Krusen, 678 S.W.2d 918 (Tex., 1984), spelling out the difficulty of proof of the elements of the cause of action for wrongful life.

94. 643 P.2d 954 (Cal., 1982).

The first wrongful life action to be upheld on appeal was probably Curlender v. Bio-Science Laboratories, 165 Cal. Rptr. 477 (1980), in which a minor born with Tay-Sachs disease brought suit through her father as guardian *ad litem* against a genetic analysis laboratory for the negligent administration of a genetic test designed to indicate whether the parents carried genes that would result in the parents' giving birth to a Tay-Sachs afflicted baby. The California appellate court found that public policy against abortions and inability to calculate damages did not stand in the way of the court's recognizing the cause of action for wrongful life. The central issue was whether the breach of duty was the proximate cause of an injury "cognizable at law," that is, plaintiff's birth with defects rather than the defect itself. Accordingly, the court approved recovery for pain and suffering to be experienced during the limited lifetime of such a child, plus any special pecuniary loss resulting from the impaired condition. It was this rationale that was sanctioned by the California Supreme Court in Turpin v. Sortini, supra.

95. Infra note 50.

96. Infra note 80.

97. 227 A.2d 589 (N.J., 1967).

98. 713 P.2d 384 (Colo. App., 1986).

99. 512 N.E.2d 691 (Ill., 1987).

100. 412 N.W.2d 232 (Mich., 1987).

101. See Hilton and Ream, "Duty to Unborn Children," *For the Defense* (September 1988) at 2–3.

102. 517 So. 2d 1019 (La. App., 1987), cert. granted 519 So. 2d 105 (1987).

103. 519 S.W.2d 846 (Tex., 1975).

104. See, inter alia, Harten v. Coons, 502 F.2d 1363 (10th Cir., 1974) (failed vasectomy); LaPoint v. Shirley, 409 F. Supp. 118 (W.D. Tex., 1976) (failed tubal ligation); Becker v. Schwartz, 60 App. Div. 2d 587, 400 N.Y.S.2d 119 (1977), modified, 46 N.Y.2d 401, 386 N.E.2d 807, 413 N.Y.S.2d 895 (1978) (failure to give parents proper genetic screening resulting in child's death after two and one half years); Stills v. Gratton, 55 Cal. App. 3d 698, 127 Cal. Rptr. 652 (1976) (negligent performance of abortion); and Troppi v. Scarf, 31 Mich. App. 240, 187 N.W.2d 511 (1971) (tranquilizers negligently given mother instead of birth control pills).

105. See Capron, "Informed Decision Making in Genetic Counseling: A Dissent to the Wrongful Life Debate," 48 Ind. L.J. 581 (1973).

106. (4th ed., 1928) at 60.

107. A.B.A.J. (1924), vol. 10, at 123.

108. 58 Misc. 2d 432 (1968).

109. Infra note 97.

110. Note that the case was overruled in 1984 by Procanik v. Cillo, infra note 57.

111. 255 N.W.2d 620 (Minn., 1934).

112. Id. at 622.

113. 11 D & C 41 (Pa., 1957).

114. 27 A.L.R.3d 916 (1969).

115. 391 P.2d 201 (Wash., 1964).

116. 251 Cal. App. 3d 303 (1967).

117. Unreported, N.W.2d—(Iowa, 1967).

118. 187 N.W.2d 511 (Mich., 1969).

119. Unreported,—N.W.2d—(Wis., 1969)

120. 358 P.2d 681 (Cal., 1961).

121. See Section 4.8. Note the following cases: McKernan v. Asheim, 102 Wash. 2d 411, 687 P.2d 850 (1984); James G. v. Caserta, 332 S.E.2d 872 (W. Va. 1985); Beardsley v. Wierdsman, 650 P.2d 288 (Wyo. 1982); Boone v. Mullendore, 416 So.2d 718 (Ala. 1982); Wilbur v. Kerr, 275 Ark. 239, 628 S.W.2d 568 (1982); Coleman v. Garrison, 349 A.2d 8 (Del. 1975); Flowers v. District of Columbia, 478 A.2d 1073 (D. C. 1984); Fassoulas v. Ramey, 450 So.2d 822 (Fla.1984); Fulton-DeKalb Hospital Authority v. Graves, 252 Ga. 441, 314 S.E.2d 653 (1984); Cockrum v. Baumgartner, 95 Ill.2d 193, 69 Ill. Dec. 168, 447 N.E.2d 385, *cert. denied sub nom*; Raja v. Michael Reese Hospital and Medical Center, 464 U.S.846 (1983); Garrison v. Foy, 486 N.E.2d 5 (Ind. App.

1985); Nanke v. Napier, 346 N.W.2d 520 (Iowa 1984); Johnston v. Elkins, 241 Kan 407, 736 P.2d 935 (1987); Schork v. Huber, 648 S.W.2d 861 (Ky. 1983); Macomber v. Dillman, 505 A.2d 810 (Me. 1986); Kingsbury v. Smith, 122 N.H. 237, 442 A.2d 1003 (1982); P. v. Portadin, 179 N.J.Super. 465, 432 A.2d 556 (1981); O'Toole v. Greenberg, 64 N.Y.2d 427, 477 N.E.2d 445, 488 N.Y.S.2d 143 (1985); Mason v. Western Pennsylvania Hospital, 499 Pa. 484, 453 A.2d 974 (1982); Smith v. Gore—S.W.2d—(Tenn. App. 1986); Hickman v. Myers, 632 W.W.2d 869 (Tex. Ct. App.—Houston 1982 writ Ref'd N.R.E.); and Miller v. Johnson, 231 Va. 177, 343 S.E.2d 301 (1986).

122. See University of Arizona Health Science Center v. Superior Court, 667 P.2d 1294 (Ariz., 1983).

123. See Ochs v. Borrelli, 445 A.2d 883 (Conn., 1982).

124. See Hartke v. McKelway, 707 F.2d 1544 (D.C.Cir., 1983), cert. denied 464 U.S. 983 (1983).

125. See 473 A.2d 429 (Md., 1984).

126. See Green v. Sudakin, 265 N.W.2d 411 (Mich. 1978).

127. 260 N.W.2d 169 (Minn., (1977).

128. 303 S.W.2d 41 (Mo., (1957).

129. 410 U.S. 113 (1973).

See Faux, *Roe v. Wade: The Untold Story of the Landmark Supreme Court Decision That Made Abortion Legal* (1988), as reviewed in 16 No. Ky. L. Rev. 411 (1988). According to the book reviewer,

> The book, written in sequential form, reads like a story. Faux begins with the selection of Norma McCorvey as Jane Roe and then probes into the decision processes of the two attorneys in the case, Weddington and Coffee. Both attorneys are women, both graduated from the University of Texas Law School, and both were motivated for the advancement of women in society. This last concern was manifested in their belief that women should have the right to decide what to do with their bodies. They searched for a year before the selection of Norma McCorvey as their plaintiff.

130. Id. at 164.

131. Id.

132. Id. at 165.

133. Id. at 153.

134. Id. at 214–15. Also, see 1986 No. Ill. U.L. Rev. 1 (1986) at 8–9.

135. See 100 Harv. L. Rev. 2017 (1987).

136. See Poelker v. Doe, 432 U.S. 519 (1977); Beal v. Doe, 432 U.S. 438 (1977); and Maher v. Roe, 432 U.S. 464 (1977).

137. 449 U.S. 297 (1980).

138. It would appear that the highest court is hardly concerned with protecting one's life-style unless there are medical aspects of prime concern; note Bowers v. Hardwick, 106 S. Ct. 2841 (1986), stating that the Constitution does not confer a right to engage in sodomy.

Abortion funding was given equal protection guarantees when necessary to preserve the mother's life or health in Right to Choose v. Byrne, 450 A.2d 925 (N.J., 1982). In Committee to Defend Reproductive Rights v. Myers, 625 P.2d 779 (Cal., 1981), funding was based on the California privacy guarantee and not on the basis of Harris v. McRae, infra. note 109. In Massachusetts v. Bowen,—F. Supp.—(Mass., March 21, 1988), the court issued a permanent injunction prohibiting the U.S Department of Health and Human

Services from enforcing regulations that would cut off funds to family planning clinics that perform abortions or offer abortion counseling. (aff. 108 S. Ct. 2722 (1988). See N.L.H. (March 21, 1988) at 3. The court observed that these federal government regulations would cause irreparable harm to women who receive services from the program and violate a woman's right to privacy and to choose to have an abortion. Note *New York Times* (January 21, 1988) at A19, and *New York Times* (August 1, 1987) at 8.

139. 428 U.S. 52 (1976).

140. Id.

141. 106 S. Ct. 2169 (1986).

142. Infra note 129.

143. 462 U.S. 416 (1983).

144. See generally Note, 100 Harv. L. Rev. 100 (1986) at 200 et seq.

145. Id. at 201–2.

146. Id. at 204.

147. Infra note 141.

148. 109 S. Ct. 3040 (1989).

149. See N.L.J. (November 27, 1989) at 29.

150. 57 U.S.L.W. 3859 (1989).

151. See *New York Times* (November 23, 1989) at 1, B13.

152. Note Greenhouse, "Abortion: A New Round," *New York Times* (November 24, 1989) at 1, A24.

153. 57 U.S.L.W. 5023 (1989).

154. See Mo. Stats., 1986, ch. 106.

155. 851 F.2d 1071 (8th Cir., 1988).

156. Infra note 129.

157. See N.L.J. (January 23, 1989) at 3, 18, and *New York Times* (July 4, 1989) at 11–14. For background material, see 100 Harv. L. Rev. 2017–34 (1987).

158. 531 N.Y.S.2d 78 (New York County, July 12, 1989).

159. Infra note 129.

160. See *Trial* (July 1988) at 85–86 (case without citation).

161. 428 U.S. 52 (1976).

162. Id.

163. See *New York Times* (December 12, 1987) at 38.

164. Infra note 139 at 71.

165. 70 N.Y.2d 697, 512 N.E.2d 538 (1987).

166. See Mohr, *Abortion in America: The Origins and Evolution of National Policy 1800–1900* (1978) at 20.

167. See 1987 Utah L. Rev. 1 (1987) at 3; also Wilson, *The American Woman in Transition: The Urban Influence 1870–1920* (1979) at 52.

168. Idaho Code §5–334 (1986); Minn Stat. §145.424 (1987); Mo. Ann. Stat. §188.130 (1987); S.D. Codif. Laws Ann. §21–55–2 (1986); and Utah Code Ann. §78–11–24 (1986).

169. 396 N.W.2d 10 (Minn., 1986).

170. Infra note 135, at 2019.

171. Id. at 2034.

172. Thornburgh v. American College of Obstetricians and Gynecologists 106 S. Ct. 2169 (1986) at 2178.

173. Planned Parenthood Association v. Ashcroft, 462 U.S. 476 (1983).

174. Planned Parenthood Association v. Harris, Dkt. C87–1405A, F. Supp. (Ga., 1987).

175. The court also pointed out that the Georgia statute violated the juvenile's right to anonymity.

176. 56 U.S.L.W. 4053 (1987) and 108 S. Ct. 479 (1987).

177. See *Hartford Courant* (December 15, 1987) at A8. Note decision at 763 F.2d 1532 (7th Cir., 1985).

178. For articles in point, see N.L.J. (October 5, 1987) at 3, 10; N.J.L. (December 21, 1987) at 10; and note the following cases striking down spousal notification: *Scheinberg v. Smith*, 550 F. Supp. 1112 (S.D. Fla., 1982); *Eubanks v. Brown*, 604 F. Supp. 141 (W.D. Ky., 1984); *Doe v. Deschamp*, 651 F. Supp. 682 (Mont., 1976); *Planned Parenthood of Rhode Island v. Board of Medical Review*, 598 F. Supp. 625 (R.I., 1984). Also N.Y.L.J. (December 15, 1987) at 1, 2

179. See generally 18 Israel L. Rev. (1983) at 415 et seq., which delineates "A Man's Right to Be Equal: The Abortion Issue."

180. See Guttmacher, "The Shrinking Non-Psychiatric Indications for Therapeutic Abortions," in H. Rosen, *Abortion in America* (1967).

181. See generally 77 Colum. L. Rev. 1216 (1977).

182. Regulations 3 and 4 of the Public Health (Examination of Amniotic Fluid) Regulations, 1980.

183. Infra note 179, at 422–23; Sec. 348 of the Israel Penal Law.

184. See 39 Vand. L. Rev. 597 (1986) at 693.

185. 462 U.S. 416 (1983).

186. 439 U.S. 379 (1979).

187. 410 U.S. 179 (1973).

188. See generally 71 Geo. L.J. 991 (1983), "Hospitalization Requirements for Second Trimester Abortions: For the Purpose of Health or Hindrance?"

189. 443 U.S. 622 (1979).

190. 450 U.S. 398 (1980).

191. See dissenting opinion of Mr. Justice Marshall at 425–26.

192. *New York Times* (August 25, 1987) at A13.

193. *New York Times* (September 15, 1987) at A24.

194. Id.

195. 820 F.2d 951 (8th Cir., June 10, 1987); for lower court, see 628 F. Supp. 676 (Ark., 1986).

196. *New York Times* (August 16, 1987) at 1, 30.

197. 514 A.2d 802 (Maine, 1986).

198. See A.B.A.J. (August 1, 1987) at 39.

199. Infra note 197, at 806, n. 3.

200. Id. The court finalized as follows:

> In the present case, the plaintiff claims to have suffered only mental and emotional distress as a result of the defendant's negligence. No physical impact occurred. Because mental distress is insufficient by itself to establish harm, an essential element of actionable negligence, no underlying tort exists. Since an underlying tort is a condition precedent to the recovery of damages for the negligent infliction of mental distress, the defendants argue that the plaintiff's claim should be barred. We hold that because of the nature of the psychotherapist-patient relationship, an action may be maintained by a patient for serious mental distress caused by the negligence of his therapist despite the absence of an underlying tort.

We are persuaded that this position is sound for the following reason. The rationale for requiring an independently actionable tort is that absent either tactile contact or the usual indicia of harm, no objective evidence exists that the defendant's negligence actually has caused the plaintiff to suffer emotional distress. There is little likelihood, however, that objective evidence of mental distress will be unavailable in a claim by a patient against his psychotherapist. Given the fact that a therapist undertakes the treatment of a patient's mental problems and that the patient is encouraged to divulge his innermost thoughts, the patient is extremely vulnerable to mental harm if the therapist fails to adhere to the standards of care recognized by the profession. Any psychological harm that may result from such negligence is neither speculative nor easily feigned. Unlike evidence of mental distress occurring in other situations, objective proof of the existence *vel non* of a psychological injury in these circumstances should not be difficult to obtain. As this case illustrates, the severity of such an injury can be medically significant and objectively supportable. We therefore conclude that the reasons for precluding recovery for mental distress are not cogent here.

Accordingly, we hold that because of the unique nature of a psychotherapist-patient relationship, a patient may recover damages for serious mental distress resulting from the therapist's negligence despite the absence of an underlying tort. Since the plaintiff's complaint does state a claim on which relief can be granted and there are genuine issues of fact regarding the elements thereof, it was error to grant summary judgment in favor of defendants.

The entry is:

Judgment vacated.

Remanded for further proceedings consistent with the opinion herein.

201. 474 N.E.2d 13 (Ill. App., 1985).
202. 445 N.E.2d 6 (Ill. App., 1982).
203. Unreported (Dkt. 74–3558),—F. Supp. (S.D.N.Y., 1978).
204. Infra note 114.
205. 65 N.Y.2d 931, 483 N.E.2d 1142 (1985).
206. 52 N.Y.2d 807, 418 N.E.2d 386 (1980).
207. 61 N.Y.2d 219, 461 N.E.2d 843 (1984).
208. 68 Cal.2d 728, 441 P.2d 912 (1980).
209. Infra note 165.
210. See Section 1.10.
211. 410 U.S. 113 (1973).
212. 381 U.S. 479 (1965).
213. Id. at 486.
214. 539 F.2d 349 (4th Cir., 1976).
215. See 1986 N. Ill. U.L. Rev. 1 (1986) at 23–24.
216. Infra note 214, at 351.
217. 405 U.S. 438 (1972).
218. See generally Skoloff, "Recent Child Custody Rulings May Jeopardize Privacy Rights," N.L.J. (April 17, 1989) at 22–23.
219. 141 A.D.2d 215 (1988).
220. 384 U.S. 757 (1966).
221. 470 U.S. 753 (1985)
222. Infra note 218, at 23.
223. Code of Ga., vol. 16, ch. 3, art. 11, sec. 19–3–1.
224. See Chance v. Chance, 5 S.E.2d 399 (Ga., 1939).
225. S.C. 1976 Code tit. 20, §1–360.
226. See Tedder v. Tedder, 94 S.E. 19 (S.C., 1917).
227. Laws 1933, ch. 606.

228. See Shea v. Shea, 294 N.Y. Rep. 909 (1980) and Cross v. Cross, 102 A.D.2d 638 (1980).

229. N.Y.L.J. (July 10, 1987) at 3, 16.

230. Unreported—F.2d—(3d Cir., 1988).

231. 405 U.S. 645 (1972).

232. Id. at 652.

233. Id. at 651.

234. Infra note 231.

235. According to the court,

But we are here not asked to evaluate the legitimacy of the state ends, rather, to determine whether the means used to achieve these ends are constitutionally defensible. What is the state interest in separating children from fathers without a hearing designed to determine whether the father is unfit in a particular disputed case? We observe that the State registers no gain towards its declared goals when it separates children from the custody of fit parents. Indeed, if Stanley is a fit father, the State spites its own articulated goals when it needlessly separates him from his family.

In *Bell v. Burson*, 402 U.S. 535 (1971), we found a scheme repugnant to the Due Process Clause because it deprived a driver of his license without reference to the very factor (there fault in driving, here fitness as a parent) that the State itself deemed fundamental to its statutory scheme. Illinois would avoid the self-contradiction that rendered the Georgia license suspension system invalid by arguing that Stanley and all other unmarried fathers can reasonably be presumed to be unqualified to raise their children. (pp. 652–653)

Bell v. Burson held that the State could not, while purporting to be concerned with fault in suspending a driver's license, deprive a citizen of his license without a hearing that would assess fault. Absent fault, the State's declared interest was so attenuated that administrative convenience was insufficient to excuse a hearing where evidence of fault could be considered. That drivers involved in accidents, as a statistical matter, might be very likely to have been wholly or partially at fault did not foreclose hearing and proof in specific cases before licenses were suspended.

We think the Due Process Clause mandates a similar result here. The State's interest in caring for Stanley's children is *de minimis* if Stanley is shown to be a fit father. It insists on presuming rather than proving Stanley's unfitness solely because it is more convenient to presume than to prove. Under the Due Process Clause that advantage is insufficient to justify refusing a father a hearing when the issue at stake is the dismemberment of his family.

The State of Illinois assumes custody of the children of married parents, divorced parents, and unmarried mothers only after a hearing and proof of neglect. The children of unmarried fathers, however, are declared dependent children without a hearing on parental fitness and without proof of neglect. Stanley's claim in the state courts and here is that failure to afford him a hearing on his parental qualifications while extending it to other parents denied him equal protection of the laws. We have concluded that all Illinois parents are constitutionally entitled to a hearing on their fitness before their children are removed from their custody. It follows that denying such a hearing to Stanley and those like him while granting it to other Illinois parents is inescapably contrary to the Equal Protection Clause. (pp. 57–658)

The dissenting opinion of Chief Justice Burger pointed out that Illinois "has not recognized common law marriages since 1905. Stanley did not seek the burdens when he could have freely assumed them":

Where there is a valid contract of marriage, the law of Illinois presumes that the husband is the father of any child born to the wife during the marriage; as the father, he has legally enforceable rights and duties with respect to that child. When a child is born to an unmarried woman, Illinois recognizes the readily identifiable mother, but makes no presumption as to the identity of the biological father. It does, however, provide two ways, one voluntary and one involuntary, in which that father may be identified. First, he may marry the mother and acknowledge the child as his own; this has the legal effect of legitimating the child and gaining for the father full recognition as a parent. Ill. Rev. Stat., c. 3, §12–8. Second, a man may be found to be the biological father of the child pursuant to a paternity suit initiated by the mother; in this case, the child remains illegitimate, but the adjudicated father is made liable for the support of the child until the latter attains age 18 or is legally adopted by another. Ill. Rev. Stat., c. 106¾, §52.

The Illinois Supreme Court correctly held that the State may constitutionally distinguish between unwed fathers and unwed mothers. Here, Illinois' different treatment of the two is part of that State's statutory scheme for protecting the welfare of illegitimate children. In almost all cases, the unwed mother is readily identifiable, generally from hospital records, and alternatively by physicians or others attending the child's birth. Unwed fathers, as a class, are not traditionally quite so easy to identify and locate. Many of them either deny all responsibility or exhibit no interest in the child or its welfare; and, of course, many unwed fathers are simply not aware of their parenthood.

Furthermore, I believe that a State is fully justified in concluding, on the basis of common human experience, that the biological role of the mother in carrying and nursing an infant creates stronger bonds between her and the child than the bonds resulting from the male's often casual encounter. This view is reinforced by the observable fact that most unwed mothers exhibit a concern for their offspring either permanently or at least until they are safely placed for adoption, while unwed fathers rarely burden either the mother or the child with their attentions or loyalties. Centuries of human experience buttress this view of the realities of human conditions and suggest that unwed mothers of illegitimate children are generally more dependable protectors of their children than are unwed fathers. While these, like most generalizations, are not without exceptions, they nevertheless provide a sufficient basis to sustain a statutory classification whose objective is not to penalize unwed parents but to further the welfare of illegitimate children in fulfillment of the State's obligation as *parens patriae*.

Stanley depicts himself as a somewhat unusual unwed father, namely, as one who has always acknowledged and never doubted his fatherhood of these children. He alleges that he loved, cared for, and supported these children from the time of their birth until the death of their mother. He contends that he consequently must be treated the same as a married father of legitimate children. Even assuming the truth of Stanley's allegations, I am unable to construe the Equal Protection Clause as requiring Illinois to tailor its statutory definition of ''parents'' so meticulously as to include such unusual unwed fathers, while at the same time excluding those unwed, and generally unidentified, biological fathers who in no way share Stanley's professed desires.'' (pp. 665–667)

236. See *New York Times* (December 4, 1987) at A18.

237. Unreported—N.Y.S.2d—(Westchester County, November 13, 1987).

238. At A13.

239. See N.L.J. (July 31, 1989) at 3, 24.

240. Braschi v. Stahl Associates, unreported,—N.E.2d—(N.Y., July 6, 1989).

241. Infra note 239, at 24.

242. See generally Case & Comment (July-August 1987) at 38 et seq.

243. See, for example, Banks v. Randle, 486 A.2d 974 (Pa., 1984).

244. 55 U.S.L.W. 5075 (1987).

245. See Alaska Stat. §25.20.045 (Supp. 1982); Ark. Stat. Ann. §61–141 (1971); Cal. Civ. Code §7005 (West Supp. 1983); Colo. Rev. Stat. §19–6–106 (1978); Conn. Gen. Stat. §§45–69f to –69n (1981); Fla. Stat. Ann. §742.11 (West Supp. 1983); Ga. Code Ann. §§74–101.1, 74–9904 (1982); Ill. Ann. Stat. ch. 40, §§1451–1453 (Smith-Hurd 1983); Kan. Stat. Ann. § §23–128 to –130 (1981); La. Civ. Code Ann. art. 188 (West Supp. 1983); Md. Est. & Trusts Code Ann. §1–206(b) (1974) and Md. Ann. Code art. 20, §212 and art. 43, §556E (1980); Mich. Comp. Laws Ann. §§333.2824, 700.111 (1980); Minn. Stat. Ann. §257.56 (West 1982); Mont. Code Ann. §40–6–106 (1981); Nev. Rev. Stat. §126–061 (1979); N.Y. Dom. Rel. Law §73 (McKinney 1977); N.C.

Gen. Stat. §49A–1 (1976); Okla. Stat. tit. 10, §§551–553 (West Supp. 1982–1983); Or. Rev. Stat. §§109.239, .243, .247, 667.355, .360, .365, .370 (1981); Tenn. Code Ann. §53–446 (Supp. 1981); Tex. Fam. Code Ann. §12.03 (Vernon 1975); Va. Code §64.1–7.1 (1980); Wash. Rev. Code Ann. §26.26.050 (West Supp. 1983–1984); Wis. Stat. Ann. §767.47(9) (West 1981), §891.40 (West Supp. 1982–1983); Wyo. Stat. §14–2–103 (1978).

246. See 73 Geo.L.J. 1283 (1985) at 1292 et seq.

247. See Section 10.2.

248. Section 4 (a)(1) of the U.P.A.

249. Section 6(a) of the U.P.A.

250. 407 A.2d 849 (N.J. Super., 1979).

251. Id at 824.

252. 333 N.W.2d 90 (Mich., 1983).

253. 478 N.Y.S.2d 679 (New York County, June 10, 1988).

254. 761 P.2d 424 (Cal., 1987).

255. Unreported,—N.Y.S.2d—(Suffolk County, October 19, 1988).

256. Unreported,—N.Y.S.2d—(Suffolk County Family Ct., August 7, 1989). See also N.Y.L.J. (October 19, 1988) at 1, 7. See Freedman, *International Products Liability* (vol. 1, 1987) at Sec. 3.14

257. 409 U.S. 535 (1973) at 538.

258. See 21 San Diego L. Rev. 1061 (1984) at 1070–72.

259. 456 U.S. 91 (1982) at 97.

260. Infra note 176.

261. See Smith v. Leflore, 437 A.2d 1250 (Pa., 1981). Also note 54 N.Y.U. L. Rev. 1131 (1979) and 16 Wake Forest L. Rev. 591 (1980).

262. 513 A.2d 733,—N.Y.S.2d—(March 30, 1987).

263. The Connecticut statute on paternity matters (Chapter 815y) begins with section 46b–160 and ends with section 46b–179d. Among the important subheadings are the petition by the mother or expectant mother, the action by the state or town, the testimony of the mother and the putative father, the availability of the blood tests, compelling disclosure of name of putative father, as well as the claim for paternity by the putative father.

264. 535 N.Y.S.2d 676 (New York County, August 11, 1988).

265. Unreported,—N.E.2d—(Ohio, September 20, 1989).

266. See N.L.J. (March 31, 1989) at 1, 7.

267. Unreported,—N.Y.S.2d—(Family Ct., Westchester County, October 24, 1989).

268. According to the court:

> This case can find no appellate authority which holds that DNA testing can be conclusive in a paternity proceeding. As no appellate court has determined that a blood test is dispositive of the issue in a paternity case, this court has the obligation to consider all factors in making its determination. Clear and convincing evidence includes blood genetic marker test results indicating high probability of paternity plus testimony as to the essential elements of proof necessary to sustain the petition (Matter of Department of Social Services v. Richard A., 121 A.D. 2d 382 [2d Dept., 1986]; see also, Matter of Harstein v. Mike S., 107 A.D. 2d 684 [2d Dept., 1985]). It is incumbent upon Family Court to consider, therefore, in addition to high probability blood test results, evidence such as the approximate date of conception, testimony that the mother and respondent had a sexual relationship during the period of conception, and lack of evidence that another man had access to the mother during such period (cf., Fannie R. H. v. Charles E., 116 A.D. 2d 576 [2d Dept., 1986].

Further, whether the presumption of legitimacy has been overcome is a question of fact which the court can determine only after a full hearing in which all evidence is considered, including blood test results, and the credibility of the litigants is assessed (Matter of Martine S. v. Anthony D., 120 Misc 2d 567, 573 [Family Ct., Kings County, 1983]). The trier of fact must have the opportunity to hear testimony and view and assess the credibility of the witnesses on these matters. No such opportunity was provided here as all the issues in the prior litigation were resolved solely on papers.

269. 539 N.Y.S.2d 617 (Westchester County, February 23, 1989).
270. See N.Y.L.J. (February 23, 1989) at 1, 7.
271. See N.Y.L.J. (May 12, 1989) at 3, 36.
272. 535 N.Y.S.2d 456 (3d Dept., 1988).
273. 536 N.Y.S.2d 767 (1st Dept., 1989).
274. 534 N.Y.S.2d 199 (2d Dept., 1988).
275. 735 P.2d 1209 (Ore., 1987).
276. See 39 Vand. L. Rev. 597 (1986) at 819–48.
277. See Chapter 6.
278. See generally 56 Nebr. L. Rev. 51 (1977), and note Canterbury v. Spence, 464 F.2d 772 (D.C. Cir., 1972), cert. denied 409 U.S. 1064 (1972).
279. Infra note 276, at 823.
280. See Prince v. Massachusetts, 321 U.S. 158 (1944); also 66 Minn. L. Rev. 459 (1982) and 52 A.L.R.3d 1118 (1973).
281. See Custody of a Minor, 379 N.E.2d 1053 (Mass., 1978) where child suffered from leukemia, and the Massachusetts court ordered chemotherapy without parental consent.
282. See Jefferson v. Griffin Spalding County Hospital, 274 S.E.2d 457 (Ga., 1981).
283. 418 U.S. 113 (1973).
284. 147 A.2d 108 (N.H., 1958).
285. 157 A.2d 497 (N.J., 1960).
286. 171 A.2d 140 (N.J. Super., 1961). Also see 23 Duq. L. Rev. 1 (1984) and 5 W. New Eng. L. Rev. 431 (1983).
287. 201 A.2d 537 (N.J. Super., 1964), cert. denied 377 U.S. 985 (1964).
288. 293 N.W.2d 736 (Mich. App., 1980); also infra note 194, at 827.
289. 446 N.E.2d 395 (Mass., 1983).
290. 489 A.2d 1130 (Md. App., 1985).
291. 301 N.W.2d 869 (Mich. App., 1980).
292. Section 43.6 of Cal. Civ. Code (1982); see Turpin v. Sortini, 643 P.2d 954 (Cal., 1982).
293. 697 F.2d 1172 (4th Cir., 1982).
294. See A.B.A.J. (August 1989) at 38 et seq.
295. 531 N.E.2d 355 (Ill., 1988).
296. 514 N.Y.S.2d 177 (April 28, 1987); see N.Y.L.J. (April 28, 1987) at 14.
297. 410 U.S. 113 (1973).
298. The New York court opined:

Confronted with similar statutes in criminal cases an overwhelming number of sister-states have likewise taken the position that it is not within judicial province, under the guise of interpretation, to encompass within the various statutory definitions of "person" an unborn fetus unless specifically included by the legislature (Meadows v. State, Ark. Sup. Ct., Jan. 26, 1987, 40 Cr.L. 2356; Keeler v. Superior Court, 2 Cal. 3d 619, 470 P.2d 617; State v. Gonzales, 467 So. 2d 723, Fla. App., 1985; People v. Greer, 79 Ill.2d 103, 402 NE2d 203, 1980; Hollis v. Commonwealth, 652 SW2d

61, Ky., 1983; State v. Brown, 378 So.2d 916, La., 1979; State v. Guthrie, 97 Mich. App. 226, 293 NW2d 775, 1980; See State v. Anonymous, 40 Conn. Supp. 498, 516 A2d 156 for further citations). Two states have reached a contrary result. Both, Massachusetts and South Carolina, are so-called common law states. The courts in both states took the position that, based on medical technology, they could change the law; and they both based their decisions in part on developments in each state in civil law tort liability involving a fetal death (Commonwealth v. Cass, 392 Mass. 799, 467 NE2d 1324, 1984; State v. Horne, 282 SC 444; 319 SE2d 703, 1984). Even in the two minority jurisdictions, due process considerations dictated that the interpretations enlarging common law standards could not be applied retroactively but could only be applied prospectively. While New York civil law recognizes that an infant injured *in utero* by the tort of another should *when born alive* be allowed to sue (Wood v. Lancet, 303 NY 349), the death of an unborn child will not support an action for wrongful death (Endresz v. Friedberg, 24 NY2d 478, 301 NYS2d 65).

The majority of states confronted with this issue have done no more than to recognize the common law rules as codified or modified by their own state's statutes. At common law it was clear that an unborn fetus, viable or otherwise, could not be the subject of homicide (3 Coke, Institutes 58 [1648] 40 CJS, Homicide s 2[b] p. 824; 40 ALR3d 444). It appears that the New York State Legislature in the 1965 revisions of the Penal Law adopted the common law rule by defining "person" as "a human being who is born and is alive." P.L. §125.05(1). Despite the following twenty-two years of development in science and medical technology there has been no revision of the definition.

The People attack as archaic the current requirement that a fetus must be born alive to be a victim of the crime charged here in light of scientific and medical knowledge that life exists before birth (see also State v. Soto, 378 NW2d 625 [Minn. 1985] [see dissent by Judge Yetka]). Many courts have rejected this argument based on the belief that such a complex and controversial subject should be addressed by the legislature and not by judicial fiat (see Keeler v. Superior Court, supra; People v. Grier, supra; State v. Dickinson, 28 Ohio St2d 65, 274 NE2d 599 [1971]; Meadows v. State, supra). What the law *ought* to be is not within this court's province but the province of the legislature. McKinney's Consolidated Laws of N.Y.- Book 1, Statutes, §73.

Indeed, a number of states have enacted feticide statutes. In Florida a statute was enacted specifically defining as a crime the willful killing of an unborn child by an injury to the mother. [§782.09, F.Stat. (1983)]. This statute of course deals with the "willful" killing; it is nevertheless an example of legislative action addressing the question of feticide in view of modern advances in scientific and medical knowledge. The California legislature has likewise amended its murder statute to include the unlawful killing of a human being *or a fetus*. The legislature of the State of New York could amend its murder and manslaughter statutes, if it chooses to do so, to include specifically the death of a fetus by willful conduct or culpable negligence. To date it has not seen fit to do so.

In view of the understandable confusion generated by the present statute particularly in light of recent scientific developments, the legislature is urged to consider the issue and determine whether as a body politic, it deems the present statute adequate to protect the unborn; or whether prospective changes in criminal liability relating to feticide are required. The legislature is uniquely qualified to address this issue, being composed of members geographically proportional throughout the state and being able to conduct hearings in a non-adversary setting. It can consider all the aspects of the issue and not only the specific facts set forth in a particular litigation. Accordingly the court is requesting the Legislature to review this serious problem and will forward copies of this decision to the Law Revision Commission and the chairman of the Judicial Committees of the Senate and Assembly.

Pursuant to the foregoing, the first and second counts of indictment #105–86 are dismissed. In so doing, this court does *not* hold that a viable fetus is not alive nor does it hold that a person should not be punished for causing its death. This decision rests on what the court perceives to be the law in this matter.

299. 467 N.E.2d 1324 (Mass., 1984).

300. See Mone v. Greyhound Lines Inc., 331 N.E.2d 916 (Mass., 1975).

301. The Connecticut statute on adoption is found in Chapter 778 and commences with section 45–61 on termination of parental rights, followed by sections on hearing of

the petition, the appointment of guardian *ad litem* for minor or incompetent parent, appointment and duties of statutory parent, placement of adoptive children by the state, and under Part II with section 45–68a delineates the availability and confidentiality of records.

302. Section 20–38.1(2) of Va. Code Ann. (1982).

303. See 69 Va. L. Rev. 465 (1983) at 498.

304. Ky. Atty. Gen. 81–18 (1981), reprinted in 7 Fam. L. Rep. 2246 (1981).

305. See 20 Colum. J. Law & Soc. Probs. 1 (1986) at 30 et seq.

306. 9 Fam. L. Rep. 2348 (Jefferson County, 1983).

307. Id.

308. 10 Fam. L. Rep. 1105 (Franklin County, 1983), rev'd sub nom. Kentucky ex rel. Armstrong v. Surrogate Parenting Association, 11 Fam. L. Rep 1359 (Ky. Ct. App., 1985).

309. Infra note 221, at 34.

310. La. Atty. Gen. Op. 83–869 (October 18, 1983).

311. 6 Fam. L. Rep. 3011 (Wayne County, 1980), aff'd 307 N.W.2d 438 (Mich. App., 1981), cert. denied 459 U.S. 1183 (1983).

312. Ohio Atty. Gen. Op. 83–001 (January 3, 1983).

313. 10 Fam. L. Rep. 1383 (D.C. Super., 1984).

314. 23 Pa. Cons. Stat. §2711(c) (1985); see generally 91 Dick. L. Rev. (Summer 1987).

315. See 23 Pa. Cons. Stat. §2511 (1985).

316. Id at §2511(b)

317. Unreported,—A2d—(Pa. Super., 1988).

318. See Tobias v. Tobias, 374 A.2d 1372 (Pa., 1977), and Commonwealth ex rel. Jordan v. Jordan, 448 A.2d 113 (Pa., 1982).

319. See *New York Times* (August 16, 1987) at K4.

320. Id.

321. Unreported,—N.Y.S.2d—(App. Div., 2d Dept., October 25, 1989).

322. 170 A.2d 199 (Md. App., 1987).

323. See N.L.J. (December 21, 1987) at 1, 18.

324. See Note, Trial (December 1987) at 65–72.

325. See Kelner and Kelner, "Trial Practice," N.Y.L.J. (November 12, 1987) at 1 et seq.

326. 333 S.E.2d 852 (Ga. App., 1985).

327. 193 Cal. Rptr. 422 (1985).

328. 538 A.2d 1175 (Md., 1988).

329. See *Time* (August 2, 1982) at 68.

330. See *New York Times* (November 17, 1988) at A25.

331. 529 A.2d 434 (N.J., 1987); also see *Trial* (December 1987) at 88–90.

332. Unreported,—N.E.2d—(Mass., 1987).

333. 730 S.W.2d 649 (Texas, 1987).

334. 30 Atl. L. Rep. 445 (December 1987).

335. 407 N.W.2d 584 (Iowa, 1987).

336. 237 Cal. Rptr. 873 (Cal. App., 1987).

337. 518 N.Y.S.2d 346 (App. Div., 2d Dept., December 30, 1988), aff'd 535 N.Y.S.2d 990 (1989).

338. Unreported,—N.Y.W.2d—(New York County, November 16, 1989).

339. 498 N.Y.S.2d 743 (1985).

340. Id.

341. 468 N.Y.S.2d 25 (App. Div., 2d Dept., 1983).

342. Infra note 338.

343. See generally Baruch, "AIDS in the Courts: Tort Liability for the Sexual Transmission of Acquired Immune Deficiency Syndrome," 22 Tort & Ins. L.J. 165–93 (Winter 1987).

344. See Freedman, *Prime Defenses to Negligence* (1986). Also, note sec. 284 (a) and (b) of *Restatement (Second) of Torts*.

AIDS is a disease characterized by a defect in a person's natural immunity against disease. Persons with AIDS are vulnerable to serious illnesses, which do not threaten those with normally functioning immune systems.

345. Infra note 344.

346. See Freedman, *The Business Tort of Fraud and Misrepresentation* 1988) at sec. 1.2(d).

347. Id. at sec. 1.1(b).

348. See Freedman, *International Products Liability* (1987) at sec. 1.08.

349. Id. at sec. 2.01. Also, supra note 372.

350. See Freedman, *Prime Defenses to Negligence* (1986) at Chap. 2.

351. Id. at Chap. 1.

352. See Freedman, *The Right of Privacy in the Computer Age* (1987).

353. Infra note 349, at Sec. 2.06.

354. Infra note 350.

355. See 100 Pub. Health Rep. 5 (September-October 1985) at 451. Also, see *Washington Post* (October 27, 1985) at A1.

356. Id.

357. Infra note 345.

358. See Edwards v. Lamb, 45 A. 480 (N.H., 1889), and Earl v. Kulko, 98 A.2d 107 (N.J., 1953), for example.

359. 450 N.Y.S.2d 350 (1982).

360. 102 A. 63 (Del., 1917).

361. 198 Cal. Rptr. 273 (1984).

362. 193 Cal. Rptr. 422 (1983).

363. Infra note 344, at 176.

364. Infra note 347.

365. Infra note 360.

366. Infra note 348.

367. Infra note 363.

368. Infra note 362.

369. Sodomy and adultery are among the crimes growing out of sexual intercourse. Note that a majority of states have by statute made homosexual conduct the crime of sodomy, even if the relationship is consensual: See ALA CODE §13 A–6–60(2) (1975); ARIZ. REV. STAT. ANN. §13–707 (1978); ARK STAT. ANN. §41–1813 (1975); D.C. CODE ANN. §22–3502 (1982); FLA. STAT. ANN. §800–02 (West 1976); GA. CODE ANN. §16–6–2 (1982); IDAHO CODE §18–6605 (1979); KAN. STAT. ANN. §21–3505 (1974); KY. REV. STAT ANN. §510.100 (Bobbs-Merrill 1975); LA. REV. STAT. ANN. §14:89 (West Supp. 1982); MD. CODE ANN. art. 27 § §553, 554 (Supp. 1982); MASS. GEN LAWS ANN. ch. 272, §34 (West 1970); MICH. COMP. LAWS ANN.

§609.293 (West Supp. 1982); MISS CODE ANN. §97–29–59 (1972); MONT. CODE ANN. §45–5–505 (1981); NEV. REV. STAT. §201.190 (1979); N.C. GEN STAT. §14–177 (1981); OKLA. STAT. ANN. tit 21, §886 (West 1983); R.I. GEN. LAWS 11–10–1 (Replacement 1969); S. C. CODE ANN. §16–15–120 (Law. Co-op. 1977); TENN. CODE ANN §39–2–612 (1982); TEX PENAL CODE ANN. §21.06 (VERNON 1974); UTAH CODE ANN. Sec. 76–5–403 (1983); VA. CODE §18.2–361 (1982); WIS STAT. ANN. §944.17 (West 1982).

370. 96 S.W.2d 245 (Texas, 1936).

371. See Crago, "The Defense of Illegality in Negligence Actions," 4 Melb. U. L. Rev. 534 (1964) at 547.

372. Infra note 362.

373. Infra note 344, at 185. See Joy v. Brown, 252 P.2d 889 (Kan., 1953) at 892.

374. See Section 496A of *Restatement (Second) of Torts*.

375. Infra note 344, at 185.

376. 164 Cal. Rptr. 618 (1980).

377. Infra note 344, at 186.

378. Infra note 363.

379. 451 N.Y.S.2d 767 (1982).

380. 405 N.Y.S.2d 438 (1972) at 453.

381. See Street v. Consumer's Mining Corp., 39 S.E.2d 271 (Va., 1946).

382. See Hercules Powder Co. v. Bannister, 171 F.2d 262 (6th Cir., 1948).

383. See Duke v. Housen, 589 P.2d 334 (Wyo., 1979).

384. Note Regina v. Clarence, 16 Cox C.C. 511 (England, 1888).

385. 390 A.2d 77 (Md., 1978).

386. See generally Turk, "AIDS: The First Decade," 14 Employee Rel. L.J. (Spring 1989) at 531–47.

387. Note Chalk v. U.S. District Court, 840 F.2d 701 (9th Cir., 1988), where the federal appellate court ruled that a public school teacher who suffered from AIDS was "qualified" for classroom duty under Section 504 of the Rehabilitation Act because current medical evidence indicated that there was no risk that AIDS could be transmitted through normal classroom contact.

The employers' responsibility toward the AIDS victim in the public or governmental sector was clarified, for the most part, by legislation and by the U.S. Supreme Court's decision in School Board of Nassau County v. Arline, 107 S. Ct. 1123 (1987). Here the public school teacher was found to be a handicapped individual because her recurrent tuberculosis was a physical impairment that substantially limited her major life activities.

388. (November 24, 1989) at A6.

8

International Aspects of the Creation of the New Family

8.1 AUSTRALIA

In 1908 the High Court of Australia in Doodeward v. Spence was confronted with a situation where the police had confiscated the corpse of a two-headed, stillborn child born in New Zealand; the plaintiff had put the corpse on public exhibition for a profit.[1] The court upheld the plaintiff's cause of action in conversion since it found that the police had interfered with his possessory right even though the purpose of the disputed possession was public and commercial display: "There is no law forbidding the mere possession of a human body, whether born alive or dead, for purposes other than immediate burial. A fortiori such possession is not unlawful if the body possesses attributes of such a nature that its preservation may afford valuable or interesting information or instruction." This eighty-year-old judicial decision apparently did not concern itself with public health or with public decency.

Today the posture on public exhibition of embryo and fetal experimentation has evidently changed, even in Australia, where the High Court had in 1908 applied a property-type enforcement rule at common law: "If one medical or scientific student may lawfully possess it, he may transfer the possession to another. . . . When a person has by the lawful exercise of work or skill so dealt with a human body or part of a human body in his lawful possession that it has acquired some attributes differentiating it from a mere corpse awaiting burial, he acquires a right to retain possession of it, at least against any person not entitled to have it delivered to him for the purpose of burial."[2]

Australia in recent times has taken bold steps in the field of artificial conception. Structured by the National Health and Medical Research Council, national ethical guidelines on IVF have been in place since 1982. One guideline places an upper time limit of ten years on the storage of embryos.[3] (There is a fascinating tale involving a married couple from Los Angeles who in 1981 participated in the IVF program at the Queens Victoria Medical Center in Melbourne. Mr. Rios, being infertile, consented to the participation of an anonymous donor whose sperm was permitted to fertilize three eggs taken from Mrs. Rios, although only one egg was then implanted in Mrs. Rios and the other two fertilized eggs were frozen for subsequent use. Shortly after, Mr. and Mrs. Rios were killed in an airplane crash in Chile. Mrs. Rios's son by a previous marriage then filed a petition in California for his right under California law to his father's share in the joint estate. The problem of the two unborn embryos in Melbourne, as possible claimants to the joint estate, was somewhat resolved in August 1984 when the Waller Committee determined that the two frozen embryos had no independent legal rights to be unfrozen and implanted in another surrogate mother. The legislature of Victoria then ordered the frozen embryos to be preserved in their liquid nitrogen container.)[4] A married woman's fertilized ovum in cryopreservation would normally be destroyed upon her death. But the prime importance of such modern reproductive technology recognition is the acceptability in Australia of scientific and medical procedures to correct infertility among married couples, the use of donor eggs in women to produce embryos, and the use of artificial insemination by anonymous male donors.[5]

The Waller Report, "On the Disposition of Embryos Produced by In Vitro Fertilization," released by the attorney general of Victoria in August 1984, recommended the cryopreservation of embryos and immediate experimental research and urged that the disposition of stored embryos should not be determined by the hospital where the embryos are stored and that such embryos should not be regarded as possessing legal rights or having rights of inheritance.[6] Accordingly, "The couple whose gametes are used to form the embryo in the context of an IVF programme should be recognized as having rights which are in some ways analogous to those recognized in parents of a child after its birth. The Committee does not consider that those rights are absolute, just as the rights of parents are limited by the rights and interests of the child, and by the larger concerns of the community in which they live."[7]

The Australian position on the legitimate purpose of human biomedical research is evident in a 1966 report, "Statement on Human Experimentation—Considerations for Guidance," issued by the National Health and Medical Research Council:[8] "Planned experimentation is essential for improving human welfare. Experiments range from those undertaken as part of patient care to those undertaken either on patients or on healthy subjects for the purpose of contribution to knowledge."[9] But on July 24, 1985, the Family Law Council of Australia issued its report, "Creating Children: A Uniform Approach to the Law and Practice of Reproductive Technology in Australia," calling for an investigation of the "social, moral, legal and ethical questions and values which cannot be easily or lightly debated—and which are not all capable of absolute and final answers. Many of these questions will need to be subject to ongoing review and community debate because of their fundamental nature."[10] The report then recommended that surrogacy arrangements be viewed as "contrary to the welfare and interests of the child"[11] and mandated that all exchanges of money for surrogate mother services be prohibited by law.[12] But the Family Law Council report approved the continuance of artificial insemination with a donor sperm unless the donor is related to the parties.[13] The report also stated that the production of human embryos should not continue solely for the purpose of research or experimentation.[14]

8.2 CANADA

The artificial insemination of a woman with the sperm of a donor as a means of alleviating male sterility has been extensively practiced in Canada since World War II.[15] However, the use of donated ova for fertilization in vivo or in vitro or of donated embryos followed by transfer to a host mother, or surrogate, "has shaken the one remaining immutable private law principle governing maternal filiation. That principle itself is based on the traditional view that a woman who gestates and delivers a child is its mother."[16] In the 1933 decision of Montreal Tramways Co. v. Leveille, the Canadian court pointed out that from conception onward, the embryo or fetus can be the subject of certain patrimonial rights, which are contingent not only on live birth but under the civil law on the viability of the child as well.[17] Prenatal injury gives the affected child a cause of action for the injury to its mother during pregnancy.[18] Where the wrongful act of a third party causes the loss of a fetus prior to birth, such a loss is not compensable without specific legislation authorizing compensation.

The Ontario Law Reform Commission report in 1985 was exceptionally liberal in many of its recommendations for modern reproductive technology.[19] Among its recommendations was not only approval of storage banks for embryos subject to regulation but also the exportation and importation of gametes and embryos subject to regulation.[20] The Canadian Medical Association in 1975 in its Code of Ethics broadly approved human biomedical experimentation and research.[21] The Human Gift Tissue Act of 1971 in Ontario fosters the "removal" of tissue from the body, provided the proper consents are obtained.[22] Article 20 of the Civil Code of the Province of Quebec permits, regulates, and validates a contract for participation in medical experimentation, providing that the experimentation does not "contravene the laws of public order and good morals."[23] The Professional Corporation of Physicians of Quebec Code of Medical Ethics states that "the physician must not diminish the physical or mental resistance of a person except for therapeutic or prophylactic reasons deemed necessary or useful."[24] It is obvious that Quebec law does not favor nontherapeutic experimentation. Canadian sensitivity to human experimentation is shown by a 1930 Alberta decision, Edmonds v. Armstrong Funeral Home Ltd., [25] which allowed damages for infliction of emotional distress against defendant for its improper handling of a dead body.[25]

Canada appears to have taken a somewhat confusing position on the right of privacy in reproductive situations, as evidenced by R v. Morgentaler, a 1985 decision by the Ontario Court of Appeal that found no fundamental right to procure an abortion; yet it concluded that the right to decide whether to have children was ''so deeply rooted in our traditions and way of life as to be fundamental.''[26] In essence, the Ontario court found that the right of personal privacy was not included under the right to life, liberty, and security of the person as found in section 7 of the Canadian Charter of Rights and Freedoms, part I of the Canadian Constitution Act, 1982. And in Eve v. Mrs. E, the Canadian court refused to authorize a hysterectomy intended to sterilize a mentally incompetent adult female because of ''the importance of maintaining the physical integrity of a human being . . . particularly as it affects the privilege of giving life.''[27]

Abortion has been a potent issue in Canada, and on January 28, 1988, the Supreme Court of Canada ruled that the restrictive abortion code passed in 1968 had denied women the right of ''life, liberty, and security of person'' guaranteed in Canada's Charter of Rights and Freedoms.[28] The highest Canadian court opined: ''Forcing a woman by threat of criminal sanction to carry a fetus to term unless she meets certain criteria unrelated to her own priorities and aspirations is a profound interference with a woman's body.''

8.3 ENGLAND

In 1982, four years after the birth in England of the world's first test-tube baby,[29] the British government structured a Committee of Inquiry into Human Fertilisation and Embryology, and mandated this Warnock committee to examine the social, ethical, and legal implications of the new reproductive technology.[30] The July 1984 report of the Warnock committee was a bold step forward in that it approved the cryopreservation of embryos under strict constraints and subject to review by a statutory licensing authority.[31] The report favored research on embryos subject to careful monitoring for a fourteen-day period; informed consent from the couple generating the embryo was, however, most desirable. Ten years was determined to be the maximum allowable time for storage of an embryo, with the right of disposal passing to the storage authority after that time. The Warnock committee sought to avoid the Australian dilemma over frozen embryos by proposing legislation that provided that any child born of an IVF process ''who was not in utero at the death of the father shall be disregarded for the purposes of succession to the inheritance from the latter.''[32] The report also proposed legislation that would impose a criminal sanction for the maintenance of surrogate mother agencies, although the other participants in the surrogacy would be exempted from criminal prosecution.[33] Nevertheless, ''all surrogacy agreements [should be declared] illegal contracts and therefore unenforceable in court.''[34] Interestingly, there were no known cases of commercial surrogate motherhood in England at the time the committee reported its findings. Yet the next year, in In re A Baby, a British court allowed a baby born to a surrogate mother to be taken outside England to live with its natural father and his wife.[35] The married couple were Americans, the husband was fertile, and his wife had a congenital defect that rendered her infertile. They found a surrogate mother in England, and the husband came to England for insemination of the British surrogate mother under the care of a qualified nurse. When the baby was born and the couple were in England, the British court ordered that in the best interests of the child, the care and control of the baby be entrusted to the natural father and his wife in the United States. Subsequently in late 1985, Parliament passed legislation outlawing commercial surrogate motherhood agencies and setting penalties up to three months' imprisonment.[36]

The English Abortion Act of 1967[37] makes the abortion decision dependent upon medical discretion and the application of statutorily mandated clinical criteria.[38] The consent of the potential father is not a legal requisite for abortion in England.[39] The act permits abortion on demand up to the end of the second trimester and limits the performance of third-trimester abortions to maternal-health-preserving situations.[40] The English secretary of state has a statutory duty to provide publicly funded abortion services under the National Health Service Act of 1977.[41]

In England the concealment of the birth of a fetus is a crime under the Offenses Against the Person Act,[42] and concealment of the performance of an abortion constitutes a breach of the Abortion Act's notification provisions.[43] But English courts consistently have denied the existence of property rights in a corpse,[44] although there is some recognition with respect to property rights for the next of kin.[45] Presumably the refusal to deliver up a dead fetus to its mother for burial or the disposition of a fetus by sale would be in violation of English common law.[46] A corpse or fetus would not be the subject of larceny under old English common law or under the English Theft Act of 1968.[47] The English Anatomy Acts of 1832 and 1871 immunize donors and researchers from any criminal liability for the donation, receipt, or possession of a corpse and presumably a fetus.[48]

The Peel Report of 1972 found no ethical or legal objection to the commercial use and commercial disposition of the placenta and retroplacental blood or fetuses, provided that the monetary payment did not exceed the "necessary costs incurred in administering those services."[49] The Peel Report also examined the issue of fetal research and established ethical standards for the self-regulating medical profession and criteria for ethical committees considering fetal research protocol.[50] Research on a dead fetus was made subject to parental consent, provided that "dissection of the dead fetus or experiments on the fetus or fetal material do not occur in the operating theatre or place of delivery, [and provided that] there is no monetary exchange for fetuses or fetal material, and full records are kept by the relevant institution." [51] If a harmed fetus were subsequently born alive, an action would lie against the researcher under the Congenital Disabilities (Civil Liability) Act of 1976.[52] The Peel Report of 1972 authorized nontherapeutic research and experimentation on the previable fetus (prior to twenty weeks or approximately 400–500 grams in bodily weight), provided that the research and experimentation conformed to certain guidelines.[53]

The 1984 Warnock committee report placed a temporary moratorium on embryo donation by lavage but otherwise furthered progress on reproductive technology. The report promoted the use of counseling for participants in human-assisted reproduction, encouraged regulation through a licensing body for research, and discouraged payments (beyond actual expenses) to semen donors.[54]

8.4 OTHER COUNTRIES

The new reproductive technologies have also received attention in other countries. The increasing secularization of society, the advance of libertarian thinking in Western democracies, and the movement toward social, economic, and even political equality for women has led to recognition of the advent of the new reproductive technology.[55]

Abortion, for example, has generally been decriminalized, as illustrated by the Israeli case of A v. B.[56] Here the statutory committee approved a married woman's application for an abortion, but at the request of her husband, the district court issued a temporary injunction pending a new hearing before the statutory committee to hear the husband's petition. The Israel Supreme Court, however, set aside the injunction, pointing out that "our law does not vest in the husband any veto or other right by virtue of which he can require abstention from making a decision as regards pregnancy." Thus, in Israel the law has not recognized a man's right to prevent abortion once the abortion has been decided upon by the woman or the court. Sterilization for therapeutic reasons, however, is treated as an assault upon the person unless the patient has given informed consent.[57] Contraceptives are freely available in Israel, but other contraceptive devices are obtainable only on prescription or upon the advice of a family planning clinic.[58] In Israel, as in many other Western-style countries, no distinction is made between legitimate and illegitimate children in view of the weakening of the institution of marriage and the traditional sex roles of the parents.[59] Artificial insemination in Israel requires the consent of both spouses, but in practice the requisite consent is not mandatory; Regulation 26 of the Israeli administrative regulations proscribes the secrecy of the identities of the donor and spouses, and Regulation 9 provides for two separate files, one of donors and one of sperm, and only the latter file is available during actual artificial insemination. Israeli medical practice is to inseminate with sperm from several donors, including the husband.[60] Artificial insemination is not restricted to married couples, but it is so implied in Israeli regulations.[61] The sperm donor has no legal relationship to the child.

Adoption in Israel does not require the father's consent when he is not married to the mother and has not recognized the child as his, or when he acknowledges paternity but the child does not live with him and he refuses without good cause to take the child into his home.[62] In practice, most Israeli children who are born out of wedlock have no identifiable father so that adoption proceeds rapidly without his consent.[63] Surrogate motherhood is generally forbidden unless effected under authority of law.[64] Jewish law in Israel is very explicit about the rights and duties arising out of marriage: the husband must provide maintenance, clothing, medical care, and burial; the husband has a right to the fruits of his wife's labor, the things she finds, the income of her property, and succession. The husband's refusal to fulfill his conjugal duties will result in entitling the wife to divorce. Infertility, as distinguished from refusal to have children, is a valid ground for divorce.[65]

The Constitution of Italy gives considerable importance to the family as an autonomous unit with its own normative structure.[66] The individual in Italy is accorded every right to organize freely the familial relationships.[67] It would thus appear that in Italy there is a constitutional right of access to modern reproductive technologies.

In France, there are apparently restrictions on medical experimentation with new reproductive technologies. For a medical experiment to be legitimate, the aim must be therapeutic for that patient; however, medical experimentation is permitted without a curative or therapeutic purpose where there is no risk, where it may be legitimate to act to save other persons, or if the medical experimentation can be classified as "d'exploration" in contrast to "physiopathologique."[68] But a court proceeding is necessary in France to determine whether a widow has a right to be artificially inseminated with the frozen sperm of her deceased husband.[69] The right to life of a fetus is restricted, especially subordinate to abortion law. [70] The interest of the French potential father is also limited in that his consent is usually not a legal prerequisite for abortion.[71]

In the Netherlands, "human experimentation . . . may be carried out to increase medical knowledge generally to achieve diagnostic or therapeutic results, or to increase the ability and experience of the investigator."[72] But "dangerous experiments are never justifiable if there is only advancement of medical knowledge; they must also entail some benefit for humanity."[73]

In Sweden storage banks are permitted to sell and purchase human gametes or embryos (and even import frozen sperm), subject to regulation, thus attesting to the generally liberal Swedish view of the modern reproductive technologies.[74] In Austria the right of the fetus to life is subject to the abortion law.[75] In Chile and in Ireland there are constitutional provisions prohibiting abortion (except to save the life of the mother).[76] The nations of Yugoslavia[77] Portugal,[78] Ecuador,[79] Mexico,[80] and Peru,[81] for example, all have constitutional provisions protecting the right of persons from intrusion by government into such human decisions as the number and spacing of children. But the duty of the state to provide medical services is not the equivalent of any constitutional right to procreate, as well illustrated in Portugal.[82]

In West Germany in January 1988, a court ordered the immediate closing of a Frankfurt surrogate motherhood center, declaring that it was contrary to the country's adoption laws and to basic moral principles.[83]

8.5 UNITED NATIONS AND INTERNATIONAL BODIES

Under principles of international human rights, the status, protection, uses, and access to human genetic material and modern reproductive technologies can be seen under such human rights as the right to marry and to raise a family, the right to life, the right to equality, the right to health, the right of privacy, and the right to family life.[84] The 1984 Universal Declaration of Human Rights[85] recognizes the right to marry and found a family, as does the International Covenant on Civil and Political Rights,[86] which requires countries to "respect and to ensure to all individuals within their territories . . . the rights recognized . . . in the Covenant, without distinction of any kind." The International Covenant on Economic, Social, and Cultural Rights proclaims that "the widest possible protection and assistance should be accorded to the family."[87]

The Declaration of Helsinki (1975) echoes this general liberality by its statements on human biomedical research and experimentation:[88] "It is essential that the results of laboratory experiments be applied to human beings to further scientific knowledge and to help suffering humanity. . . . The purposes of biomedical research involving human subjects must be to improve diagnostic, therapeutic and prophylactic procedures and the understanding of the aetiology and pathogenesis of disease.[89]

The European Commission of Human Rights in 1960 heard an application by a Norwegian citizen against a resolution passed by the Norwegian Parliament providing for the interruption of pregnancy under certain conditions and circumstances. The petitioner requested the commission to decide whether the human right to have offspring is an inalienable human right or, if not, under what conditions and circumstances this human right can be forfeited; another issue was "whether human rights are fully applicable to the human embryo from the time of conception, or if not, at what stages in the development of the human individual these rights take part and full force."[90] Since the petitioner himself was not subject to the Norwegian legislation, the European Commission of Human Rights did not consider itself competent to resolve the issues. But in 1980 in X v. United Kingdom, the commission ruled that "everyone's right to life" did not include the unborn.[91] Subsequently, in 1981, the Inter-American Commission on Human Rights upheld the right to life for every human being, but Article 4 of the American Convention on Human Rights was stated to protect the right "in general, from the moment of conception."[92] The American Declaration on Human rights, however, does not identify the precise moment of the commencement of the right to life. [93]

The United Nations has been embroiled in conflict over abortion, as evidenced by the August 1987 public announcement of the U.S. Agency for International

Development, that it would again withhold its contribution to the U.S. Fund for Population Activities because the fund allegedly supports coerced abortion in the People's Republic of China.[94] In 1986 the Agency for International Development withheld $25 million, despite denials by the Chinese government that their programs force abortions.

The United Nations continues its profound concern for the protection and welfare of children around the world, evidenced by the 1986 General Assembly Resolution adopting the Declaration of Social and Legal Principles Relating to the Protection and Welfare of Children, with Special Reference to Foster Placement and Adoption.[95] Previously the Council of Europe,[96] the Hague Conference on Private International Law,[97] and the Inter-American Specialized Conference on Private International Law[98] have adopted conventions concerning the welfare of children. The 1986 U.N. document stresses the observation that "the first priority for a child is to be cared for by his or her own parents," but adoption practices are necessary for the welfare of children.[99]

The November 20, 1989, U.N. Convention on the Rights of the Child is an unusual instrument in that it protects the broad-spectrum rights of an unusually vulnerable social group, children.[100] Indeed, the preambles of both the Declaration of Geneva of 1924 and the 1959 Declaration state that "mankind owes to the child the best that it has to give."[101] It should be noted that throughout the twentieth century, international law has granted special protection to children. Some of the earliest international agreements protecting children involved the white slave trade. In 1904 the International Agreement for the Suppression of White Slave Traffic[102] addressed the government's role in preventing international traffic in women and girls, and its companion, the International Convention for the Suppression of the White Slave Traffic,[103] was adopted in 1910 and provided for procurers severe criminal sanctions. Over the years, at least twenty conventions have been adopted to protect working children. The roots of the Draft Convention on the Rights of the Child can be traced to the first Declaration of the Rights of the Child in Geneva in 1923 and adopted by the League of Nations in 1924. The result was the 1959 U.N. Declaration of the Rights of the Child.[104] The convention consists of fifty-four substantive articles covering the spectrum of rights of the child.[105] The convention does not extend its protections to imprisonment for contractual obligation or to the right to participate in government. It should be noted that the U.N convention was initiated by Poland and that it took ten years of negotiation to bring the convention to the vote on November 20, 1989.[106]

The U.N. Convention on the Rights of the Child calls for a child's right to a name, survival, education, and protection against exploitation and abuse. It provides safeguards against violations, including the forcible separation of children from their parents. The convention is deliberately vague on abortion, adoption, and child labor in order to avoid offending any country.

The Hague Convention on the Civil Aspects of International Child Abduction,[107] ratified by the U.S. Senate in October 1986, was implemented in April

1988 when Congress passed the International Child Abduction Remedies Act.[108] The thrust of the act is to empower U.S. courts to determine only rights under the convention and not the merits of any underlying custody claims.[109] The act creates a central authority and grants concurrent jurisdiction to federal and state courts to enforce the Hague Convention. (As of June 1989 the convention was in force only in Australia, Austria, Canada, France, Hungary, Luxembourg, Norway, Portugal, Spain, Sweden, Switzerland, the United Kingdom, and the United States.) The convention seeks the prompt return of children wrongfully removed to or retained in any jurisdiction of a contracting state and to ensure that rights of custody and visitation under the law of one contracting state are effectively respected in the other contracting states. The convention applies only to children under 16 years of age who have been ''habitually residing'' in a contracting state immediately before the breach of custody or access rights.[110]

NOTES

1. 6 C.L.R 406 (Australia, 1908). Also see 39 Vand. L. Rev. 419 (1986) at 434.
2. 6 C.L.R. at 414.
3. See 21 Gonz. L. Rev. 395 (1985–1986) at 412 et seq.
4. See Lawson, Molloy, Jobson, and Walley, The Life and Strange Times of Elsa Rios,'' *Australian Bulletin* 25 (July 3, 1984), as delineated in note 3 at 418–19.
5. See generally 59 Australian L.J. 379 (July 1985).
6. Infra note 3 at 413–14.
7. Waller Report, section 2.8, as summarized in note 3 at 415.
8. See (1966) 2 Med. J. Australia 325.
9. Id. Also see generally 3 Legal Med. Q. (Australia) (1979) at 83 et seq.
10. Family Law Council report at 101, as delineated in note 3 at 416 et seq.
11. Id. at xiii.
12. Id.
13. Id.
14. Id. at xiv.
15. See generally 32 McGill L.J. (1987) at 339.
16. Id. at 339–40.
17. (1933) S.C.R. 456 (1933) 4 D.L.R. 337.
18. Infra note 15, at 340.
19. Infra note 15, at 346.
20. Id.
21. Infra note 9, at 87–88.
22. See S.O. 1971 ch. 83, Sec. 3, subsec. 1.
23. Infra note 9, at 88.
24. 2d ed, June 1976 (formerly Decree No. 3391, October 6, 1971).
25. (1931) 1 D.L.R. 676 (Alta Sup Ct., 1930).
26. (1985) 52 O.R. (2d) 353 at 377, 22 D.L.R. (4th) 641 (C.A.).
27. (1986) 2 S.C.R. 388 at 434; sub nom. Re Eve, 31 D.L.R. (4th) 1.
28. See *New York Times* (February 21, 1988) at 6.
29. See 21 Gonz. L. Rev. 395 (1985–1986) at 419.

30. See 48 Mod. L. Rev. 73 (1985) and 289 Brit. Med. J. 207 (1984).
31. See 289 Brit. Med. J (1984) at 238.
32. Infra note 4.
33. Infra note 28, at 420–21.
34. See 20 Colum. J.L. Soc. Probs. 1 (1986) at 42.
35. 135 New L.J. 104 (1985).
36. Infra note 34, at 42.
37. See 39 Vand. L. Rev. 419 (1986) at 422 et seq.
38. The Abortion Act provides:

(1) Subject to the provisions of this section, a person shall not be guilty of an offense under the law relating to abortion when a pregnancy is terminated by a registered medical practitioner if two registered medical practitioners are of the opinion, formed in good faith—

(a) That the continuance of the pregnancy would involve risk to the life of the pregnant woman, or of injury to the physical or mental health of the pregnant woman or any existing children of her family, greater than if the pregnancy were terminated; or

(b) that there is a substantial risk that if the child were born it would suffer from such physical or mental abnormalities as to be seriously handicapped.

(2) In determining whether the continuance of a pregnancy would involve such a risk of injury to health as is mentioned in paragraph (a) of subsection (1) of this section, account may be taken of the pregnant woman's actual or reasonably foreseeable environment.

(3) Except as provided by subsection (4) of this section, any treatment for the termination of pregnancy must be carried out in a hospital vested in the Minister of Health or the Secretary of State under the National Health Service Acts, or in a place for the time being approved for the purposes of this section by the said Minister or the Secretary of State.

(4) Subsection (3) of this section, and so much of subsection (1) as relates to the opinion of two registered medical practitioners, shall not apply to the termination of a pregnancy by a registered medical practitioner in a case where he is of the opinion, formed in good faith, that the termination is immediately necessary to save the life or to prevent grave permanent injury to the physical or mental health of the pregnant woman.

39. See Paton v. British Pregnancy Advisory Service Trustees (1978) 2 All E.R. 987, 3 W.L.R. 687 (Q.B.).
40. Infra note 37, at 424.
41. Ch. 49, sec. 3(1).
42. (1861), 24 & 25 Vict., ch. 100, sec. 60.
43. Infra note 38.
44. See The Queen v. Sharpe, 169 Eng. Rep. 959 (1987).
45. See Rees v. Hughes (1946), 1 K.B. 517.
46. See The King v. Cundick, 171 Eng. Rep. 900 (1822).
47. Ch. 60, sec. 1(1); also note 4 Anglo-Am. L. Rev. 412 (1975).
48. 2 & 3 Will 4, ch. 75, and 34 & 35 Vict., ch. 16.
49. Infra note 37, at 438.
50. Infra note 37, at 442 et seq.
51. Id. at 443.
52. Ch. 28, sec. 1(1).
53.

(ii) Only fetuses weighing less than 300 grammes are used;

(iii) The responsibility for deciding that the fetus is in a category which may be used for this type of research rests with the medical attendants at its birth and never with the intending research worker;

(iv) Such research is only carried out in departments directly related to a hospital and with the direct sanction of its ethical committee;

(v) Before permitting such research the ethical committee satisfies itself: (a) on the validity of the research; (b) that the required information cannot be obtained in any other way; and (c) that the investigators have the necessary facilities and skill.''

54. See generally Law Med. & Health Care (October 1984) 192 et seq.

55. See generally 18 Israel L. Rev. 381 (1983).

56. (1981) 35 (iii) P.D. 57. See Skalev, ''A Man's Right to Be Equal: The Abortion Issue,'' 18 Israel L. Rev. 381 (1983).

57. See sec. 378 of the Israel Penal Law (1977) and sec. 23 of the Israel Civil Wrongs Ordinance (2 L.S.I. (N.V.) 5).

58. Infra note 55, at 392.

59. Id. at 398.

60. See Shifman, ''Determination of Paternity of a Child Born Through Artificial Insemination,'' 10 Mishpatim 63 (1980) at 67–75.

61. See Israel Regulations 19, 22–26; infra note 54, at 400.

62. See sec. 13(2) of the Israel Adoption of Children Law, S.H. 293; also note 12 Israel L. Rev. 194 (1977).

63. Infra note 55, at 404.

64. Sec. 33 of Israel Adoption of Children Law.

65. See generally 15 Israel L. Rev. 109 (1980); also infra note 55, at 407. See also Shifman, ''Marriage and Cohabitation in Israeli Law,'' 16 Israel L. Rev. 439 (1981), concluding that there is an Israeli phenomenon ''according to which the legal significance of lawful marriage is diminishing, whereas that of extra-marital cohabitation is growing to the extent that the distinction is becoming blurred.''

66. Articles 29–31.

67. Infra note 15, at 349–50.

68. See Legal Med. Q. (1979) at 92: ''G. Boyer Chammard, P. Monzein, La responsabilité médicale 124 (Paris: Presses Universitaires de France, 1974); L. Kornprobst, S. Dephin, Le contract de soins medicaux, no. 123 (Paris: Sirey, 1970); J. Vidal, J.P. Carlotti, *Le consentment du malade à l'act médicale*. Rapports, Ordre National des Médecins, Paris, 1955; X. Ryckmans and R. Meert-van de Put, *Les droits et les obligations des médecins*, at T 1, no 593 2ed., Bruxelles: Maison Ferdinaud Larcier, SA, 1971; P. Lombard, P. Macaigne and B. Oudin, Le médecin devant ses juges 224 (Paris, Editions Robert Laffont, 1973); P. Laget, *Expérimentation et médecin* 301, 314–15, in Le médecin face aux risques et à la responsabilité, textes recueillis par M Eck, Paris: Fayard, 1968; and A. Decocq, Essai d'une théorie générale des droits sur la personne, Paris: Librarie Générale de Droit et de Jurisprudence, R. Pichon et R. Durand-Auzias, 1960, at no 107.''

69. See Hastings Center Rep. (December 1984) at 20.

70. See French Cons. Const, January 15, 1975, J.O. January 16, 1975.

71. See Cons d'Etat, October 31, 1980, L. J.C.P. 1982 II, 1973.

72. See Report of the Public Health Council, published in 4 World Med. J. 299 (1957); also infra note 67, at 85–86

73. Id.

74. See Swedish Law No. 1140, December 20, 1984, on Insemination at 336–36; also infra note 15, at 346.

75. See Verfassungsgerichtshof, 2 Eu. G.R.Z. 74 (1975).

76. See 14 Colum. Human Rts. L. Rev. 311 (1982–83) at 339–50.
77. See Article 191 of Constitution of the Socialist Federal Republic of Yugoslavia.
78. See Article 67 of the Constitution of the Republic of Portugal.
79. See Article 25 of the Constitution of Ecuador.
80. See Article 4 of the Constitution of Mexico.
81. See (1985) 36 Int. Dig. Health Leg. 980–83.
82. See Portugal Law No. 3184 of March 24, 1984.
83. See *New York Times* (January 7, 1988) at 7. Also (January 4, 1988) at All.
84. Infra note 15, at 350 et seq.
85. GA Res 217A, 3 U.N. G.A.O.R. pt. I, UN Doc. A/810 (1948), Article 16 (1).
86. 999 UNTS 171 (December 16, 1966), Article 23(2).
87. 993 UNTS 3 (December 16, 1966), Article 10(1).
88. Infra note 68, at 83–84.
89. Id.
90. See X v. Norway, 6 C.D. 34, 4 Y.B. Conv. H.R. 270 (Decision of May 29, 1961), No. 867/60.
91. 19 D.R. 244, sub nom. Paton v. United Kingdom, 3 E.H.R.R. 408, infra note 39.
92. See Case 2141, decided March 6, 1981, O.A.S./ser. L/V/II.52, doc. 48.
93. Infra note 15, at 353.
94. See *New York Times* (August 14, 1987) at A7.
95. 26 I.L.M. 1096 (1987).
96. See the 1967 European Convention on Recognition and Enforcement of Decisions Concerning Custody of Children and on Restoration of Custody of Children, 7 I.L.M. 211 (1968) and 19 I.L.M. 273 (1980).
97. See the 1965 Hague Convention on Jurisdiction, Applicable Law, and Recognition of Decrees Relating to Adoptions, 4 I.L.M. 338 (1965), and the 1980 Hague Convention on the Civil Aspects of International Child Abduction, 19 ILM 1501 (1980).
98. See the 1984 Inter-American Convention on Conflict of Laws Concerning the Adoption of Minors, 24 I.L.M. 460 (1985).
99. Note the U.N. General Assembly Resolution on Declaration on Social and Legal Principles Relating to the Protection and Welfare of Children, with Special Reference to Foster Placement and Adoption Nationally and Internationally. Res 41/85, 41st Sess, Agenda item 136.
100. 43 UN E.S.C.O.R. Comm. on Human Rights, UN Doc. E/CN.4/87/25 (1987).
101. See Cohen, "Elasticity of Obligation and the Drafting of the Convention on the Rights of the Child," 3 Conn. J. Internat. L. 71 (1987) at 109.
102. 1 L.N.T.S. 83 (March 18, 1904).
103. 3 L.N.T.S. 278 (May 4, 1910).
104. G.A. Res 1386, 14 UN G.A.O.R. Supp. (No. 16) at 19, UN Doc. A/4354 (1959). Also infra note 99, at 90.
105. Infra note 101, at 91:

> By the end of its January 1987 session, the Working Group had adopted the following articles: article 1 (definition of the word "child"); article 2 (right to a name and nationality); article 3 (protection during legal or administrative proceedings); article 4 (non-discrimination); article 5 (state implementation); article 6 (family unity and place of residence); article 6 *bis* (family reunification and communication); article 6 *ter* (intra-familial kidnapping); article 7 (free expression of opinion); article 7 *bis* (freedom of religion); article 8 (parental duties in child-rearing); article 8 *bis* (abuse

and maltreatment); article 9 (mass media); article 9 *bis* (preservation and identity); article 10 (emergency and foster care); article 11 (adoption); article 11 *bis* (refugees); article 12 (disabled); article 12 *bis* (health care services); article 12 *ter* (periodic review of placement); article 13 (social security); article 14 (standard of living); article 15 (compulsory education); article 16 (preparation for a responsible life); article 16 *bis* (indigenous populations); article 17 (leisure and recreation); article 18 (economic exploitation); article 18 *bis* (protection from illegal use of narcotics); article 18 *ter* (sexual exploitation); article 18 *quarter* (traffic in children); article 18 *quinto* (other exploitation); article 19 (penal provisions); article 20 (armed conflict); article 21 (protection of previously given greater rights); article 21 (dissemination of information about rights).

106. See *New York Times* (November 21, 1989) at A6.

107. P.L. 100–300.

108. 42 U.S.C. 11601 to 11610.

109. See Freed and Brandes, ''The Hague Convention,'' N.Y.L.J. (November 28, 1989), at 3, 4.

110. Id.

9

Governmental Regulation and the New Family

9.1 THE RIGHTS OF SINGLE MEN AND SINGLE WOMEN

In general, there has been much unlawful discrimination against single men and single women with respect to benefits available under the new reproductive technologies. For example, many physicians will not perform artificial insemination with single women,[1] and many statutes openly state that the particular IVF procedure is available only for married couples.[2] Even sperm donors do not offer their services where single women are involved, possibly for fear that donors might be held legally responsible for the support of the child conceived by an unmarried woman.[3] The U.S. Supreme Court in Eisenstadt v. Baird ruled in 1972 that the Massachusetts statute restricting the availability of contraceptive to married persons was unconstitutional;[4] furthermore, it was not rational to allow married persons access to contraceptives and deny that access to unmarried persons.[5] Two years later in Cleveland Board of Education v. La Fleur, the Court found that a state statute that required pregnant school teachers to take a mandatory five-month unpaid leave of absence for childbirth was invalid.[6] That statute was said to burden the basic rights of marriage and family life unreasonably in discriminating against pregnant school teachers.

The U.S. Supreme Court in August 1989 refused to rehear Michael H. v. Gerald D.,[7] thus scuttling the paternity rights for a California man who apparently sired a child by a woman married to someone else.[8] (The plaintiff is the cofounder of a national organization, Equality Nationwide for Unwed Fathers, seeking to strengthen the legal status of single fathers and their children). The highest court in a plurality opinion by Mr. Justice Scalia rejected plaintiff's claim that he possessed a due process of law right or ''liberty interest'' to establish a parental relationship with the child conceived during his sexual affair with Carole D. Mr. Justice Scalia pointed out that the 1872 California statute creating a presumption that the husband is the child's father protects against undue intrusion into the integrity and privacy of the family.[9] The concurring opinion of Mr. Justice Stevens would recognize the "liberty interest" under another California statute that permitted visitation rights for those with an interest in the child's welfare.[10] It should be noted that the California Superior Court had found that plaintiff's regular visitations with the child during eight years violated "the intention of the Legislature by impugning the integrity of the family unit."[11] The twenty-two-page dissenting opinion of Mr. Justice Brennan stated that "in construing the Fourteenth Amendment to offer shelter only to those interests specifically protected by historical practice . . . the plurality opinion ignores the kind of society in which our Constitution exists. . . . We are not an assimilative, homogeneous society, but a facilitative, pluralistic one, in which we must be willing to abide someone else's unfamiliar or even repellent practice because the same tolerant impulse protects our own idiosyncrasies."

Single women and single men may receive a shot in the arm from a 1987 Massachusetts statute (effective January 6, 1988) requiring insurance companies to pay for medical care in the nature of infertility treatments.[12] Infertility is not a cosmetic problem; in 1985 Maryland passed the first law on infertility coverage applicable, however, only to IVF procedure.

Legislation "protecting legitimate family relationships" as well as both the regulation and protection of the family unit are "venerable State concerns."[13] Statutes limiting the availability of artificial insemination, for example, to married women and statutes that might be drafted to limit the use of the IVF procedures to married women would appear to fall within this classification.[14] Under Maher v. Roe[18] it can be argued that the unmarried woman's decision to be artificially inseminated or to participate in an in vitro fertilization procedure does not fall within the gambit of any recognized fundamental right.[15]

In England the problem of children of unmarried parents or single persons has plagued the English courts. In Spence v. Dennis, the court held that the children, born some twenty years before the marriage, could not be said to be the children of the marriage, but instead were the children of their biological parents, that is, single persons, the English Legitimacy Act of 1976 notwithstanding.[16] According to the court, "In view of the delay between the birth of the children and the marriage in this case, it could hardly be said that the marriage served to protect them from the stigma of illegitimacy during their upbringing."

9.2 GOVERNMENT STERILIZATION POLICIES

Democratic governments seldom establish eugenic policies, although there are many state statutes on sterilization, a surgical procedure to render an individual incapable of procreating.[17] The U.S. Supreme Court has spoken in Skinner v. Oklahoma,[18] where the Oklahoma statute called for mandatory sterilization for "habitual criminals"; the statute offends the basic rights of marriage and of procreation and furthermore must be subjected to a rational basis test.[19] However, in the New York case of Avila v. New York City Health and Hospitals Corp., the court ruled that an institution receiving federal funds may not arbitrarily prevent a mentally competent and freely consenting individual from having a sterilization operation.[20] The plaintiff was a 37-year-old mildly retarded woman who at the age of 20 had a child who was significantly retarded and today resides with his grandmother. Under federal regulations, an institution may perform a sterilization only if the individual is at least 21 years of age, is not mentally incompetent, has voluntarily given informed consent, and at least 30 days and not more than 180 days have passed from the date of the consent: "New York courts recognize an individual's right to determine medical treatment. . . . Mrs. Avila has complied with the federal requirements and would be entitled to the requested operation."[21]

9.3 CHILD WELFARE CONCERNS

Every court at one time or another has articulated the public concern for child welfare, even at the expense of other participants in the creation of the new family. In Cramer v. Morrison, the California appellate court expressed the state's interest in "protecting children from the stigma of illegitimacy, preservation of the family, and insuring that individuals, rather than the government, bear responsibility for child support."[22] A single parent or the nontraditional family, it is argued, is not financially able to care for the child and will undoubtedly create a burden on the state welfare system. However, it must be noted that single parenthood is not necessarily a financial hardship, nor is marital status correlated with income level.[23] A lesbian family falls into the same categorization, for there may be wealth and also stable, loving care far more than in proportion to that of a married couple. The presence of a legal father is no guarantee that child support obligations will be met. Divorce and illegitimacy are the largest source of children without financial support and of child welfare concerns.

The U.S. Supreme Court in Zablocki v. Redhail in 1978 had ruled that the state may not prevent indigents from marrying based on outstanding child support obligations from prior relationships.[24] Indeed, a woman is free "to bring the child into life to suffer the myriad social, if not economic disabilities that the status of illegitimacy brings."[25] There is no stability in a family relationship where the government defines marriage narrowly and discriminately, or spells out uniform child-rearing obligations. There may be no stability in the family relationship even where the child is raised by his or her biological parents. The psychological parent may be more important than the biological parent, as shown in Smith v. Organization of Foster Families for Equality and Reform, [26] where the highest court observed: "Biological relationships are not the exclusive determination of the existence of a family. . . . The importance of the familial relationship, to the individuals involved and to society, stems from the emotional attachments that derive from the intimacy of daily association."[27] And in Quilloin

v. Walcott, the highest court concluded that the biological father was not entitled to veto a stepparent adoption for his child where the biological father had never lived with the child or taken on any parental responsibilities and therefore did not have a psychological relationship with the child.[28]

Child welfare concerns are not necessarily served by two parents, for one parent or a nontraditional family can and does do the job. Unlike child abuse or child neglect, a child growing up with a single parent or in a nontraditional family is not the kind of a situation that merits government intervention. There can be no guarantee of a normal home or normal environment under the guise of the state's interest in the protection of child welfare.[29]

On June 29, 1988 the U.S. Supreme Court in Bowen v. Kendrick[30] upheld the facial constitutionality of the Adolescent Family Life Act (AFLA),[31] authorizing federal grants to public and private organizations for service and research in the area of premarital adolescent sexual relations and pregnancy. The Court, however, remanded the case to the federal district court to determine whether, in its application, AFLA violates the establishment clause of the First Amendment.[32] Congress had enacted AFLA in 1981 in response to the social, health, and economic problems caused by teenaged sexuality, pregnancy, and parenthood. AFLA is a scheme for providing grants to sectarian and nonsectarian organizations to provide two types of services to adolescents: care services, for the provision of care to pregnant adolescents and adolescent parents, and prevention services, for the prevention of adolescent sexual relations. The grants are intended to serve several purposes, including the promotion of "self-discipline and other prudent approaches to the problem of adolescent premarital sexual relations" and the support of research projects "concerning the societal causes and consequences of adolescent premarital sexual relations, contraceptive use, pregnancy, and child rearing." However, AFLA imposes certain limitations on the use of funds by grant recipients. It expressly provides that no funds may be used for family planning services unless appropriate family planning services are not otherwise available in the community. Furthermore, AFLA restricts grants to programs or projects that do not provide abortions or abortion counseling or referral, unless such counseling or referral is specifically requested by the adolescents, and the AFLA states that grants may be made only to projects or programs that do not "advocate, promote, or encourage abortion." At the time of the Supreme Court's decision, the secretary of health and human services had received 1,088 grant applications and had awarded 141 grants under AFLA.

The Second U.S. Court of Appeals in State v. Sullivan[33] proclaimed that abortion may not be mentioned as an option to women seeking family planning services in agencies receiving funding under Title X of the Public Health Service Act.[34] The regulations were deemed to mirror congressional intent and are permissible construction of the statute that does not violate women's constitutional rights. According to the court, the government has only a duty to protect the exercise of free choice; the government does not have to subsidize it. Clinic workers' freedom of speech is not violated if the curtailment occurs within the scope of their employment. The dissenting opinion called the new regulations "capricious and arbitrary," self-admittedly adopted for shifts in political climate and depriving women of the right to make an informed choice.

The definition of family is most important in child welfare laws. One definition delineates the "alternative family," which embraces two or more adults, not related by blood, marriage, or adoption, who are involved in a mutually supportive, committed relationship and who are voluntarily registered publicly in order to be considered as a family, together with their dependents.[35] But alternative families are denied many rights accorded the traditional family. Indeed, the legal system might be utilized to extend meaningful benefits to all families so that all will receive the same recognition, protection, and benefits.[36]

Child welfare concerns were paramount in the recent New York decision on Paul T. v. Maria S., where the best interests of the child required that the father be granted sole custody.[37] The court considered the credibility, the interest of the parties, fitness, financial ability, emotional stability, and the testimony of an expert witness that the mother was unable to meet the child's needs. As the court expressed it:

> In making a custody determination, the court must determine which parent is entitled to custody of the child. Sections 70(a) and 240(1) of the Domestic Relations Law provide that neither parent has a prima facie right to thc custody of the child. The court begins a custody determination with the presumption that both parents are equally qualified to have custody of the child.
>
> In determining which parent is better qualified, the court weighs numerous factors. The issue of paramount concern to this court in a custody proceeding is the best interest of the child. (Friederwitzer v. Friederwitzer, 55 NY2d 89; Matter of Nehra v. Uhlar, 43 NY2d 242). However, no single factor is determinative, and, in rendering its decision, the court considers the totality of the circumstances (Eschbach v. Eschbach, 56 NY2d 167).
>
> The criteria a court utilizes in determining custody are guidelines which do not bind the court, but rather assist and guide it in determining what is in the child's best interest (Eschbach v. Eschbach, supra; Friederwitzer v. Friederwitzer, supra). The court considers the following, among other factors: care and affection shown for the child; ability and availability of the parents; atmosphere of the home; lifestyle; availability of educational advantages; effect of custodial change; financial standing; stability; and credibility (Eschbach v. Eschbach, supra; Friederwitzer v. Friederwitzer, supra; Wallinger v. Wallinger, 96 AD2d 988; McIntosh v. McIntosh, 87 AD2d 968; Saunders v. Saunders, 60 AD2d 701).
>
> In the instant matter, the court considered the conduct of both parties, both with reference to each other and to the child. What is of great concern to this court is the extent to which respondent was incapable of controlling her anger which she vented by utilizing, and, in some cases, endangering, this child. The court has also had the opportunity to observe the mother's lack of control of her feelings, especially anger, by her behavior in the courtroom. The court gives credence to respondent's witnesses who testified that she loves and has great affection for the child. However, these feelings

apparently did not enable her to deal with her anger in a manner which did not endanger the child nor threaten the child's welfare.[38]

9.4 ADMINISTRATIVE REGULATION

Modern reproductive techniques such as IVF[39] and ET[40] have not been prohibited by any administrative regulation or governmental agency.[41] The battle against infertility and the importance of medical research and experimentation are deemed important.[42] Surrogacy is a frequent subject before state legislatures, but little has been done in administrative or other regulation.[43] Perhaps there is a sense of futility in attempting to regulate even administratively these necessary and vital activities. Childless couples would otherwise take recourse to surreptitious purveyors of unhealthy and dangerous reproductive services. The constitutional right of privacy would be invaded[44] unless thoroughly reasonable regulation is available.[45] In Dronenburg v. Zech, the District of Columbia Court of Appeals limited the right of privacy with respect to consenting adults participating in homosexuality.[46]

Administrative regulation can profitably handle the preservation of the confidentiality of the records. Most states that require record keeping for donor insemination, for example, allow access to those records only by court order.[47]

NOTES

1. See Chapter 2.
2. See Chapter 4.
3. See 21 San Diego L. Rev. 1061 (1984) at 1073 et seq.
4. 405 U.S. 438 (1972).
5. Id. at 447.
6. 414 U.S. 632 (1974).
7. 109 S. Ct. 233 (1989).
8. See Note A.B.A.J. (December 1989) at 24.
9. Cal. Civ. Code sec. 621.
10. Cal. Civ. Code sec. 4601.
11. Infra note 8.
12. See *Hartford Courant* (October 10, 1987) at B2.
13. See Weber v. Aetna Casualty & Surety Co., 406 U.S. 164 (1972).
14. Note 21 Gonz. L. Rev. 395 (1985/1986) at 406.
15. 432 U.S. 464 (1976).
16. See *Butterworth Family Law Service Bulletin* 65 (1989).
17. Note Connecticut legislation on sterilization, found in ch. 779b, beginning with sec. 45–78p, and followed by sections on appointment of counsel to represent respondent if he or she is unable to give informed consent.
18. 316 U.S. 535 (1942).
19. Infra note 3, at 1074; also note 4 Harv Women's L.J. 1 (1981).
20. 518 N.Y.S.2d 574 (Bronx County, August 11, 1987).
21. 42 CFR sec. 50.201 et seq.

22. 88 Cal. App.3d 873, 153 Cal. Rptr. (1979).

23. See generally 15 Clearinghouse Rev. 925 (1982).

24. 434 U.S. 374 (1979).

25. Id. at 386.

26. 431 U.S. 816 (1978).

27. Id. at 843–44.

28. 434 U.S. 246 (1978).

29. See Zepeda v. Zepeda, 190 N.E.2d 849 (Ill. App., 1963) at 856; cert. denied 379 U.S. 945 (1964).

30. 108 S. Ct. 1 (1988).

31. 42 U.S.C. 300z.

32. On the religious issue, note Committee for Public Education v. Nyquist, 413 U.S. 756 (1973): governmental involvement in programs concerning religion: "may be so direct or in such degree as to engender a risk of politicizing religion. . . . Religious groups inevitably represent certain points of view and not infrequently assert them in the political arena, as evidenced by the continuing debate respecting birth control and abortion laws. Yet history cautions that political fragmentation on sectarian lines must be guarded against. . . . Government participation in certain programs, whose very nature is apt to entangle the state in details of administration and planning, may escalate to the point of inviting undue fragmentation.

33.—F.2d—(2d Cir., November 1, 1989).

34. 42 U.S.C. 300 et seq.

35. See Cox, "Choosing One's Family: Can the Legal System Address the Breadth of Women's Choice of Intimate Relationship?" 8 St. Louis U. Pub. L. Rev. 275 (1989).

36. Id. at 334.

37. Unreported,—N.Y.S.2d—(Westchester County Family Ct., November 13, 1989).

38. Note the Connecticut statute dealing with termination of parental rights under chap. 778 of Conn. Gen. Stat.

39. See Section 1.3

40. See Section 1.4.

41. See 18 U. Mich. J.L. Ref. 4 (Summer 1985) at 880.

42. According to the *Hartford Courant* (November 30, 1989) at El, a vaccine has been developed using genetic engineering techniques; it produces long-term contraception in female mice. The vaccine works by preventing fertilization of eggs by sperm rather than by interfering with the development of the fetus after conception or inducing abortions.

43. See 11 Fam. L. Rep. 3001 (1985).

44. See Section 1.10.

45. See 73 Geo. L.J. 1283 (1985) at 1296 et seq.

46. 741 F.2d 1388 (D.C. Cir., 1984).

47. Cal. Civ. Code sec. 7005(a); Conn. Gen. Stats sec. 45–69h; and Ore. Rev. Stat. sec. 677.365(2) and (3).

10

Forms, Contracts, and Statutes: Creation of the New Family

10.1 FORMS OF AGREEMENT AND CONTRACTS

The American Medical Association as early as 1957 issued a series of medico-legal forms designed to protect physicians performing artificial insemination.[1] The AMA then stressed the need for a written agreement between the physician and the plaintiff, which should cover the following:

> (1) The wife should consent in writing to the procedure, because otherwise its accomplishment would constitute an Assault and Battery; (2) The written consent of the husband should be obtained because the procedure seriously affects and involves the marital relationship; (3) The donor should consent in writing to the unrestricted use of the semen he supplies and should certify that he will make no effort to ascertain the identity of the husband and wife involved; (4) Although the possibility of suit by the donor's wife is remote, her written consent to the giving of the semen may also be desirable, inasmuch as her marital interests are affected; and (5) The physician should have permission to use his own best judgment in selecting the outside donor.[2]

The AMA guidelines also urged physicians to "use reasonable care in selecting a healthy donor who has no knowable transmissible disease"; furthermore, "the physician should establish to his own satisfaction that, from the medical point of view, the husband is sterile; and, where possible, the semen used should be 'pooled' and include semen of the husband and donor."[3] The AMA was aware that "in all probability it would be the physician, rather than the donor, who would be regarded as the guilty party in any criminal prosecution instigated to ban the practice of artificial insemination. Therefore, it urged its members to act in a reasonable manner at all times: "It is the physician who, by his own voluntary act, has actually interfered with the wife's reproductive faculties and caused the birth of any child that may result. If the performance of artificial insemination should be held to be a criminal offense, the fact that the patient consented may not be a defense to the physician. It has generally been held that consent to perform a criminal act is a nullity.''[4]

It would appear that all of these AMA forms of agreement[5] are still effective, and their importance lies in their flexibility (or alternative choices therein), which makes these forms of agreement meaningful today. The acknowledgment by the husband and wife of ''hazards, risks and possible consequences involved'' is an appropriate safety valve that should stand up to judicial scrutiny.[6] AMA Form 32-A signed by the donor may, however, contain preclusive data in paragraph 2 by its representations as to the donor's race, religion, and nationality. Form 32-B signed by the wife of the donor may require some paid consideration to be effective, and Form 31 is but an expanded copy of Form 30 with the inclusion of an effective indemnification agreement.

The *Journal of Family Law* (1986–1987) recommended several forms of surrogate motherhood contracts,[7] including a paternity suit settlement contract,[8] which might be filed with a court prior to the making of the surrogate motherhood contract.[9] The contract contains a clause calling for the father's custody of the child[10] and even details on the custody of the child after birth.[11] Child support, delineated in Article IV, would be subject today to federal guidelines set forth in the Child Support Enforcement Amendments (passed by Congress in 1984),[12] which mandated that every state by October 1, 1987, come up with formulas for determining child support awards to be submitted to the Office of Child Support Enforcement in the U.S. Department of Health and Human Services.[13]

10.2 UNIFORM PARENTAGE ACT

The Uniform Parentage Act (UPA)[14] has been adopted by only fifteen states,[15] with many variations in language. Section 5 addresses artificial insemination:

> (a) If, under the supervision of a licensed physician and with the consent of her husband, a wife is inseminated artificially with the semen donated by a man not her husband, the husband is treated in law as if he were the natural father of the child thereby conceived . . . ; and (b) The donor of semen provided to a licensed physician for use in artificial insemination of a married woman other than the donor's wife is treated in law as if he were not the natural father of the child thereby conceived.[16]

The thrust of section 5 is to relieve the donor of any legal liability and to legitimize the child so conceived, provided that the artificial insemination is performed by a licensed physician. Many states outside UPA unfortunately restrict legitimacy of such children born by donor insemination to married women only.[17] Of the fifteen states enacting the UPA, perhaps only six have enacted statutes addressing the paternity of children born to unmarried women.[18] In two states, at least the donor of semen to an unmarried woman is not the legal father of the child unless a written contract between the parties states otherwise.[19]

The UPA guarantees equal treatment under the law for all children born of artificial insemination; a child whose mother was so inseminated will not be deprived of a right to a legal father.[20] California has gone further than the UPA in shielding the donor of semen from any legal-paternal responsibility;[21] however, its statute deals with married women and therefore does not uphold the rights of the illegitimate child born of artificial insemination to a single woman since the statute completely severs the legal relationship between the child and his natural father. (Section 5(b) of the UPA therefore is at variance with section 7005(b) of the California Civil Code.) Ohio's version of the UPA[22] determines parentage based on biological or adoptive relationships, and the parent-child relationship ''extends equally to all children and all parents, regardless of the marital status of the parents.''[23]

Under the UPA, the father (not the semen donor) of a child born out of wedlock is liable for the expenses of the mother's pregnancy and delivery, and for the support, education, and funeral expenses of the child, whether or not the child is born alive.[24]

10.3 THE AID STATUTE

An article appearing in the 1985 *San Diego Law Review*[25] called for state legislatures to enact a model statute on artificial insemination because ''action by the medical profession would not adequately deal with the problems presented; after all, the medical profession . . . has allowed A.I.D. to continue in its current state. With a vast majority of doctors opposed to mandatory record-keeping and a large number actively attempting to confound any recording efforts, it would be unwise to leave the establishment of a regulatory system to them.''[26] Legislatures, on the other hand, ''would be capable of weighing the interests of the various parties.''[27] The proposed model statute places much emphasis on donor screening and on record keeping.[28] Both of these important procedures are admittedly absent from most state statutes, as perhaps exemplified by the Connecticut statute on Children Conceived Through Artificial Insemination,[29] which deals with legitimacy of the child, the person who may perform AID and the requisite consent, the filing of the request and consent with probate court, the lack of rights in the donor of sperm, and inheritance rights of the child.[30]

According to the U.S. Congressional Office of Technology Assessment report in August 1988, only 44 percent of the nation's 11,000 physicians who perform artificial insemination do tests on the donated semen for the AIDS virus.[31] However, the physicians surveyed said that husbands or sexual partners of the women being artificially inseminated were the sources of the sperm in 54 percent of the cases.

10.4 PROPOSED UNIFORM SURROGATE PARENTHOOD ACT

The proposed Uniform Surrogate Parenthood Act,[32] expressing the ''intent of the Legislature'' that ''surrogate parenthood arrangements are in accord with the public policy of this State and to facilitate the use of such surrogate parenthood arrangements,'' was carefully annotated in the 1985 *Georgetown Law Journal*.[33] The comments there are especially useful in understanding the need for state regulation.

Obviously, there is nothing in section 1 that limits surrogate parenthood to infertile couples; for single men who desire to have a child without marrying or having sexual intercourse, surrogate parenthood is available. Single women who desire to have a child without marrying or having sexual intercourse are beyond the pale of the availability of surrogate motherhood contemplated by the Uniform Surrogate Parenthood Act. Note that the surrogate mother herself need not be married; all parties identified must be at least 18 years of age.

§2. In all matters relating to surrogate parenthood arrangement and surrogate parenthood contract, different counsel shall represent the natural father (with his wife) and the surrogate (with her husband).

§3(a) As soon as is practicable after execution of the surrogate parenthood contract, but not later than ten business days after such execution, the parties shall file with the court a notice of the surrogate parenthood arrangement. The notice shall contain: (1) the names and addresses of the parties; and (2) the name and address of the licensed physician who will perform the insemination.

(b) At the time of filing the notice of the surrogate parenthood arrangement, the parties shall file with the court:

(1) an original executed copy of the surrogate parenthood contract;

(2) the written consent of the surrogate terminating in favor of the natural father and his wife all her parental rights and responsibilities to the child;

(3) the certificate of a person who is a [registered or licensed] marriage counselor, a licensed psychologist, or a licensed psychiatrist that such person had counseled the natural father and his wife on the consequences and responsibilities of surrogate parenthood and that, in such person's informed professional opinion, the natural father and his wife understand such responsibilities, are prepared to take on such responsibilities, and are capable of taking on such responsibilities;

(4) the certificate of a person who is a licensed psychologist or a licensed psychiatrist, but not the same person described in paragraph (3) of this subsection, that such a person has counseled the surrogate on the potential psychological consequences of her performance of her responsibilities under the surrogate parenthood contract and that, in such person's informed professional opinion, the surrogate understands such potential psychological consequences and is capable of performing her responsibilities under the surrogate parenthood contract;

(5) the separate opinions of legal counsel for the natural father (with his wife) and for the surrogate (with her husband), stating that in each case the client entered into the surrogate parenthood arrangement and executed the surrogate parenthood contract voluntarily and under no physical or psychological compulsion;

(6) evidence that the natural father and his wife have deposited the funds described in section 4(g) of this Act in an escrow account or an attorney trust account;

(7) evidence that the natural father and the surrogate are both at least eighteen years of age;

(8) if the surrogate is married, a written acknowledgement by her husband that he is

aware of the surrogate's participation in the surrogate parenthood arrangement and of his potential obligations and responsibilities under this Act, and his written consent to undergo the blood and/or tissue typing tests required by section 9(b) of Act;

(9) the written consent of the natural father to undergo the blood and/or tissue typing tests required by section 9(b) of this Act.

(c) When notice of the surrogate parenthood arrangement is filed, the natural father and his wife shall post with the court a surety bond of a surety company registered to do business in [this state] to indemnify [this state] (or any of its agencies, instrumentalities, or subdivisions) for any cost, up to $250,000, incurred in the care and/or placement of the child.

(d) As soon as is practicable after filing of the notice of the surrogate parenthood arrangement, but not later than sixty calendar days after such filing, the court shall determine whether the parties have filed all the documentation that this section requires. If the court determines that the parties have filed all necessary documentation, it shall issue an order verifying that the surrogate parenthood arrangement complies with the provisions of law and directing that the insemination may proceed as the surrogate parenthood contract provides.

(1) If the court determines that the filing is incomplete, it shall allow the parties thirty days to complete the filing. When thirty days elapse, the court will again make the determination described in the first sentence of this subsection within the sixty-day period that such sentence requires.

(2) If the court determines that the filing includes documentation that is false or misrepresented, the court shall issue an order voiding the filing. The voiding of a filing will have the effect of making the proposed surrogate parenthood arrangement illegal. Any party to a voided filing, including the counsel of each party, shall not be a party to, or counsel representing a party to, a surrogate parenthood arrangement for one year from the date of the order voiding the filing.

(e) The court shall retain jurisdiction over the surrogate parenthood arrangement from the filing of the notice of the surrogate parenthood arrangement until the court's issuance of the order described in section 9(c) of this Act.

Section 3 in subparagraph (a) insists upon the licensed physician's performing the artificial insemination because of the health and safety factors. Subparagraph (b) speaks in terms of a prerequisite that both the natural father and his wife and the surrogate herself undergo psychological counseling before becoming parties to a surrogate arrangement. Subparagraph (c) is a troublesome requirement in that the natural father and his wife must post a surety bond up to $250,000 to indemnify the state if anything goes wrong, such as a child born with a serious impairment or disability. On the other hand, as set forth in paragraph (d), the courts are ever-present to curb abuses in the surrogacy and to give stability to the relationship; courts also serve as a repository for documentation and can resolve paternity disputes.

§4. The surrogate parenthood contract shall include, but shall not be limited to, the following terms:

(a) that the surrogate agrees to conceive the child through artificial insemination with the natural father's semen, to bear the child, and to terminate all her parental rights and responsibilities to the child effective immediately on the child's birth through a written consent executed at the same time as the surrogate parenthood contract;

(b) that the surrogate agrees to submit to reasonable medical evaluation and treatment and to adhere to reasonable medical instructions about her prenatal health and the child's health, including abstention from any act prohibited by the surrogate parenthood contract and related to the prenatal health and development of the child;

(c) that the natural father and his wife agree to pay all reasonable expenses related to the inseminations and the surrogate's preinsemination medical evaluation and examination;

(d) that the natural father and his wife agree to pay all reasonable expenses of the surrogate, whether legal, medical, psychological, or psychiatric, related to the surrogate parenthood arrangement and incurred during the preinsemination counseling process, the pregnancy, and the six-week period following the child's birth;

(e) that the natural father and his wife agree to provide life insurance and health insurance for the natural father and his wife and the surrogate over the term of the pregnancy and the six-week period following the birth of the child, in amounts that the surrogate parenthood contract shall specify;

(f) that the natural father and his wife agree to compensate the surrogate reasonably for her services, living expenses, and lost wages, in an amount not to exceed $25,000;

(g) that the natural father and his wife agree to deposit the compensation amount in an escrow account or attorney trust account as soon as is practicable after execution of the surrogate parenthood contract, but no later than ten business days after execution of such contract, and that the parties agree that such funds be distributed as the contract shall specify, except that no more than one-half of such compensation amount shall be distributed before the court issues the order described in section 9(c) of this Act, unless the pregnancy terminates spontaneously, in which instance section 4(h) of this Act shall apply;

(h) that the compensation amount shall not be reduced if the child is stillborn or is born impaired, except that the surrogate parenthood contract may stipulate that if the pregnancy terminates spontaneously within the first thirteen weeks of gestation, the surrogate shall receive a compensation amount not less than one-third of the specified compensation, and that if the pregnancy terminates spontaneously between the fourteenth and twenty-seventh weeks of gestation, the surrogate shall receive a compensation amount not less than two-thirds of the specified compensation;

(i) that the natural father and his wife agree to accept custody of, and to assert full parental rights and responsibilities for, the child immediately upon the child's birth, regardless of any impairment to the child;

(j) that the natural father and his wife shall have the right to choose reasonably the blood and/or tissue typing tests required by section 9(b) of this Act, from among the alternatives provided therein, such reasonable choices to be specified in the surrogate parenthood contract; and

(k) that the parties shall have available all legal and equitable remedies, including specific performance, in the event of a breach of the surrogate parenthood contract, notwithstanding any contrary provision of law.

Section 4 details what provisions should be included in the surrogate parenthood contract. Subparagraph (a) spells out the consideration the surrogate mother gives in exchange for the payment from the natural father, while subparagraph

(b) delineates her code of behavior during the surrogacy and when specific performance, as stated in subparagraph (k), can be had. Subparagraph (c) states that financial resources are available to complete performance under the contract, and the onus rests squarely upon the natural father and his wife. Subparagraph (e) provides for life insurance and also for health insurance for the surrogate for any injury or even death caused by the pregnancy. Fair compensation for the surrogate is established by subparagraph (f), even at the risk of labeling the surrogacy "baby selling";[34] the statutory maximum of $25,000 makes the risk of exploitation of the surrogate mother less likely. The escrow account contemplated in subparagraph (g) ensures all parties to the contract of good faith performance, and subparagraph (h) mandates that the surrogate must be paid in full whether the child is stillborn, impaired, or healthy, because in each instance the surrogate's services have been the same and she has been exposed to the same risks and inconveniences. Reduced compensation for a spontaneous abortion is rational, based on the foregoing considerations. Acceptance of custody of the child is ensured under subparagraph (i), regardless of the outcome of the birth, unless the court subsequently determines that the man who contracted with the surrogate is not the biological father of the child. Paternity testing is discussed under subparagraph (j), and subparagraph (k) assures the parties of all legal and equitable remedies under law.

§5. The surrogate parenthood contract may include the following provisions, notwithstanding any other contrary provision of law:

(a) that by participating in the surrogate parenthood arrangement and by executing the surrogate parenthood contract, the surrogate waives her right to terminate the pregnancy resulting from her insemination with the natural father's semen, unless such termination is medically necessary to preserve the surrogate's life or material health; and

(b) that the surrogate agrees to return all of the compensation amount that she has received from the escrow account or attorney trust account, to repay to the natural father and his wife all of the amounts they have paid for her legal and medical expenses relating to the preinsemination period, the insemination (including her preinsemination medical evaluation and examination) and the pregnancy, and to reimburse all of the legal and medical expenses of the natural father and his wife relating to the surrogate parenthood arrangement and surrogate parenthood contract in the event of any nonspontaneous termination of the pregnancy necessary to save the life or material health of the surrogate.

Section 5 describes other provisions that might be included in the contract. The waiver by the surrogate of her right to abortion appears to be valid because the waiver would be the product of her voluntary act, which encompasses her estimate of the costs and benefits.[35]

§6. (a) The written consent of the surrogate terminating all her parental rights and responsibilities to the child, which she files with the court as specified in section 3(b)(2) of this Act, shall be effective immediately on the child's birth unless, within fourteen days after the child's birth, but not before the child's birth, the surrogate both files with the court a written revocation of her consent and petitions the court to determine paternity of the child.

(b) If the court determines that the child was not conceived through the insemination that was part of the surrogate parenthood arrangement, the court shall terminate all of the parental rights and responsibilities of the natural father and his wife and shall grant to the surrogate and her husband full parental rights to and responsibilities for the child, including custody. In such case, the surrogate's husband shall be the child's legal father.

(c) In making the determination described in subsection (b) of this section, the court shall consider all relevant evidence, including the results of the blood and tissue typing tests required by section 9(b) of this Act.

(d) If the court determines that the child was not conceived through the insemination that was part of the surrogate parenthood arrangement, the surrogate shall return all of the compensation that she has received from the escrow account or attorney trust account, shall repay to the natural father and his wife all of the amounts that they have paid for her legal and medical expenses relating to the preinsemination period, the insemination (including her preinsemination medical evaluation and examination), and the pregnancy, and shall reimburse all of the legal and medical expenses of the natural father and his wife relating to the surrogate parenthood arrangement and surrogate parenthood contract.

Section 6 proclaims that the surrogate mother should not have the right to withdraw her consent to the termination of her parental rights and responsibilities unless the purported natural father is not the actual biological father of the child.

§7. The natural father may petition the court having jurisdiction over the surrogate parenthood arrangement to determine paternity of the child within fourteen calendar days of the child's birth. Sections 6(b) and 6(c) of this Act shall apply to determinations under this section. If the natural father has died before this fourteen-day period has expired, *but only in such a case*, the wife shall have standing to petition the court to determine paternity of the child.

Section 7 delineates the issue of paternity as requested by the natural father, provided same is raised with fourteen calendar days of the birth of the child.

§8. The court having jurisdiction over the surrogate parenthood arrangement shall seal all records of determinations described in sections 6 and 7 of this Act.

Section 8 concerns disclosure of information but apparently does not restrict the child's access to relevant personal health information.

§9. (a) As soon as is practicable after the child's birth, but not later than seventy-two hours after the birth, the parties shall file with the court a notice of the child's birth, certifying the birth date and time and the child's weight, length, and physical condition at birth in reasonable detail and providing the child's footprints.

(b)(1) Unless paragraph (2) of this subsection applies, at the time the parties file the notice of the child's birth, the parties shall file with the court the results of blood and/or tissue typing tests of the child, the natural father, and the husband. The natural father shall have the right to select the tests to be employed, but he may select only as many tests as would provide a reasonably sure indication of paternity. The natural father may select from, but shall not be limited to, the following tests:

(A) red cell antigens;
(B) red cell isoenzymes;
(C) human leukocyte antigens;
(D) serum proteins; and
(E) any other blood and/or tissue typing test accepted into evidence by the courts of [this state].

The tests that this subsection requires shall be performed within twenty-four hours of the child's birth. The results of the tests shall be made available to the parties as soon as is practicable.

(2) If the physician with primary care responsibility for the child notifies the court in writing at the time that the notice of the child's birth is filed that performance of the tests that paragraph (1) of this subsection requires would endanger the child's life or material health, such tests shall be performed on the child within twenty-four hours of that physician's certification that performance of such tests no longer endangers the child's life or material health. The results of such tests shall be filed with the court within seventy-two hours of such certification.

(c) Within forty-eight hours of the filing of the results of the blood and/or tissue typing tests, the court shall issue an order granting custody of the child to the natural father and his wife and shall direct that the [instrumentality having responsibility for issuance of birth certificates in the jurisdiction where the child is born] issue the child's birth certificate naming the natural father and his wife as the child's parent(s). This order shall become final and irrevocable fourteen calendar days after the child's birth, unless the surrogate withdraws her consent and petitions the court to determine paternity of the child under section 6 of this Act or the natural father petitions the court to determine paternity of the child under section 7 of this Act.

Section 9 pertains to record-keeping functions such as birth certificates and blood and/or tissue typing tests, that are mandatory, and also provides for the child's custody to the natural father and his wife.

§10. From the child's birth until the order of the court described in section 9(c) of this Act becomes final, the natural father and his wife shall have custody of the child, unless the court, in its discretion and in the best interests of the child, orders otherwise, but the court may so order only in the event that the natural father or surrogate petitions the court to determine the child's paternity.

Section 10 precludes the court from interfering with the surrogate motherhood contract unless the parties request otherwise.

§11. The natural father shall be the child's legal father, unless the surrogate or the natural father petitions the court under section 6 or section 7 of this Act to determine the child's paternity and the blood and/or tissue typing tests indicate that the natural father is not the child's biological father. If such tests indicate that the natural father is not the child's biological father, the husband shall be the child's legal father. The provisions of this Act shall prevail over any other conflicting provisions of law.

Section 11 ensures the child of legitimacy by the presumption of legitimacy; indeed, the husband of the surrogate will be the child's legal father if the natural father is not the child's biological father.

§12. Payments that the natural father and his wife make to the surrogate under the terms of the surrogate parenthood contract and pursuant to section 4 of this Act are not illegal, notwithstanding any other contrary provision of law.

State laws or policies against baby selling or even black-market adoptions do not affect the operation of the Uniform Surrogate Parenthood Act, according to section 12.

§13. (a) Reasonable actions of agents, finders, and intermediaries, including attorneys or physicians, on behalf of the parties in structuring a surrogate parenthood arrangement and in negotiating a surrogate parenthood contract are not illegal, notwithstanding any other contrary provision of law. Any unreasonable action shall be punishable under section 16 of this Act.

(b) Reasonable payments that the natural father and his wife make to agents, finders, and intermediaries, including attorneys or physicians, are not illegal, notwithstanding any contrary provision of law.

Section 13 authorizes payments to agents in adoption procedures as well as other persons necessary for the surrogacy; reasonable compensation is therefore fully authorized.

§14. The court shall have the power to award any legal or equitable relief, including specific performance, upon any breach of the surrogate parenthood contract, except that the court shall not order the surrogate to terminate the pregnancy.

Section 14 sets forth the obvious powers of the court except for the terminancy of the pregnancy.

§15. The terms of the surrogate parenthood contract shall govern any and all disputes relating to the surrogate parenthood arrangement, unless the court determines that extraordinary circumstances require otherwise.

§16. (a) Any insemination of a surrogate that takes place before the court issues its order directing that the insemination may take place, and any violation of any other provision of this Act, shall be a [misdemeanor]. The parties, the physician who performs the insemination, and any agents, finders, and intermediaries involved in the arrangement, including the parties' counsel, shall be guilty of a [misdemeanor] in the event of any violation punishable according to the provisions of this section.

(b) All other provisions of this Act will apply in the event of an insemination described in subsection (a) of this section.

Sections 15 and 16 provide for criminal liability in the event of violation of the act, and ensure compliance with the provisions of the act.[36]

For the New York view, see Miller and Swidler, ''In Support of the Surrogate Parenting Act,'' N.Y.L.J. (April 28, 1989) at 1, 7:

> The Surrogate Parenting Act, advanced by the New York State Task Force on Life and the Law, reflects a growing consensus that public policy should discourage surrogate parenting. The proposal does not interfere with the arrangements when they are voluntary and non-commercial. It does, however, protect the interests of children and ensures that they will not be the subject of commercial arrangements. It also preserves basic values about the dignity of women and human reproduction. The Surrogate Parenting act thus subjects the novel practice of surrogacy to the same principles that have long been embodied in our laws on the relationship between parent and child.

Another uniform act is the Uniform Status of the Children of the New Biology Act, which the National Conference of Commissioners on Uniform State Laws was considering in August 1988.[37] The conference recommended that surrogate mother contracts are void and that a court must give its approval of the contract before conception. However, the surrogate mother would be given 180 days after the court approval to repudiate, if she so desires, the contract.

10.5 OTHER STATUTES AND OTHER LAWS

Child abuse and child neglect statutes have also been applied in new reproductive technology disputes, although they have frequently come under attack for being unconstitutionally vague and thus fail to ensure sufficient parental autonomy in family affairs.[38] These statutes have also been criticized as distortions of the state's *parens patriae* authority.[39] Statutes delineating child neglect run a similar pattern, and both statutes should not be allowed to interfere with family autonomy, which must be preferred over state intervention, as expressed in 1982 by the U.S. Supreme Court in Santosky v. Kramer,[40] which held that the burden of proof for terminating parental rights must be ''clear and convincing'' rather than simply supportive of the ''preponderance of the evidence'' standard.

Screening of donors of eggs, sperm, and adoptive parents is relatively untouched by statutes or by administrative rulings. The American Fertility Association in 1980 recommended to state legislatures that family medical history, a medical examination, and a full investigation for sexually transmitted diseases become mandatory for any potential donor of sperm or eggs other than the spouse of the recipient.[41] Adoptive parents should similarly be screened to determine if their interest in adoption is generated by the hope that a child will save their marriage; such adoptive parents are a poor risk for adoptive parentage[42]

''Private ordering'' or private contracting of domestic relations is being extended today to child support, child custody, and visitation rights, and the courts are frequently divested of much of their authority in this area.[43] Hence the need for statutes and laws is lessened, but the fact remains that the state does have compelling interests, which must be satisfied. Deregulation in the field of family law is not in the offing. No state is prepared to take a laissez-faire role in regulating the family picture. Procreative liberty and noncoital technology will require continuing state concern and interest.[44]

NOTES

1. See Freedman, *Society on Trial: Current Court Decisions and Social Change* (1965) at 84
2. Id.
3. Four of the most popular AMA forms are (1) Agreement for Artificial Insemination; (2) Consent of Wife of Donor; (3) Application to Serve as Donor of Semen; and (4) Agreement for Artificial Semen.
4. Infra note 1, at 85.
5. Infra note 3.
6. See AMA Form 30, infra note 3.
7. 25 J. Fam. L. (1986–1987) at 522 et seq. and at note 19 therein. Also see section 10.4.
8.

PATERNITY SUIT SETTLEMENT CONTRACT

Mary Doe and John Doe, wishing to avoid litigation and for their mutual benefit and the welfare of their unborn child, now on this ______ day of __________, 19 ___, freely and voluntarily enter into this contractual agreement to resolve all present legal disputes between them.

WHEREAS, Mary is now in her [first, second] month of pregnancy, as confirmed by her physician, Dr. _________ on the ______ day of _________, 19___; and

WHEREAS, John and Mary believe John to be the father of her unborn child; and

WHEREAS, Mary does not want to raise their child and wishes to avoid the burdens of custody and visitation; and [additional parental shortcomings of Mary may be listed here.]

WHEREAS, John does want to raise their child and wants to enjoy the benefits and burdens of custody; and

WHEREAS, Mary and John believe him to be a fit and proper person to have sole legal custody of their child commencing at birth and sole physical custody commencing when the child leaves the hospital [or other facility] providing immediate post-natal care; and

WHEREAS, John and Mary agree that John's wife (consort), Jane Roe, is also a fit and proper person to assist John in caring for their child and understand her to be willing and desirous of doing so; and

WHEREAS, Mary presently expects to relinquish her parental rights, after their child is born, [in the hope that Jane will seek a stepparent adoption of their child]; and

WHEREAS, John is well able to provide generous support to Mary during her pregnancy; and

WHEREAS, John wants to provide the best possible care for their unborn child by the furnishing of such support and to assist Mary, on their child's behalf, with all expenses related to her pregnancy and their child's birth; and

WHEREAS, John and Mary agree that, during her pregnancy, she should be free of the anxieties of employment, etc., etc.; and

WHEREAS, Mary and John agree that their child will be best served by Mary's, during her pregnancy, refraining from smoking and from drinking alcoholic beverages; living in the nature retreat at Moose Lake, which is near Moose Heart Hospital; etc.; etc.;

NOW, THEREFORE, John Roe and Mary Doe voluntarily and freely agree, contract, and bind themselves and their legal representatives and assigns, as appropriate, to the following articles of agreement:

Article I: Paternity

A. John hereby acknowledges and admits that he [may be and probably] is the father of the child with whom Mary is now pregnant, and that he bears all legal duties and privileges of parenthood to that child.

B. John and Mary agree that, at the earliest reasonably possible time after their child's birth, based upon competent medical advice, each of them and their child shall undergo appropriate blood tests to determine John's paternity with reasonable certainty and, if the child be his or if such tests cannot be made for any reason beyond Mary's control, shall continue to carry out and perform all agreements herein contained and reasonably inferred herefrom. If the child shall be not John's, then Article IA and Article II of this agreement shall be null and void, and Mary shall return to John or to his estate, as soon as she reasonably may, [two-thirds of] all monies paid to her for support and for her and her child's medical care under this agreement except those covered by health insurance carried by John and actually paid by such insurance and not recoverable by any insurance company [but shall not reimburse John for legal fees already then incurred by either of them in relation to the subject of this agreement and chargeable to him by its terms nor the costs of the blood tests required by this paragraph].

Article II: Custody

A. Mary and John hereby agree that John shall have sole legal and actual custody of their child after the child's birth. They believe this to be in the best interests of their child because Mary does not want the child [and would procure an abortion were John not desirous of raising their child] and because John does want their child and is a fit and proper person to care for and support their child. [The willingness of John's wife (consort), Jane Roe, to help John to care for the child is a factor considered by the parties hereto but is not a necessary condition to John's custody rights hereunder.]

B. Should John die or become incapacitated before their child's birth, Mary agrees to make the best arrangements she can for the care of their child [and, if Jane Roe be willing, to consult with Jane Roe about those arrangements], and Mary acknowledges her parental responsibility in that event.

C. Mary agrees to follow all competent medical advice during her pregnancy and childbirth and to provide the best possible care for the parties' unborn child. [Further, she agrees to refrain from smoking or drinking alcoholic beverages during pregnancy; to live in the nature retreat at Moose lake; etc.; etc.] [She agrees to refrain from choosing to abort their fetus unless it be medically necessary and hereby waives, insofar as is legally possible, her right to do so, unless John shall consent in writing to her procuring an abortion.]

Article III: Child Support

A. John agrees to pay to Mary the sum of [$2,500] per month from the date of this agreement until her recovery from, and discharge from the hospital [or other facility] after the birth of their child, the first payment to be made on the date of this agreement and the total number of payments expected, but not guaranteed, to be eight. These payments to Mary are for the support and care of their unborn child during Mary's pregnancy and for her support as necessitated thereby.

B. John further agrees to pay all Mary's medical expenses incident to this pregnancy and the birth of their child except for those actually paid by health insurance carried by either of the parties [or by Mary's husband, Joe Doe].

C. John further agrees to pay all medical bills incurred by or on behalf of their child at and after the child's birth except for those actually paid by health insurance carried by either of the parties [or by Mary's husband, Joe Doe].

D. John further agrees to pay all legal fees for this agreement and its enforcement, including those incurred by Mary in preparation or enforcement of this agreement

E. The parties recognize that the child support payments made to Mary are not taxable to her, and, should any I.R.S. or court ruling to the contrary require her to pay federal income tax thereon, John agrees to pay the amount of such tax that is attributable to those payments at the rate that would be applicable if she had no other income during the months in which those payments were received and as though she had received a like amount each month of the tax year(s) in question, but in no event shall he pay more than her actual tax liability incurred because of the child support payments made hereunder.

F. John further agrees that, should he die or become disabled before the birth of their child, the payments required under this agreement shall be made by and from his estate or other property. [He further agrees to make a will leaving (one-third, one-fourth, etc.) of his net estate to their child] [unless blood tests show that the child is not his.]

G. John agrees never to seek any child support from Mary for their child, and hereby forever waives his right to claim such support from her.

Article IV: Miscellaneous Provisions

A. Mary and John hereby agree that the child support payments provided for herein are not to be a measure of either their child's post-birth needs or of John's ability to pay, should payments of child support after birth be sought for any reason. Because the pre-natal welfare of their child is of particular concern and importance to him, John has agreed to payments beyond the capacity of his normal budget and well beyond the needs of a baby or young child, although not beyond those of an unborn child.

B. This agreement shall be immediately effective when signed and shall bind the parties, their heirs, and their assigns forever. The parties recognize that they cannot legally, and do not wish to, foreclose any legal rights of their child by this agreement, but they do hereby intend fully to settle all matters pending or disputed, now and hereafter, between themselves and pertaining to this child, Mary's pregnancy, or the child's birth.

C. Each party hereby agrees to execute any and all documents necessary to perform her and his obligations under this agreement and, upon suit by the other party, to have such documents executed for them by order of a court of competent jurisdiction should either of them fail for any reason to do so, so long as the party plaintiff is not in breach of this contract.

We hereunto set our signatures this ______ day of __________, 19___, and agree freely and voluntarily to each and every provision of this agreement and to all facts recited herein.

________________ ________________

John Roe Mary Doe

Before me appeared this ______ day of __________, 19___, Mary Doe and John Roe, known to me to be the persons herein named, and, each of her and his own free will signed this agreement in my presence and in the presence of each other.

____

NOTARY PUBLIC

My commission expires

____

The foregoing Contract might have an accompanying affidavit of the wife of the biological father and also a waiver by the husband of the surrogate mother, as follows:

Father's Wife's or Consort's Affidavit

Being informed that Mary Doe is pregnant by my husband (consort) John Roe, I, Jane Roe, hereby, under oath and subject to penalties for perjury, express my full willingness to assist John in raising his child. I hope that I may adopt his child as a step-parent after the child's birth, but I am, in any event, willing and able to help him to raise the child and agree whole-heartedly to his taking sole legal and actual custody of his child when born and to his paying generous child support until then.

____
Jane Roe

State of _______________
County of _______________
Signed and sworn to before me
this _____ day of ________, 19__.
NOTARY PUBLIC
MY commission expires _______________

Surrogate Mother's Husband's Waiver

I, Joe Doe, husband of Mary Doe, forever waive any and all legal claims of marital fault or otherwise against my wife, Mary Doe, for or in connection with her becoming pregnant by, and bearing the child of, John Roe, whether such claims arise under past, current, or future law of this or any other jurisdiction. I hereby voluntarily intend to bind myself, my heirs, and my assigns forever. I reserve, however, all rights to deny paternity of her child by John Roe, if the child is, in fact, established to be his.

____
Joe Doe

State of _______________
County of _______________
Signed and sworn to before me
this _____ day of ________, 19__.

____
NOTARY PUBLIC
My commission expires _______________

9. See Am. Jur. Legal Forms 2d sec. 90:1–90:50 (1972) and Model Legal Forms sec. 4510–4548.5 (1977).

10. Infra note 8, Art. IIA thereof.

11. Infra note 8, Art. III thereof, and note the proposed agreement:

THIS AGREEMENT is made this _____ day ________, 198[ ], by and between ________ (hereinafter referred to as ''Surrogate'') and her husband, ________ (hereinafter referred to as ''Husband'') and ________ (hereinafter referred to as ''Natural Father'').

RECITALS

THIS AGREEMENT is made with reference to the following facts:

(1) The Natural Father is a married individual over the age of eighteen (18) years who is desirous of entering into the following agreement.

(2) The Natural Father desires to have a child who is biologically related to him.

(3) The Surrogate and her Husband are a married couple each over the age of eighteen (18) years who are desirous of entering into the following agreements in consideration of the financial remuneration incident hereto. . . .

NOW, THEREFORE, in consideration of the mutual promises contained herein and with the intentions of being legally bound, hereby the parties agree as follows:

SECTION I. The Surrogate represents that she is capable of conceiving children, but agrees that she will not form or attempt to form a parent-child relationship with any child she may conceive pursuant to the provisions of this contract and shall freely and readily, in conformance with applicable statutory regulations, terminate all parental rights to said child pursuant to this agreement. . . .

SECTION II. The Surrogate and her Husband have been married since ________ and the Husband is in agreement with the purposes, intents, and provisions of this agreement and agrees that his wife, the Surrogate, shall be artificially inseminated pursuant to the provisions of this agreement. The Husband will not form a parent-child relationship with any child the Surrogate may conceive by artificial insemination as described herein and agrees to freely and readily terminate all parental rights to said child and acknowledges he will do all acts necessary to rebut the presumption of paternity (including blood testing) . . . .

SECTION III. The Natural Father is hereby entering into a written contractual agreement with the Surrogate and her Husband, whereby the Surrogate shall be artificially inseminated, with the semen of the Natural Father, by ________, M.D. The Surrogate, upon her becoming pregnant, shall carry said embryo/fetus(s) (hereinafter referred to as "child") until delivery. Delivery shall occur in the state of ________. The Surrogate and her Husband agree that they will on the fifth day after delivery of the child, or as soon thereafter as is medically possible, institute proceedings in [________] to terminate their respective parental rights to said child and sign any and all necessary affidavit documents, etc., in order to further the intent and purposes of this agreement. The Surrogate and her Husband agree to sign all necessary affidavits, prior to the birth of the child in order to have the Natural Father's name placed on said child's birth certificate as the biological father. . . .

SECTION IV. The Natural Father and the Surrogate and her Husband recognize and acknowledge that the Attorney(s) for the Natural Father shall act as agent for the Natural Father in all matters pertaining to this agreement in order to maintain complete confidentiality.

SECTION V. The consideration for this agreement, in addition to other provisions contained herein, shall be as follows: (a) $ ______shall be paid to the Surrogate and her Husband upon entry of the judgment fully terminating the parental rights of the Surrogate and her Husband as defined by the law in [] to the child to be born pursuant to these provisions between the Surrogate and the Natural Father.

12. See *New York Times* (November 11, 1987) at Cl et seq.

13. Three popular payment formulas are delineated:

The Wisconsin formula, in use in that state since 1983, is straightforward. The noncustodial parent pays a percentage of his or her gross income, calculated by how many children are involved: 17 percent for one child, 25 percent for two children, 29 percent for three, 31 percent for four and 34 percent for five or more. This plan has been criticized for not taking into account the income of the custodial parent; the assumption is that that parent is already paying a percentage of his or her income, to which the noncustodial parent is now being forced to add.

The Delaware Melson formula, named for the judge in Delaware who developed it, has been in use in that state since 1979. It sets aside a specific sum, in most cases $450 a month, for the subsistence of each parent. The combined income of the parents that exceeds the total, $900, is then used for the basic needs of the child in the following amounts: $180 a month for the first child, $135 for the second and third and $90 for the fourth through sixth, with each parent contributing proportionate to his or her net income.

After those amounts have been allocated, 15 percent of the remainder of each parent's net income goes to additional child support for one child. For each of the second and third children, 10 percent is added, while 5 percent is added for each of the fourth, fifth and sixth children.

The Income Shares model, developed by the federally financed Child-Support Guidelines Project of the National Center for State Courts, is based on the idea that the child is entitled to the proportion of parental income that he would have received had the family remained intact.

Basic child support is computed on the basis of the parents' combined incomes. The specific amount of monthly or weekly support is set according to tables indicating what intact families in equivalent income brackets spend on their children. Each parent's income then determines what proportion of the support he or she must pay. (At C12, infra note 12)

14. 9A U.L.A. 587 et seq. (1979).

15. Ala. Code § §26–17–1 to 26–17–21 (1975); Cal. Civ. Code § §7000–7018 (1976);

Colo. Rev Stat. § §19–6–101 to 19–6–129 (1977); Del. Code Ann. tit. 13 § §801–18 (1983); Hawaii Rev. Stat. § §584–1 to 584–26 (1976); Ill. Ann Stat. ch. 40, § §2501–2526 (Smith-Hurd 1985); Minn. Stat. Ann. § §257.51–.74 (West 1980); Mont. Code Ann. § §40–6–101 to 40–6–134 (1975); Nev. Rev. Stat. § §126.011–.391 (1979); N.J. Rev. Stat. Ann. § §9:17–38 to 9:17–59 (West 1983); N.D. Cent. Code § §14–17–01 to 14–17–26 (1975); Ohio Rev. Code Ann. § §3111.01–.19 (Page 1982); R.I. Gen. Laws §§15–8–1 to 15–8–27 (1979); Wash. Rev. Code Ann. § §26.26.010–.905 (1976); Wyo. Stat. § §14–2–101 to 14–2–120 (1977).

16. See 9A U.L.A. 592–593 (1979). Note the Connecticut statute on artificial insemination. Also note the Connecticut statute on children conceived through artificial insemination under Chapter 778b and consisting of but four sections, to wit:

Sec. 45–69f. Child born as a result of artificial insemination legitimate. (a) It is declared that the public policy of this state has been an adherence to the doctrine that every child born to a married woman during wedlock is legitimate.

(b) This chapter shall be construed as a codification and clarification of such doctrine with respect to any child conceived as a result of heterologous artificial insemination.

Sec. 45–69g. A.I.D. Who may perform. Consent required. (a) The technique known as heterologous artificial insemination, or artificial insemination with the semen of a donor, referred to in this chapter as A.I.D., may be performed in this state only by persons certified to practice medicine in this state pursuant to chapter 370.

(b) A.I.D. shall not be performed unless the physician receives in writing the request and consent of the husband and wife desiring the utilization of A.I.D. for the purpose of conceiving a child or children.

Sec. 45–69h. Request and consent to be filed in probate court. Confidentiality. (a) Whenever a child is born who was conceived by the use of A.I.D., a copy of the request and consent required under subsection (b) of section 45–69g, together with a statement of the physician who performed the A.I.D., that to the best of his knowledge the child was conceived by the use of A.I.D., shall be filed with the judge of probate in the district in which the child was born or in which the child resides.

(b) The information contained in such statement may be disclosed only to the persons executing the consent. No other person shall have access to the information except upon order of the probate court for cause shown.

Sec. 45–69i Status of child born as result of A.I.D. Any child or children born as a result of A.I.D. shall be deemed to acquire, in all respects, the status of a naturally conceived legitimate child of the husband and wife who consented to and requested the use of A.I.D.

17. See Alaska Stat., § 25.20.045 (1982); Ark. Stat. Ann. §61–141(c) (1983); Conn. Gen. Stat. Ann. §45–69(f)-(n) (West 1980); Fla. Stat. Ann. §742.11 (West Supp. 1985); Ga. Code Ann. § §74–101.1, 74–9904 (1981); Idaho Code §39–5401 (1984); Kan. Stat. Ann. §23–128 to §23–129 (1974); La. Civ. Code Ann. art. 188 (West 1980); Md. Est. & Trusts Code Ann. §1–206(b) (1981); Mass. Gen Laws Ann. ch. 46, §4B (West 1985); Mich. Comp. Laws Ann. § §333.2824(6), 700.111(2) (West 1980); N.Y. Dom. Rel. Law §73 (McKinney 1977); N.C. Gen. Stat. §49A–1 (1984); Okla. Stat. Ann. tit. 10, §551–53 (West 1980); Or. Rev. Stat. §109.243 (1983); Tenn. Code Ann. §68–3–306 (1983); Tex. Fam. Code Ann. §12.03(a) (Vernon 1975); Va. Code §64.1–7.1 (1984).

18. See statutes of California, Colorado, New Jersey, Oregon, Washington, and Wyoming, as set forth, infra note 15.

19. New Jersey and Washington, infra note 15.

20. See 21 San Diego L. Rev. 1061 (1984). Of more than passing interest is the Connecticut statute on abortion, §53–29, –30, –31, and –31a, all of which were declared

unconstitutional and an injunction was issued in Abele v. Markle, 369 F Supp. 807 (Conn., 1973):-

Sec. 53–29. Attempt to procure miscarriage or abortion. Any person who gives or administers to any woman, or advises or causes her to take or use anything, or uses any means, with intent to procure upon her a miscarriage or abortion, unless the same is necessary to preserve her life or that of her unborn child, shall be fined not more than one thousand dollars or imprisoned in the State Prison not more than five years or both.

Sec. 53–30. Abortion or miscarriage. Any woman who does or suffers anything to be done, with intent thereby to produce upon herself miscarriage or abortion, unless necessary to preserve her life or that of her unborn child, shall be fined not more than five hundred dollars or imprisoned not more than two years or both.

Sec. 53–31. Encouraging the commission of abortion. Any person, who, by publication, lecture or otherwise or by advertisement or by the sale or circulation of any publication, encourages or prompts to the commission of offenses described in section 53–29 or 53–30, or who sells or advertises medicines or instruments or other devices for the commission of any of said offenses except to a licensed physician or to a hospital approved by the department of health services, or who advertises any so-called monthly regulator for women, shall be fined not more than five hundred dollars or imprisoned not more than one year or both.

Sec. 53–31a. Abortion or miscarriage. The public policy of the state and the intent of the legislature is to protect and preserve human life from the moment of conception and in order to effectuate this public policy and intent:

(a) No person shall give or administer to any female person, advise or cause her to take or use anything, or use any means, with intent to procure upon her a miscarriage or abortion, nor shall any female person do or suffer anything to be done, with intent thereby to produce upon herself a miscarriage or abortion.

(b) No person shall sell or advertise medicines or instruments or other devices for the commission of a miscarriage or abortion, except to a licensed physician or a hospital licensed by the state of Connecticut.

(c) The provisions of subsections (a) and (b) of this section shall not apply to an abortion or miscarriage performed by a licensed physician when such abortion or miscarriage is necessary to preserve the physical life of the mother and when such abortion is performed in a hospital licensed by the state of Connecticut.

(d) A violation of this section shall be a class D felony.

21. See Cal. Civ. Code Sec. 7005(b).
22. Ohio Rev. Code Ann. §3111.01 et seq. (1982).
23. Sec. 3111.01(B), infra note 22.
24. Sec. 1, 9A U.L.A. 587 (1979).
25. 22 San Diego L. Rev. 1193 (1985).
26. Id at 1214.
27. Id.
28. Id.
29. Conn. Gen. Stats. ch. 778b (1987).
30.

Sec. 45–69f Child born as a result of artificial insemination legitimate. (a) It is declared that the public policy of this state has been an adherence to the doctrine that every child born to a married woman during wedlock is legitimate.

(b) This chapter shall be construed as a codification and clarification of such doctrine with respect to any child conceived as a result of heterologous artificial insemination.

Sec. 45–69g A.I.D. Who May Perform. Consent Required. (a) The technique known as heterologous artificial insemination, or artificial insemination with the semen of a donor, referred to in this chapter as A.I.D., may be performed in this state only by persons certified to practice medicine in this state pursuant to chapter 370.

(b) A.I.D. shall not be performed unless the physician receives in writing the request and consent of the husband and wife desiring the utilization of A.I.D. for the purpose of conceiving a child or children.

Sec. 45–69h Request and consent to be filed in probate court. (a) Whenever a child is born who was conceived by the use of A.I.D., a copy of the request and consent required under subsection (b) of section 45–69g, together with a statement of the physician who performed the A.I.D., that to the best of his knowledge the child was conceived by the use of A.I.D., shall be filed with the judge of probate in the district in which the child was born or in which the child resides.

(b) The information contained in such statement may be disclosed only to the persons executing the consent. No other person shall have access to the information except upon order of the probate court for cause shown.

Sec. 45–69i Status of child born as result of A.I.D. Any child or children born as a result of A.I.D. shall be deemed to acquire, in all respects, the status of a naturally conceived legitimate child of the husband and wife who consented to and requested the use of A.I.D.

Sec. 45–69j. *No rights in donor of sperm.* A donor of sperm used in A.I.D., or any person claiming by or through him, shall not have any right or interest in any child born as a result of A.I.D.

Sec. 45–69k. *Status of child determined by jurisdiction of birth.* (a) Any child conceived as a result of A.I.D. performed in Connecticut and born in another jurisdiction shall have his status determined by the law of the other jurisdiction unless the mother of the child is domiciled in Connecticut at the time of the birth of the child.

(b) If a child is conceived by A.I.D. in another jurisdiction but is born in Connecticut to a husband and wife who, at the time of conception, were not domiciliaries of Connecticut, but are domiciliaries at the time of the birth of the child, the child shall have the same status as is provided in section 45–69i, even if the provisions of subsection (b) of section 45–69g and section 45–69h may not have been complied with.

Sec. 45–69l. *Inheritance by child conceived as a result of A.I.D.* (a) A child born as a result of A.I.D. may inherit the estate of his mother and her consenting spouse or their relatives as though he were the natural child of the mother and consenting spouse and he shall not inherit the estate from his natural father or his relatives.

(b) The mother and her consenting husband or their relatives may inherit the estate of a child born as a result of A.I.D., if the child dies intestate, and the natural father or his relatives shall not inherit from him.

Sec. 45–69m. *Words of inheritance to apply to child conceived through A.I.D.* (a) The words "child," "children," "issue," "descendant," "descendants," "heir," "heirs," "unlawful heirs," "grandchild," and "grandchildren," when used in any will or trust instrument, shall, unless the document clearly indicates a contrary intention, include children born as a result of A.I.D.

(b) The provisions of this section shall apply to wills and trust instruments whether or not executed before, on or after October 1, 1975, unless the instrument indicates an intent to the contrary.

Sec. 45–69n. *Status of child conceived through A.I.D., born prior to October 1, 1975.* Nothing in this chapter shall be construed as a change or modification of the rights or status of children born before October 1, 1975, but shall be construed as a clarification and codification of the rights and status which the children had on said date.

31. See *New York Times* (August 11, 1988) at A23.

32. See 1980 So.Ill.U.L.J. 147 (1980), 70 A.B.B.J. 50 (1984), and Wadlington, *Cases and Other Materials on Domestic Relations* 443 (1984).

33. 73 Geo L.J. 1283 (1985).

34. See Chapter 5.

35. See Michel v. Louisiana, 350 U.S. 91 (1955) at 99.

36. See generally: Coleman, "Surrogate Motherhood: Analysis of the Problems and Suggestions for Solutions," 50 Tenn. L. Rev. 71 (1982); Handel & Sherwyn, "Surrogate Parenting," Trial, Apr. 1982, at 57; Rushevsky, "Legal Recognition of Surrogate Gestation," 7 Women's Rts. L. Rptr. 107 (1982); Comment, "Contracts to Bear a Child," 66 Calif. L. Rev. 611 (1978); Comment, Parenthood by Proxy: Legal Implications of Surrogate Parenting, 67 Iowa L. Rev. 385 (1982); Comment, "The Surrogate Child: Legal Issues and Implications for the Future," 7 J. Juv. L. 80 (1983); Note, "In Defense of Surrogate Parenting: A Critical Analysis of the Recent Kentucky Experience," 69 Ky. L.J. 877 (1981); Comment, "Surrogate Mother Agreements: Contemporary Legal Aspects of a Biblical Notion," 16 U. Rich. L. Rev. 467 (1982); Note, "Surrogate Motherhood: Contractual Issues and Remedies under Legislative Proposals," 23 Washburn L.J. 601 (1984); and Comment, "Surrogate Motherhood: A Nursery Full of Unresolved Problems," 17 Willamette L.J. 913 (1981).

37. See NLJ (August 29, 1988) at 6.

38. See Alsager v. District Court, 406 F. Supp. 10 (SD Iowa, 1975), aff'd. 545 F.2d 1137 (8th Cir., 1976).

39. See generally 93 Harv. L. Rev. 1156 (1980) at 1224.

40. 455 U.S. 745 (1982).

41. See 69 Va. L. Rev. 465 (1983) at 503.

42. Id. at note 145.

43. Id. at 508–9.

44. See 59 S. Cal. L. Rev. 939 (1986) at 1039. Also note the following pertinent articles: American College of Obstetricians and Gynecologists, *Ethical Issues in Surrogate Motherhood* (statement of policy from the Executive Board) (May 1983); L. B. Andrews, "The Stork Market: The Law of the New Reproduction Technologies," A.B.A.J. 70(8): 50–56 (August 1984); G. J. Annas, "Surrogate Embryo Transfer and the Perils of Parenting," Hastings Center Report 14(3): 25–26 (June 1984); G. J. Annas, and S. Elias, "In Vitro Fertilization and Embryo Transfer: Medicolegal Aspects of a New Technique to Create a Family," Fam. L.Q. 17(2): 199–223 (Summer 1983); G. G. Blumberg, "Legal Issues in Nonsurgical Human Ovum Transfer," A.M.A 251(9): 1178–81 (March 2, 1984); M. Bostillo, et al., "Nonsurgical Ovum Transfer as a Treatment in Infertile Women," J.A.M.A. 251(9) 1171–73 (March 2, 1984); M. Drori, "Reflections on the Effect of Modern Techniques of Fertility on Family Law," Med. L. (1): 15–28 (1982); D. M. Flannery, et al., "Test Tube Babies: Legal Issues Raised by In Vitro Fertilization," Geo. L.J. 67(6): 1295–1346 (August 1979); S. R. Gersz, "The Contract in Surrogate Motherhood: A Review of the Issues," L. Med. & Health Care 11(3): 107–14 (June 1984); C. Grobstein. "External Human Fertilization," Sci. Am. 240(6): 57–67 (June 1984); A. R. Holder. "Surrogate Motherhood: Babies for Fun and Profit," L. Med. Health Care 12(3): 115–17 (June 1984); A. R. Holder, "Legal Issues at Conception and during the Prenatal Period," in A. R Holder, *Legal Issues in Pediatrics and Adolescent Medicine* (Wiley Medical Publications, New York, 1985); H. T. Krimmel, "The Case against Surrogate Parenting," Hastings Center Report 13(5) 35–39 (October 1983); G. Kritchevsky, "The Unmarried Woman's Right to Artificial Insemination: A Call for an Expanded Definition of Family," Harv. Women's L.J. 4(1): 1–42 (Spring 1981); J. R. Lieberman and V. Insler, "Physicians' Right to Refuse Treatment of Infertility: Preserving Quality of Life?" Med. L. 1(1): 33–38 (1982); T. Ooms, and S. O'Brien, "AID and the Single Mother," Hastings Center Report 13(1): 22–23 (February 1983); P. J. Parker, "Moti-

vation of Surrogate Mothers: Initial Findings,'' Am. J. Psych. 140(1): 117–18 (January 1983); J. A. Robertson, ''Procreative Liberty and the Control of Conception, Pregnancy, and Childbirth,'' Va. L. Rev. 69(3): 405–65 (April 1983); J. A. Robertson, ''Surrogate Mothers: Not So Novel After All,'' Hastings Center Report 13(5): 28–34 (October 1983); J. J. Schlesselman, ''How Does One Assess the Risk of Abnormalities from Human In Vitro Fertilization?'' Am. J. Obstet. and Gynecology 135: 135–48 (September 1, 1979); G.P. Smith II and R. Iraola, ''Sexuality, Privacy and the New Biology,'' Marq. L. Rev. 67(2): 263–91 (Winter 1984); W. J. Sweeney and L. S. Goldsmith, ''Test Tube Babies: Medical and Legal Considerations,'' J. Legal M. 1(4): 1–17 (April 1980); W. Wadlington, ''Artificial Conception: The Challenge for Family Law,'' Va. L. Rev. 69(3): 465–514 (April 1983); L. Walters, ''Ethical Aspects of Surrogate Embryo Transfer,'' J. Am. Med. Assn. 250(16): 2183–84 (October 28, 1983).

Index to Cases

Subject Index

About the Author

WARREN FREEDMAN was Liability Counsel and Assistant Secretary for Bristol-Myers Squibb Corporation prior to his retirement in 1980. He is the author of numerous Quorum books on legal topics, as well as many leading legal treatises.